国家汉办/孔子学院总部
Hanban/Confucius Institute Headquarters

Mencius

Collection of Critical Biographies of Chinese Thinkers

(Concise Edition, Chinese-English)

Editors-in-chief: Zhou Xian, Cheng Aimin

Author: Xu Xingwu
Translator: David B.Honey
Expert: Li Ji

Nanjing University Press

《中国思想家评传》简明读本 - 中英文版 -

主 编 周 宪 程爱民

孟 子

著 者 / 徐兴无 Xu Xingwu

译 者 / David B. Honey

审 读 / 李 寄 Li Ji

南京大学出版社

Editor: Rui Yimin
Cover designed by Zhao Qin

First published 2010
by Nanjing University Press
No. 22, Hankou Road, Nanjing City, 210093
www.NjupCo.com

©2010 Nanjing University Press

Chinese Library Cataloguing in Publication Data
The CIP data for this title is on file with the Chinese Library.

ISBN10: 7-305-07583-4(pbk)
ISBN13: 978-7-305-07583-4(pbk)

Books available in the collection

Confucius
《孔子》
978-7-305-06611-5

Laozi
《老子》
978-7-305-06607-8

Emperor Qin Shihuang
《秦始皇》
978-7-305-06608-5

Li Bai
《李白》
978-7-305-06609-2

Cao Xueqin
《曹雪芹》
978-7-305-06610-8

Du Fu
《杜甫》
978-7-305-06826-3

Zhuangzi
《庄子》
978-7-305-07177-5

Sima Qian
《司马迁》
978-7-305-07294-9

Mencius
《孟子》
978-7-305-07583-4

Mozi
《墨子》
978-7-305-07970-2

总序

General Preface

China is one of the cradles of world civilization, enjoying over five thousand years of history. It has produced many outstanding figures in the history of ancient thought, and left a rich philosophical heritage for both the Chinese people and the entire humanity. The fruit of these thinkers was to establish unique schools that over the long course of history have been continuously interpreted and developed. Today much of these thoughts are as relevant as ever and of extreme vitality for both China and the rest of the world. For instance, the ideal of "humaneness" and the concept of "harmony" taught by Confucius, the founder of Confucianism, have been venerated without ceasing by contemporary China as well as other Asian nations.

Ancient Chinese dynasties came and went, with each new dynasty producing its own scintillating system of thought. These rare and beautiful flowers of philosophy are grounded in the hundred schools vying for attention in pre-Qin times and the broad yet deep classical scholarship of Han and Tang times and in the simple yet profound occult learning of the Wei and Jin dynasties together with the entirely rational learning of Song and Ming Neo-Confucianism. The fertile soil of religious belief was Buddhism's escape from the emptiness of the sensual world and Daoism's spiritual cultivation in the search for identification with the immortals. The founders of these systems of thought included teachers, scholars, poets, politicians, scientists and monks— they made great contributions to such disparate cultural fields in ancient China as philosophy, politics, military science, economics, law, handicrafts, science and technology, literature, art, and religion. The ancient Chinese venerated them for their wisdom and for following moral paths, and called them sages, worthies, saints, wise men, and great masters, etc. Their words and writings, and sometimes their life experiences, constitute the rich matter of ancient Chinese thought distilled by later generations. The accomplishments of Chinese thought are rich and varied, and permeate such spiritual traditions as the harmony between humans and nature, the unification of thought and action, and the need for calmness during vigorous action, synthesizing the old and innovating something new.

Nanjing University Press has persisted over the last twenty years in publishing the 200-book series, *Collection of Critical Biographies of Chinese Thinkers*, under the general editorship of Professor Kuang Yaming, late honorary president of Nanjing University. This collection is the largest-scale project of research on Chinese thinking and culture undertaken since the beginning of the twentieth century. It selected more than 270 outstanding figures from Chinese history, composed their biographies and criticized their

中国是世界文明的发源地之一，有五千多年的文明史。在中国古代思想史上，涌现出了许许多多杰出的思想家，为中华民族乃至整个人类留下了丰富的思想遗产。这些思想成果独树一帜，在漫长的历史中又不断地被阐释、被发展，很多思想对于今天的中国乃至世界而言，仍然历久弥新，极具生命力。比如，儒家学派创始人孔子"仁"的理念、"和"的思想，不仅在当代中国，在其他亚洲国家也一直备受推崇。

古代中国朝代更迭，每一个朝代都有灿烂夺目的思想文化。百家争鸣的先秦诸子、博大宏深的汉唐经学、简易幽远的魏晋玄学、尽心知性的宋明理学是思想学术的奇葩；佛教的色空禅悦、道教的神仙修养是宗教信仰的沃土；其他如经世济民的政治、经济理想，巧夺天工的科技、工艺之道，风雅传神、丹青不老的文学艺术……都蕴涵着丰富的思想。这些思想的创造者中有教师、学者、诗人、政治家、科学家、僧人……他们在中国古代的哲学、政治、军事、经济、法律、工艺、科技、文学、艺术、宗教等各个文明领域内贡献巨大。古代中国人尊敬那些充满智慧、追求道德的人，称呼他们为圣人、贤人、哲人、智者、大师等，他们的言论、著作或被后人总结出来的经验构成了中国古代思想的重要内容，在丰富多彩中贯穿着天人合一、知行合一、刚健中和等精神传统，表现出综合创新的特色。

南京大学出版社坚持20余年，出版了由南京大学已故名誉校长匡亚明教授主编的《中国思想家评传丛书》，这套丛书共200部，是中国20世纪以来最为宏大的中国传统思想文化研究工程，选出了中国历史上270余位杰出人物，为他们写传记，

intellectual accomplishments; all in all, it is a rigorous and refined academic work. On this foundation, we introduce this series of concise readers, which provides much material in a simple format. It includes the cream of the crop of great figures relatively familiar to foreign readers. We have done our best to use plain but vivid language to narrate their human stories of interest; this will convey the wisdom of their thought and display the cultural magnificence of the Chinese people. In the course of spiritually communing with these representative thinkers from ancient China, readers will certainly be able to apprehend the undying essence of thoughts of the Chinese people.

Finally, we are deeply grateful for the support from Hanban/ Confucius Institute Headquarters, and the experts from home and abroad for their joint efforts in writing and translating this series.

Editors

November 2009

评论他们的思想成就，是严肃精深的学术著作。在此基础上推出的这套简明读本，则厚积薄发，精选出国外读者相对较为熟悉的伟大人物，力求用简洁生动的语言，通过讲述有趣的人物故事，传达他们的思想智慧，展示中华民族绚烂多姿的文化。读者在和这些中国古代有代表性的思想家的心灵对话中，一定能领略中华民族思想文化生生不息的精髓。

最后，我们衷心感谢国家汉办/孔子学院总部对本项目提供了巨大的支持，感谢所有参与此套丛书撰写和翻译工作的中外专家学者为此套丛书所做的辛勤而卓有成效的工作。

编者
2009年11月

目录

Contents

一　当今之世，舍我其谁——生平、抱负和著作

Chapter I　During the Present Age Nobody Can Achieve It, but I!Life, Aspirations, and Works

In ancient China the greatest persons were called "sages." The original meaning of "sage" was "clever." Only those who possessed the greatest wisdom and virtue, and who were able to invent culture, implements, and institutions or who were able to save the people in deep water were worthy of being called "sages." In ancient Chinese records and legends, Fuxi, Nüwa, and Shennong were the so-called sages since the creation of the world, who were collectively termed the "Three August Ones." Following them came Huangdi, Zhuanxu, Diku, Yao and Shun, known as the "Five Emperors." Afterwards appeared Yu of Xia, Tang of Shang, and King Wen of Zhou, called the "Three Kings" and then Confucius, who lived between 551 B.C. to 479 B.C. He deeply felt the crisis in the ancient cultural tradition created by political turbulence and moral decay, and so self-consciously took upon himself the burden of assuming the tradition of moral governance transmitted since the times of Yao and Shun. His self-appointed task was thus to elucidate the civilization based on ritual and music that had been the legacy of King Wen of Zhou, King Wu of Zhou, and the Duke of Zhou. Confucius termed this tradition of civilization or culture of approximately 2500 years in duration "culture" (*wen*). He travelled all around the various kingdoms promoting his own positions. Once he went to a place called Kuang, where he was mistaken by the populace for a nobleman who had once pillaged the place. This led to him becoming besieged. Yet he was full of confidence as he spoke to his disciples, saying: "After the death of King Wen, hasn' t 'culture' fallen to me to transmit? If Heaven above desired to destroy 'culture' , then why would it choose me to inherit it? If Heaven does not desire this to happen, then what could the people of Kuang do to me?" ❶

Although Confucius was unable to become a sage king, his lifetime of itinerant teaching, education, and method of composition preserved the ancient writings, elucidated the ancient culture, and criticized the amoral government. He also founded private teaching and the Confucian school of thought; therefore he was venerated by later generations as a "sage," and called "the Most Holy First Teacher." The meaning of this title is the greatest sage and the earliest teacher. Because he was the explainer of culture to Chinese people, the ancients said: "If Heaven had not created Confucius, all time would have been one long night of darkness." In world history, Confucius, together with Socrates who lived from 469 to 399 B.C., and Sakyamuni, who lived between 560 B.C. to 480 B.C. as well as Jesus Christ who lived later, from the turn of the era until 30 A.D., became four great philosophers who created models of

在中国古代，最伟大的人物被称为"圣人"。"圣"的原意是聪明。只有那些最有智慧和道德，并能发明文化、器物、制度或者拯救民众于水深火热之中的人才能被称为圣人。在中国古代文献或传说中所谓自天地开辟以来的圣人，有伏羲、女娲、神农，称为"三皇"；接着有黄帝、颛顼、帝喾、尧、舜，称为"五帝"；以后还有夏禹、商汤、周文王，称为"三王"。而生活在公元前551年至479年间的孔子，深切地感受到古代文化传统因为政治的动荡和道德沦丧而产生的危机，便自觉地承担起继承尧、舜以来的德治教化传统，以阐释周文王、武王及周公以来的礼乐文明为己任。孔子称这样一个具有2500年左右的文明或文化传统叫做"文"。他周游列国，推行自己的主张。一次走到一个叫匡的地方，被民众误认为是某个掠夺过当地的贵族，因而遭到围困。他却非常自信地对弟子们说："周文王死了，'文'不都承担在我的身上吗？如果上天想要灭绝'文'，哪就不会选中我来承担它；如果上天不想这样做，这些匡地的民众能拿我怎样？"❶

虽然孔子没有能够成为一个帝王，但他一生以游说、教育和著述的方式保存古代的文献，阐释古代的文化，批评不道德的政治，开创了私人讲学和儒家学派，因此被后人推尊为"圣人"，称之为"至圣先师"，意思是最了不起的圣人和最早的教师。因为他是中国人的文化启蒙者，所以古人说："天不生仲尼，万古如长夜"。在世界史上，孔子与生活在公元前469年至公元前399年间的苏格拉底、与生活在公元前560年至480年间的释迦牟尼以及迟至公元元年至公元30年间的耶稣并称为四位

---

❶《论语·子罕第九》5章。按，本书引述古代文献，均译为现代汉语。

❶ *Analects*, "Zihan," 9.5. In this work all citations from ancient works will be translated into modern Chinese.

thought for humanity❶. From Confucius until the present, the Chinese cultural tradition has developed for another 2500 years. Despite several periods of transformation, compared to other world civilizations, the continuity of Chinese culture is quite obvious. Credit must be given to Confucius as the creative model. We may say, then, that Confucius was a cultural hero.

After Confucius, no other sage appeared in the Chinese historical record. Outstanding men have been called "worthies" in terms of their moral cultivation, meritorious achievements, and knowledge or intelligence, and the two appellations "Sages and Worthies" have often been employed together. Despite the historical use of the terms "sage king," "sage ruler," or "sage lord" by subjects to flatter their monarchs or emperors, they never lightly called them "sages." Nevertheless, one man was greater than the general run of worthies, and approached being a sage himself. Therefore he was called a "Secondary Sage." ❷ This man was none other than Mencius.

Mencius was the inheritor of Confucius as a cultural hero. Modern Chinese philosopher Feng Youlan said, ❸

> Confucius' position in Chinese history is similar to Socrates' position in western history; Mencius' position in Chinese history is similar to Plato's position in western history. Their clear, soaring styles are similar.

Modern Chinese archaeologist Li Ji further stated , ❹

> The primary contribution made to world civilization by China is her humanism. This was led primarily by Confucius and Mencius, who lived

创造人类思想范式的大哲学家❶。从孔子到我们现在，中国文化传统又发展了2500多年，尽管其间历经多次变革，但与世界其他文明相较，中国文化的延续特征是非常明显的，这不能不归之于孔子创造的范式。可以说，孔子是一位文化英雄。

孔子之后，中国的文献中再也没有出现圣人。在道德、事功、知识或智能方面杰出的人物被称为贤人，并以"圣贤"并称。尽管历代臣民们都阿谀奉承他们的国君或帝王是圣王、圣主、圣君，但从不轻易地称他们为圣人。不过，有一个人比一般的贤人要伟大一些，最接近圣人，因而被称为亚圣、大贤❷。这个人就是孟子。

孟子是继孔子之后的文化英雄。中国现代哲学家冯友兰说❸：

> 孔子在中国历史中的地位，如苏格拉底之在西洋历史；孟子在中国历史中之地位，如柏拉图之在西洋历史，其气象之高明亢爽亦似之。

中国现代考古学家李济又说❹：

> 古代中国对世界文化的首要贡献是她的人文主义。

❶ 见卡尔·雅斯贝尔斯（Karl Jaspers）《大哲学家》"思想范式的创造者"。李雪涛主译，北京，社会科学文献出版社，2005。
❷ 东汉赵岐《孟子章句题辞》称孟子为"命世亚圣之大才者也"，又称《孟子》这本书是"大贤拟圣而作"。宋孙奭《孟子正义》，《十三经注疏》下册，北京，中华书局影印清阮元校刻本，1980，第2662页。
❸ 冯友兰《中国哲学史》上册，上海，华东师范大学出版社，2000，第86页。
❹ 李济《中国早期文明》，上海，上海世纪出版集团，2007，第61页。

❶ See Karl Jaspers, "Four Creators of Models of Thought," in *Great Philosophers*, Trans, Li Xuetao, et al.(Beijing: Social Sciences Academic Press, 2005)
❷ The great worthy from the Eastern Han period Zhao Qi termed Mencius the "world renowned secondary sage of great ability" in his work *Chapters and Verses of Mencius*, "Introduction," and furthermore described the book *Mencius* as "written by a great worthy in imitation of a sage." Sun Shi (Song Dynasty), *The Orthodox Interpretation of Mencius*, in *The Thirteen Classics, with Commentary and Sub-Commentray*, vol. 2 (Beijing: Zhonghua Book Company Photocopy of Ruan Yuan [Qing] edition, 1980), p. 2662.
❸ Feng Youlan, *A History of Chinese Philosophy*, vol. 1 (Shanghai: East China Normal University Press, 2000), p. 86.
❹ Li Ji, *Early Chinese Civilization* (Shanghai: Shanghai Century Publishing Group, 2007), p. 61.

at the end of the Chinese bronze age and the beginning of the Chinese iron age respectively.

Mencius' experiences were similar to those of Confucius. He too was full of ideals, he too roamed around the various states; after encountering setbacks at every hand he returned home to write and teach. Therefore, he strongly identified with Confucius and with the tradition inherited from Confucius.

Mencius felt that the sages were the teachers for a hundred generations, that they accomplished much through their struggles a hundred generations earlier, and that after a hundred generations all who heard or read of their accomplishments were inspired thereby. If they had not been sages, could they have exerted such an influence? ❶ According to Chinese tradition one generation amounts to thirty years, so what Mencius said about exerting influence across one hundred generations amounts to at least three thousand years of influence.

Mencius considered Confucius as the greatest of the sages; he said : ❷

Anciently there was a sage called Boyi who would not even listen to or look at an immoral thing. He would not serve a lord who was not his conception of an ideal ruler; he would not govern a commoner whom he did not like. When rule was upright then he would serve; when it was chaotic he would retire to his hometown. He would never settle in a region with a tyrannical regime or where mob rule prevailed. He felt that associating with uneducated country folk was like donning his ritual garb and headwear but sitting in the mud or among ashes. During the age of King Zhou of Shang, he lived as a hermit on the shore of Beihai, waiting for peace to prevail in the world. His integrity was able to turn the greedy honest, and make the cowardly turn resolute.

Another sage called Yi Yin said, "What kind of ruler cannot be served? What type of people cannot be governed?" Regardless of whether the world was ordered or chaotic, whether the ruler was good or evil, he would shoulder the burden of taking up office. He said, "Heaven gave birth to the people for a man such as I who was first enlightened to teach them. As a first enlightened one, I will employ the way of Yao and Shun to open their eyes." As long as one male or female remained unenlightened, it was like he pushed them into the ditch. Therefore, Yi

中国的人文主义的主要倡导者是孔子和孟子，他们分别生活在中国青铜时代的末期和中国铁器时代的初始。

孟子的经历与孔子很相似，他满怀理想，周游列国，四处碰壁后回到家乡著书立说。所以，他对孔子和孔子承担的传统有着非常强烈的认同。

孟子认为，圣人是百世之师，他们在百世以前奋发有为，百世以后，听到他们言行的人没有不被他们感发的。如果不是圣人，能够有这样的影响力吗？❶按照中国的传统，以30年为一世计算，孟子所说的百世之师至少具有三千年的影响力。

孟子认为孔子是最伟大的圣人。他说❷：

> 古时候有个叫伯夷的圣人，对不道德的东西，听也不听，看也不看。不是他理想中的君主，决不侍奉；不是他喜欢的百姓，决不治理。政治清明，就出来做事；政治混乱，就退居乡野。暴政流行、暴民聚集的地方决不去居住。他觉得与没有教养的乡巴佬在一起，就好像穿着礼服，戴着冠冕却坐在泥地或炭灰上。商纣王的时候，他隐居在北海之滨，等待天下太平。他的气节，能让贪心的人变得廉洁，让懦夫变得坚强。

> 另一位圣人叫伊尹，他说："哪个君主不可以侍奉呢？哪个百姓不可以治理呢？"无论天下是治是乱，也不管君主是好是坏，都任劳任怨地出来做官。他说"上天生育了人类，就是让我这样先懂得道理的人来教导他们。我是先知先觉者，所以我要用尧、舜之道来启发他们。"只要有一个男人或女人没有蒙受到教化，就像是自

---

❶《孟子·尽心下》15章。
❷《孟子·万章下》1章。

❶ *Mencius*, "Jinxin," Ⅱ 15.
❷ *Mencius*, "Wanzhang," Ⅱ 1.

Yin took the entire empire as his personal duty.

There was another sage called Liuxia Hui who was not ashamed to serve a tyrant, and was not embarrassed regardless of how low his position was. Yet he fulfilled his duties according to his own principles, and was not resentful when he was driven off by his lord; and when mingling with country folk he was able to get along harmoniously. According to his view, you are you and I am I, and even if you bare your arm to me, nothing you do can contaminate me. His deportment would cause the petty person to turn tolerant, and the harsh to turn lenient.

Yet Confucius was completely different. When he was in the state of Qi conversing with the ruler with whom he did not get along, he did not wait hardly a second to leave. And when he departed from the state of Lu, he stated to his students: "This is my homeland, let's not leave so fast!" This was Confucius—when he had to move fast he moved fast, when he had to move slow he moved slow; when it was appropriate to be an official he served as an official; when it was not appropriate he refused to serve. All in all, Boyi was a lofty sage; Yi Yin was a responsible sage; Liuxia Hui was an accommodating sage; and Confucius was a sage who knew when it was time to serve. Confucius can be termed as one who was the summation of the tradition. What is the "summation of the tradition?" Compare it to the performance of music. During the prelude the bronze bells are struck; during the coda the jade chimes are struck. The bronze bells begin by setting the rhythm; the jade chimes are the culmination of the rhythm. One's moral state similarly has a beginning and a conclusion; at the beginning one possesses wisdom; at the conclusion one achieves saintly virtue. Wisdom is like a skill, while saintly virtue is comparable to strength. It is like shooting at an archery target from beyond one hundred paces. Hitting the target depends on one's strength; but hitting the bull's eye is not a matter of strength.

Mencius' disciple Gongsun Chou asked him which one of Confucius' disciples he was most like. Mencius responded reluctantly, "We won't talk about this now." Gongsun Chou again asked how he would judge Boyi, Yi Yin, and Confucius, and whether the two were comparable to Confucius. Mencius said, "They were all sages, what a pity that I do not come up to their level. But my personal aspiration is to follow the example of Confucius. Boyi and Yi Yin cannot be compared to Confucius; in fact, no one has ever been able to come up to Confucius since mankind first appeared." ❶

己将他们推下了沟壑。于是，伊尹便以天下为己任了。

还有一位圣人叫柳下惠，给暴君做事不感到羞辱，官做得再小也不觉得难堪。可他做官时就按照自己的原则做事，被君主赶走也不怨恨。即使同乡巴佬在一起，他也能与之相处得很融洽。在他看来，你是你，我是我，即使你在我身边光着胳膊，也不能沾染我。他的风度，能让小气的人变得宽容，让刻薄的人变得敦厚。

而孔子又不一样了，他在齐国，与国君谈得不投机，连淘米的功夫都等不及，赶紧离开了。而离开鲁国时，却对学生说："这是我的父母之邦，慢些走吧！"这就是孔子，该快就快，该慢就慢，该做官就做官，不该做官就不做。所以，伯夷是个清高的圣人，伊尹是个负责的圣人，柳下惠是个随和的圣人，而孔子是个识时务的圣人。孔子可以算得上集大成的人。什么叫"集大成"呢？演奏音乐时，序曲敲金钟，尾声击玉磬。金钟是音乐节奏条理的开始，玉磬是音乐节奏条理的结束。人的道德境界也是这样有始有终，开始的时候具有智慧，最后成就圣德。智慧如同技巧，圣德好比力量。就像站在百步以外射箭，射到靶子，是你的力量；射中靶心，并不是你的力量。

孟子的弟子公孙丑问他以哪一位孔门弟子自居？孟子似乎不屑回答，说："我们暂时不谈这个。"公孙丑又问他如何评价伯夷、伊尹和孔子？伯夷、伊尹能否与孔子相比？孟子说："他们都是圣人，可惜我不能达到他们的境地。不过我个人的愿望，是学习孔子。伯夷、伊尹不能与孔子比肩，自从有人类以来，没有人比得了孔子。"❶

❶《孟子·公孙丑上》2章。

❶ *Mencius*, "Gongsun Chou," I 2.

There are several aspects of Mencius' spirit and character that are close to that of Confucius. He was similar in that he likewise shouldered responsibility. This type of responsibility actually was a lofty sense of mission. He stated, "One who waits for a King Wen of Zhou to appear before exerting himself to act is nothing more than an ordinary commoner. As for bold members of the gentry, even though no King Wen appears, they will exert themselves to act!" ❶

Mencius truly venerated Confucius, but the facts of his life are more vague than those of Confucius who predated him by some one hundred years. The great historian of the Western Han, Sima Qian, placed Mencius together with another great Confucian master who was his junior by some fifty years, Xunzi, in the work he compiled *Historian's Records* in a chapter titled "Biographies of Mencius and Xun Qing." This is the earliest biography of Mencius, but Mencius' biography in this chapter only amounted to 137 characters. It neither records the dates of Mencius' birth and death nor describes his appearance or life experience, and misplaces in the narrative the Mencius' visit to King Xuan of Qi before his visit to King Hui of Liang. This is possibly due to the chaotic social conditions during the Warring States Period that led to the destruction of quite a few records concerning Mencius. But more importantly, the book *Mencius* was possibly compiled jointly by Mencius and his disciples, and emphasized his expositions and debates, and devoted even more space to explaining the thought of Mencius. According to common sense, Mencius would not describe his own appearance and deportment or the scenes of his own life in any detail. This is strikingly different from the *Analects* of Confucius, which was compiled by Confucius' disciples based on their memory of the words and deeds of their master. Although the content of the *Analects* is shorter than that of *Mencius*, the voice and likeness of Confucius and the living conditions of both master and disciples are lifelike and vivid. Some say that *Mencius* is similar to a record of conversations, and that the *Analects* are more of a memoir, so their methods of narrating personalities, viewpoints, and contents naturally are different. Therefore, scholars of later generations are only able to extrapolate information from the historical events and kings that appear in the *Mencius*, from the chapter "Biographies of Mencius and Xun Qing" of the *Historian's Records* and from historical sources of the Warring States, Qin and Han periods.

Mencius' name was Ke, some said that his style name was Ziju or Ziyu; both were fabricated based on the meaning of his name. In his *Chapters and Verses of Mencius*, "Introduction," the Eastern Han scholar Zhao Qi declared that he had never heard of Mencius having a style name; he further said that

孟子的精神气质也有几分接近孔子，他像孔子一样自负。这种自负其实是崇高的使命感。他说："一定要等到周文王出世才能奋发有为的人不过是凡夫俗子。至于那些豪杰之士，即使没有文王出来，他们也会奋发有为的！"❶

孟子如此推崇孔子，可是他的生平事迹比早于他一百来年的孔子要模糊得多。西汉时期的大史学家司马迁在他撰写的《史记》中，将孟子与比孟子小约五十来岁的另一位儒家大师荀子合写为《孟子荀卿列传》。这是最早的孟子传记，可其中孟子的生平只写了137个字，既没有记录他的生卒年，也没有描绘他的容貌、身世，而且错将孟子见齐宣王放在见梁惠王之前。这可能因为战国时代社会动荡，毁坏了不少孟子学派的历史记录，但更重要的是《孟子》这本书很可能是孟子和他的弟子们合作编撰的，重在记录孟子的言说与辩论，更多地表述孟子的思想。按照常理，孟子不会去刻意描绘自己的容貌风度与生活场景。这与孔子的弟子通过追忆老师的言行而编成的《论语》大不相同。《论语》的文字篇幅虽比《孟子》短小，但孔子的音容笑貌与师生们的生活场景却栩栩如生。或者说，《孟子》如同谈话录，《论语》如同回忆录，叙述者的身份、叙述的角度和内容自然是不同的。因此，后世学者只能根据《孟子》这本书中提到的史事与国君，再根据《史记·孟子荀卿列传》及诸多战国秦汉时期涉及孟子的史料作推断。

孟子名轲，有人说孟子字"子车"或"子舆"，都是根据他的名字杜撰出来的。东汉人赵岐在《孟子章句·题辞》中声称从未听说过孟子的字，又说孟子是鲁国公族孟孙氏的后裔，

❶《孟子·尽心上》10章。

❶ *Mencius*, "Jinxin," Ⅰ10.

Mencius was a descendant of the Mengsun clan, nobility of the state of Lu. Although he was said to be from the state of Zou, he buried his mother in Lu. Zou was a minor state during the Warring States Period on the southwestern border of Lu, corresponding to the stretch of territory in modern Zou in Shandong province, only 20 kilometers from the capital of Lu and Confucius' hometown of Qufu. Mencius said, "I am so close to the homeland of sages," ❶ therefore he studied with the disciples of Zisi. Zisi was the grandson of Confucius and the student of Zengzi. According to tradition, the "Great Learning" and "Doctrine of the Mean" chapters of the Confucian classic *Record of Rites*, were composed by Zengzi and Zisi respectively, or at least recounts their thought by later Confucians. In the *Mencius*, in addition to 26 places that mention the words and deeds of Confucius, Zengzi appears in 22 places, and Zisi appears 16 times, while Yan Hui appears 7 times and Zilu 6 times. Others, such as Zixia, Ziyou, Zigong, Zizhang, Ran Qiu et al. only appear one, two, or three times ❷. This confirms that Mencius truly emerged from the school of Zisi; therefore he knew a lot concerning the words and deeds of his former masters. But Mencius certainly did not slavishly adhere to the teachings of his own school. He said, "The residual effects of the fine virtues of gentleman do not dissipate until five generations; the bad conduct and influence of petty persons also end after five generations. I was not able to be one of Confucius' followers, but I have learned privately from the example of former worthies." ❸

As for when Mencius was born, there have been nine historical theories or conjectures throughout from as early as 444 B.C. and as late as 372 B.C., separated by 72 years. The most influential among them date from the 12th year of King An of Zhou (390 B.C.), the 17th year (385 B.C.), and the 37th year of King Ding of Zhou (372 B.C.). If we knew Mencius' date of birth, then we could extrapolate the date of his death. Legend has it that Confucius lived 73 years, and Mencius lived 84 years. The ancients took these two life-spans as standards of life expectancy; it is epitomized in the folk saying "At 73 or 84, depart life on your own even though not summoned by the King of Hell." We cannot know for certain whether Mencius lived until 84, but it was close to that age. The first chapter in *Mencius*, "King Hui of Liang," records that as soon as the king saw Mencius he exclaimed, "Old Man, you have not shirked coming a

他虽说是邹国人，但将母亲归葬于鲁。邹国是战国时代的末等小国，就在鲁国的西南边境上，相当于现今山东省邹城市一带，与当时鲁国的国都、孔子的故乡曲阜相距仅20公里。孟子说："距离圣人的家乡如此之近"❶，所以他便跟从子思的门人学习。子思是孔子的孙子，曾子的学生。据说儒家经典《礼记》里的《大学》和《中庸》分别是曾子和子思所作或是后世儒学对他们思想的追述。在《孟子》书中，除了孔子的言行出现了26处之外，曾子出现了22处，子思出现了16处，颜回出现了7处，子路出现了6处，其他如子夏、子游、子贡、子张、冉求等仅出现1处或3处❷。这说明孟子的确出自于子思学派，因此对先师们的言行知道得较多。但是孟子决非固守门户的学究，他说："君子的美德余韵五代以后便断绝了，小人的败德风气五代以后也断绝了。我没有能成为孔子的门人，我是私下向贤人们学来的。"❸

关于孟子的生年，历史上有9种说法或推测，早到公元前444年，迟至公元前372年，相差72年之多。其中周安王十二年（公元前390）、周安王十七年（公元前385年）、周定王三十七年（公元前372年）三种说法影响最大。知道孟子的生年，便可据此推算孟子的卒年。传说孔子的年寿是73，孟子的年寿是84岁，古人将他们的年寿作为人生的寿命标准，民间俗语称："七十三，八十四，阎王不请自己去。"孟子是否活到84岁，我们不得确知，但也差不多。《孟子》书中的第一章是"孟子见

---

❶ 《孟子·尽心下》38章。
❷ 据杨泽波《孟子评传》（南京，南京大学出版社，1998，第26页）的统计。
❸ 《孟子·离娄下》22章。

❶ *Mencius,* "Jinxin," Ⅱ 38.
❷ According to the statistics of Yang Zebo, *Critical Biography of Mencius* (Nanjing: Nanjing University Press, 1998), p.26.
❸ *Mencius,* "Lilou," Ⅱ 22.

thousand *li* to visit me, you certainly must have something to benefit the state, right?" ❶ This passage revealed some information on the age of Mencius, because the term "Old Man" is a term of respect for seniors. The state of Wei was a strong state of that period, and King Hui was a feudal prince of the house of Wei. He transferred the state capital from Anyi to Daliang, and set himself up as a king; later generations called him King Hui of Liang. His reign lasted 50 years, and he died in 318 B.C. In the course of Mencius' audiences with the king, King Hui mentioned being slighted by the southern state of Chu ❷. This would have been around 323 B.C. ❸, during the waning years of his reign. In *Mencius* it records that when Mencius visited King Hui's successor King Xiang of Wei, he said, "At first glance he do not appear to be a lord of men." ❹ Afterwards, Mencius set off for the state of Qi. Therefore, when Mencius saw King Hui of Liang, it would have been in the last year of his reign. When he left the state of Wei, it was around 318 B.C., after the king's death. According to the above mentioned three theories on Mencius' date of birth, in this year of 318 Mencius would have been either 72, 67, or 55 years old. When the aged king saw Mencius, he called him "old man;" therefore we may posit that at that time Mencius was either 72 or 67 as the most reasonable age. After leaving, he dwelt in Qi for five or six years, then returned home to compile his book. Therefore, it is possible that he did live 80 years or so. Probably we may never know Mencius' dates of birth or death, but this does not at all prevent us from understanding Mencius' thought, and it did not at all hinder his influence on later generations. All we must do is to extract hints from his work or his travels, and to select birth and death years that will reasonably accommodate these events to serve as coordinates for investigating the chronology of Mencius' life and thought.

From the book *Mencius* we may infer the date of the first time he became an official in the state of Zou. *Mencius* records Zang Cang, the favored minister of Duke Ping of Lu, slandering Mencius for the lavish burial he provided for his mother, which exceeded the one he provided for his father who had died previously; this was contrary to ritual propriety. Mencius' disciple Yuezhengzi said to Duke Ping of Lu that when Mencius' father died, Mencius was just had achieved the status of a scholar, and so could only bury

梁惠王"，梁惠王一见孟子便说："叟！您不辞千里之远来到我这里，一定会给我国带来利益吧？"❶这里透露出孟子的年龄信息，因为"叟"是对长者的尊称。魏国是当时的强国，梁惠王就是魏侯。他将国都从安邑迁到了大梁，并自封为王，后人称他为梁惠王。他执政长达50年，卒于公元前318年。在与孟子的谈话中，梁惠王说到被南方楚国欺辱的事❷，这是公元前323年的事❸，已在他执政的晚期。《孟子》中还记载孟子看见梁惠王的嗣君魏襄王时说："一看就不像人君的样子。"❹接着孟子便去了齐国。因此，孟子见梁惠王时，应当是惠王末年；离开魏国的时间，大概在公元前318年惠王薨后。按照上述三种孟子生年推算，此年孟子或为72岁，或为67岁，或为55岁。年老的梁惠王见到孟子时，还尊称他为"叟"，所以我们假定孟子此时为72岁或67岁更为合理。他后来在齐国居住了五、六年，又回家著书。因此他活到80岁左右是可能的。我们可能永远算不出孟子的生卒年，不过这丝毫不妨碍我们了解孟子的思想，也丝毫不妨碍他对后代的影响。我们只需从《孟子》书中考察出他的游历线索，再选择一个能够合理容纳这些事迹的生卒年，作为考察孟子生平和思想的时间坐标。

从《孟子》书中，我们可推考出他首次出仕是在邹国。《孟子》书中记载鲁平公的宠臣臧仓曾经诽谤孟子厚葬母亲，超过安葬先死的父亲，有违礼制。孟子的弟子乐正子对鲁平公说，

---

❶《孟子·梁惠王上》1章。
❷《孟子·梁惠王上》5章。
❸ 参见杨宽《战国史》附录三《战国大事年表》，上海，上海人民出版社，1983。第568页—第570页。
❹《孟子·梁惠王上》6章。

❶ *Mencius*, "King Hui of Liang," Ⅰ 1.
❷ *Mencius*, "King Hui of Liang," Ⅰ 5.
❸ See Yang Kuan, *History of the Warring States*, appendix 3, "Chronology of Major Events During the Warring States Period" (Shanghai: Shanghai People's Press, 1983), pp. 568-570.
❹ *Mencius*, "King Hui of Liang," Ⅰ 6.

his father according to the rites appropriate for a literatus; but when his mother died, Mencius had already become a grandee, and so of course employed the rites appropriate to a grandee to bury his mother❶. Mencius' mother died while he was travelling in the state of Qi, therefore when he buried his father he had attained to the status of a scholar, and had disciples who followed him.

Here it would be appropriate to mention Mencius' mother.

In the book of *Mencius* he never mentions his own father, but he had deep feelings for his mother. He sent his mother back for burial to Lu in a coffin. While en route to Qi, his disciple stated with worry, "A little while ago I was indebted to you master for esteeming me highly by letting me take care of the coffin. I your disciple feels that the coffin used to bury your mother is a little too expensive." Mencius answered "In ancient times, there were no requirements as to size for coffins; it was only more recently that inner coffins were required to be seven inches thick, and outer coffins commensurate with it. Actually, everyone from the Son of Heaven to the common folk are very meticulous when it comes to coffins. This is not only for the sake of aesthetics, but to express the sentiments of filial sons as well. If it were only due to ritual constraints that the finest wood could not be obtained, this of course would be regrettable. Yet if one could purchase the finest wood but had no money to spend, this would likewise be regrettable. If one could purchase the best wood and could also afford to do so, this is the way of the ancients, so why cannot I act this way? How much more so that the body of a close relative is at least kept from contact with the mud and that a filial son ease his mind? I have heard that a gentleman does not stint on using any fine thing that is available in the world to bury his father or mother!" ❷Later persons fabricated the name of Mencius' mother to be Lady Zhang or Lady Li, the name of his father to be Mengsun Ji, with a style name of Gongyi, and the like; none of these names are proven. On the contrary, five extremely moving stories date from the Western Han period which have profoundly impacted the creation of educational tradition of the Chinese as well as women's culture. Whether or not these stories are based on historical events is not important because they truly impacted later views on history.

The first one is the story of Mencius' mother breaking the strings of her loom, seen in the Western Han work by Han Ying, *The Unofficial Commentary*

孟子父亲死的时候，孟子还是个士，只能用士的礼制来安葬父亲，而他母亲死的时候，孟子已经是个大夫了，当然用大夫的礼制来安葬母亲了❶。孟子的母亲是在他游历齐国时死的，因此，他在邹葬父时已经有了士的身份，而且有了随从的弟子。

这里顺便说一下孟子的母亲。

《孟子》书中，孟子从未说到过自己的父亲，倒是对母亲感情极深。他将母亲的灵柩从齐国送回鲁国安葬，在返至齐国的路上，弟子充虞说："前些时承蒙老师看得起我，让我办理老夫人的棺椁。当时很忙，没敢请教，今天希望能得到您的赐教。弟子觉得，您葬母亲用的棺木似乎太贵重了。"孟子回答说："上古的时候，人们对棺椁的尺寸并没有规定，到了中古才规定棺木厚七寸，外椁的厚度与之相称。其实从天子到平民百姓，对棺木都很讲究，这不仅是为了美观，而是要尽一尽孝子的心意。如果只是因为礼制的限制而不能取用上等的木料，这当然有遗憾；而能够取用上等的木料，却没有钱买，同样有遗憾。既能取用上等的木料，又能买得起，古人都能这样做，我为什么不能呢？何况仅仅让亲人的尸体不与泥土相沾，就能让孝子安心了吗？我曾经听人说：君子从不吝惜用天下人所能享用的一切东西来安葬父母！"❷后世的人们伪造孟子的母亲叫仇氏或李氏，父亲叫孟孙激，字公宜等等，皆不足为凭。倒是西汉人讲述的五个极为生动的故事，对中国人的教育传统以及女性文化产生了深刻的影响。这些故事是否真实的历史事件已不重要，因为它们已经具有真实的历史影响。

一是孟母断机的故事，见于西汉韩婴的《韩诗外传》。孟

---

❶《孟子·梁惠王下》16章。
❷《孟子·公孙丑下》7章。

❶ *Mencius,* "King Hui of Liang," Ⅱ16.
❷ *Mencius,* "Gongsun Chou," Ⅱ7.

of Han on the Book of Poetry. When Mencius was young, one time he suddenly quit memorizing passages, then after a while resumed memorizing. At that time Mencius' mother was weaving at her loom. She called him over and asked him, "Why did you stop?" Mencius answered, "I forgot a word, then later I remembered it." Mencius' mother picked up her clothing scissors and cut up the cloth that she had labored so hard to weave. This served to warn Mencius that he should not interrupt whatever he was laboring over. Ever afterwards, Mencius never again forgot any words❶.

The second one is the story of the neighboring slaughter house, also found in the *The Unofficial Commentary of Han on the Book of Poetry*. When Mencius was young, the neighbor to the east operated a slaughter house. Mencius asked his mother, "Why is the neighbor slaughtering pigs?" Mencius' mother responded, "To provide food for you!" After she finished speaking, she felt guilty and was at a loss for words. After reflecting a moment, she thought to herself, "When I was carrying him, I would not sit in a seat that was not straight, and would not eat meat that was not cut properly, this was part of educating him while still in the womb. Now he has some knowledge yet I deceive him, isn't this a case of not being sincere?" Thereupon, she went to the neighbor and bought some pork to cook for him ❷.

The third story is about Mencius' mother moving three times, as seen in the *Biographies of Virtuous Women* of the Western Han scholar Liu Xiang. When Mencius was young, his house was near to a cemetery, so Mencius naturally liked to imitate how people buried the dead and how they cried in mourning for them. Mencius' mother said, "This is no place for my son to live;" so she moved to a market place. But Mencius liked to imitate sellers hawking their wares. So Mencius' mother once again moved her household, this time to the vicinity of a school. Mencius liked to imitate the rituals he observed there of bowing with clasped hands. Mencius' mother said, "This then is the place where my son should live." ❸

The fourth is the story of Mencius wishing to divorce his wife, as seen in *The Unofficial Commentary of Han on the Book of Poetry*. Once when Mencius' wife was sitting by herself, she sat with her legs apart in a relaxed manner looking around. When Mencius entered the house and saw her, he ran off to tell his mother, saying, "My wife is not concerned with ritual propriety, I want to divorce her." Mencius' mom said, "Why is this?" Mencius replied, "She sits with her legs apart." Mencius' mother said, "How do you know?" Mencius answered, "I personally saw her doing it." Mencius' mother said, "This means that you lack ritual propriety, not your wife. Doesn't it say in the

子幼时，有一次背书当中突然停下来，过了一会儿又背。孟母正在织布，便叫孟子来问道："为什么停了下来？"孟子说："忘了词，后来又想起来了。"孟母拿起割布刀将自己辛辛苦苦织好的布划裂，以此警诫孟子不能中断自己的努力。从此孟子再也不忘词了❶。

二是东邻杀豚的故事，见于《韩诗外传》。孟子幼时，东面的邻居家里杀猪。孟子问母亲："他家杀猪干什么？"孟母说："要给你吃呀！"说完便后悔失言。自思道："我怀孕期间，坐席不正则不坐，肉切得不方也不吃，对孟子进行胎教。现在他有了智识，我反而欺骗他，这不是教他不诚实吗？"于是到邻家买了肉回来煮给孟子吃❷。

三是孟母三迁的故事，见于西汉刘向《列女传》。孟子幼时，家住在墓地附近，孟子便喜欢模仿人们下葬、哭拜之事。孟母说："这不是我儿子应该住的地方。"便迁至市场。可孟子又喜欢模仿商人叫卖东西。孟母又将家迁到学校附近，这下孟子喜欢模仿揖让行礼之事了，孟母说："这才是我儿子该住的地方啊！"❸

四是孟子去妻的故事，见于《韩诗外传》。孟子的妻子独处时，便伸开双腿随便放松地坐着。孟子进内房时看见了，跑去告诉母亲说："妻子不讲究礼仪，我要把她休弃了。"孟母问："为什么？"孟子回答说："她伸着腿坐。"孟母问："你怎么知道的？"孟子说："我亲眼见到的。"孟母说："这就是你无礼

---

❶ 许维遹《韩诗外传集释》卷九第一章，北京，中华书局，1980，第306页。
❷《韩诗外传集释》卷九第一章，第306页。
❸ 西汉刘向《列女传》卷一"邹孟轲母"，沈阳，辽宁教育出版社，1998，第7页。

❶ Xu Weiyu, *Collected Explanations on the Unofficial Commentary of Han on the Book of Poetry* (Beijing: Zhonghua Book Company, 1980), p. 306.
❷ *Collected Explanations on the Unofficial Commentary of Han on the Book of Poetry*, vol. 9.1, p.306.
❸ Liu Xiang, *Biographies of Virtuous Women*, chapter 1, "The Mother of Meng Ke of Zou" (Shengyang: Liaoning Education Press, 1998), p. 7.

Ritual Ceremonies that 'When one enters a gate, one must inquire whether anyone is inside, when one climbs up to a hall, one must first sound a greeting, and when one first enters a woman's quarters, one must first lower one's eyes'? This means that one should not come upon others when they are unaware. Now you have entered your wife's private quarters, and did not call out and sound a greeting, this let somebody who was relaxing alone in private suddenly be seen by another, this is precisely why it is you who are lacking in ritual propriety, not your wife." Thereupon Mencius reproached himself and no longer brought up the matter of divorcing his wife. ❶

The fifth is the story of Mencius taking office in the state of Qi as seen in the *Biographies of Virtuous Women*. Once when Mencius was in Qi he looked worried, and leaned on a pillar on the porch moaning and groaning. Mencius' mom asked him to tell her about it. Mencius said, "I have heard that a gentleman depends on his own personal abilities to be an official, and does not casually accept rewards, does not seek glory or high salary. If a feudal prince does not want to listen to one's opinion, then one should not go to explain himself; if a feudal prince does not accept what one says even after hearing it, then one should not attend court. Now my ambitions cannot be realized in Qi, and when I see you I see an aged mother, so I am worried." When Mencius' mother heard this, she said, "The obligations of we women are only to worry about daily cooking chores, to take care of our fathers and mothers-in-law, to sew and mend the clothing worn by the members of the household, and to do our duties the best we can. I have never thought of something beyond my duties, and have never made my own decisions; rather, I only know about being obedient. Before I was married off I obeyed my parents; after being married off I obeyed my husband; after my husband died I obeyed my son. All this for me is ritual propriety. You now have become an adult, but I have turned old. You should only pay attention to acting according to correct principles, and I should only pay attention to act according to my own obligations." ❷

Becoming an adult, getting married, and taking office are the three most important stages in the lives of gentlemen in ancient times, and these three stages for Mencius were inseparable from the teachings of his mother.

The first time Mencius set out to travel among the feudal states he went to Qi, during the 23rd year of King Wei of Qi (approximately 335 B.C.). At this time Mencius was about 50 years old. Qi was a great state in the eastern part of China. During the Spring and Autumn Period, rites were neglected and music had fallen into disuse, hegemonic rulers arose on all sides, and feudal princes swallowed up each other. Grandees from aristocratic clans in the feudal states

了，不是你妻子无礼。《礼仪》上不是说吗：'进门时，要问问里面有没有人；登堂时，要先打招呼；进闺房时，眼光要向下看。'这是说不要乘人不备。现在你进入夫妇私密之处，进房不出声打招呼，让人家独处随便的样子突然被人看见，这恰恰是你无礼，不是你妻子无礼啊！"于是孟子自我责备起来，不敢提休妻的事了。❶

五是孟子仕齐的故事，见于《列女传》。孟子在齐国的时候，面有忧色，在家靠着廊柱，长吁短叹。孟母问他原委，孟子说："我听说，君子凭自身的能力做官，不随便接受赏赐，不贪图荣华厚禄。诸侯不听自己的意见就不去说，听了不采纳就不去上朝。现在我的志向不能在齐国实现，回头看看您年事又高，所以我内心忧虑啊！"孟母听了，说："我们妇道人家的规矩是只管做好每天的饭菜，侍奉好公婆，浆洗缝补好家里的衣服，认真尽自己的本份，从没有非分之想，从不会自作主张，只知道顺从。未嫁出去时听从父母，嫁出去听从丈夫，丈夫死了听从儿子，这就是礼啊！现在你已经成人了，而我却老了。你应该只管按照你的道理去做事，我也只管按照我的规矩去做事罢了。"❷

成人、婚姻和出仕，是古代君子一生中最重要的三个环节，而孟子这三个环节与伟大的母教是分不开的。

孟子首次出游的诸侯国是齐国，大约在齐威王二十三年（约公元前335年）前后，此时孟子已是50岁左右了。齐国是东方大国。春秋时代，礼崩乐坏，霸主崛起，诸侯兼并。诸侯国内贵族大夫掌控政治，弑君弑父的情况不断发生。因此周天子

---

❶《韩诗外传集释》卷九第十七章，第322页。
❷《列女传》卷一"邹孟轲母"，第8页。

❶ *Collected Explanations on the Unofficial Commentary of Han on the Book of Poetry*, vol. 9.17, p. 322.
❷ Liu Xiang, *Biographies of Virtuous Women*, chapter 1, "The Mother of Meng Ke of Zou," p. 8.

held political power, regicide and patricide occurred one after the other. The king of Zhou had fallen from his position as the commonly recognized king to becoming a tool coerced by the hegemonic overload. By the age of the Warring States, the position of the Son of Heaven had fallen from bad to worse. Previous to this, in the year 403 B.C., the king of Zhou recognized the fact that the state of Jin had been divided by the grandees into the three smaller states of Zhao, Wei and Han; afterwards, Tian He, the prime minister of Qi, had Duke Kang of Qi removed to the seashore. In 386 B.C. the king of Zhou once again recognized him as the Lord of Qi. In 374 B.C., the son of Tian He Tian Wu, who was Duke Huan of Qi, killed the sons and grandsons of Duke Kang of Qi and proclaimed himself as the lord, This then is the famous story from Warring States history of the Tian family replacing the Qi nobility.King Wei of Qi was precisely the son of Duke Huan of Qi. When he first ascended the throne he spent his days drinking and did not inquire after state affairs. A Qi court jester, the debater Chunyu Kun, presented a riddle for him, "A large bird lived in Qi, which flew to the household of a great prince. For three years it neither flew nor cawed. Do you know what it wanted?" King Wei of Qi answered, "This bird did not fly but then changed; with one flight it soared to heaven. It did not caw, but then changed; with one caw it startled men." After speaking he roused himself to action, and devoted himself to governing. He defeated the feudal princes and invigorated the state of Qi. In *Mencius* there is no mention of any dialogue between Mencius and King Wei of Qi; it only records that when he departed, he rejected a rich present of money. He explained to his disciples the reason for rejecting the gift was that he had not served in office in Qi[1] . While still in Qi he said to his disciples, "I did not serve in office, nor did I have the duty of offering words of counsel." [2] It seems to indicate that he was not highly regarded by King Wei.

However, this trip to Qi proved to be highly beneficial to the development of Mencius' thinking and intellect. Duke Huan of Qi had built an academy outside the gate of Ji in the capital of Linzi, established the fame of his grandees, and recruited worthy people from around the state and treated them with great esteem and favor. Later generations called it Jixia or the Jixia Academy. King Wei and King Xuan both also delighted in wandering scholars who were well-versed in literature, presenting them with spacious quarters, honoring them with appointment as grandees with no obligation to serve in office. They merely had to deliberate over state affairs and pursue learning. At its height, over one thousand of these figures were in residence[3] . Therefore, although when Mencius was in Qi during the reign of King Wei he did not

已从天下共主沦为霸主们要挟的工具。到了战国时，天子的地位更是江河日下。先是在公元前403年，周天子承认晋国被大夫们分成赵、魏、韩三国；后来齐国的相国田和将齐康公迁居到海上。公元前386年，周天子又承认他为齐侯。公元前374年，田和之子齐桓公田午杀了齐康公的子孙自立为侯，这便是战国史上著名的田氏代齐事件。齐威王正是齐桓公的儿子，他即位之初整天饮酒，不问国事。齐国的小丑辩士淳于髡出了个谜语让他猜："齐国有大鸟，飞到大王家。三年不飞又不鸣，您可知它要干嘛？"齐威王答道："此鸟不飞则已，一飞冲天；不鸣则已，一鸣惊人。"说完便振奋精神，励精图治，打败诸侯，振兴了齐国。《孟子》书中没有孟子与齐威王的对话，只是记载他离开齐国时，拒绝了威王馈赠他的一笔丰厚的礼金。他对弟子解释拒绝的理由是在齐国并没有做官❶。在齐国时，他还曾对弟子说过"我没有官职，我也就没有进言的责任"这样的话❷。看来他并没有得到齐威王的重视。

不过，这次游历齐国对孟子的思想学术大有裨益。齐桓公在齐国首都临淄的稷门之外建构了一座学宫，设立大夫的名号，招致天下贤人，尊宠优待。后人称之为稷下或稷下学宫。齐威王、齐宣王又非常喜欢文学游说之士，赐给他们宽敞的府第，尊为上大夫，不担任具体的官职，只议论国事，探讨学问，兴盛的时候达到上千人❸。所以孟子在齐威王时虽然没有担任官职，但他是稷下先生，享受大夫的待遇。在孟子来到齐国以前，

❶《孟子·公孙丑下》3章。
❷《孟子·公孙丑下》5章。
❸《史记·田敬仲完世家》，北京，中华书局，1959。

❶ *Mencius*, "Gongsun Chou," Ⅱ3.
❷ *Mencius*, "Gongsun Chou," Ⅱ5.
❸ *Historian's Records*, "Hereditary House of Tian Jingzhong" (Beijing: Zhonghua Book Company, 1959).

serve in office, still he was a master in residence at Jixia, enjoying the treatment of being accorded a grandee. Before Mencius arrived at Qi, scholars of Taoist persuasion or scholars of both Confucian and Mohist leanings such as Chunyu Kun, Peng Meng, Tian Pian, Shen Dao, Song Xing, Yin Wen, Er Yue, and Gaozi had all arrived at the Jixia Academy. The *Mencius* records dialogues between Mencius and Chunyu Kun and Song Xing. Mencius' teachings on the mind and cultivating the nature were profoundly influenced by Song Xing et al. Yet Mencius' debate with Gaozi regarding human nature is the most brilliant component of Mencian thought. Mencius took upon himself the mission of defending Confucianism and of attacking the dual heresies of Taoism and Mohism. His talent for powerful eloquence should be related to his experiences at Jixia. The establishment of an academy in Qi promoted the development and veneration of the scholar class. Mencius' travels amid the various states, although failing to fulfill his mission, and spiritually he remained in an impoverished condition, still in terms of affecting his life with added resources, his journeys brought rich results. In Mencius there is no record of his being in difficulties❶. It is not like when Confucius was besieged, threatened with murder, or when he was without food supplies between Chen and Cai, or when he was described by someone as down and out, wandering around like a lost dog. Disciple Peng Geng once asked Mencius, "Do you regard as excessive the fact that several scores of chariots follow you in retinue, several hundreds of men accompany you, and you feast from one state to the next?" Mencius responded, "If doing something was not commensurate with morality, then accepting even one basket of food would be wrong. If something were in accordance with morality, similar to Shun accepting the entire world from the hand of Yao, it would not be considered excessive. Do you still find all this excessive?" ❷ His attitude towards feudal princes and the nobility was rather arrogant. He told his disciples, "When speaking with feudal princes, one must look down on them, do not regard them as being remote and above all things. Their palaces are lofty and capacious, but if I attained my own ambitions, I would be quite different. Their viands may fill the feast mats with delicacies, and wives and concubines may number in the hundreds, but if I attained my own ambitions I would be quite different. They drink and make merry all day long, hunting and sporting, with chariots in the thousands; but if I attained my own ambitions, I would be quite different. I do not pursue anything of what they like; my ideals are in accord with rites of

淳于髡、彭蒙、田骈、慎到、宋钘、尹文、儿说、告子这些带
有道家、名家的学术色彩，或兼有儒家、墨家思想的学者都来
到了稷下学宫。《孟子》书中载有孟子与淳于髡、宋钘的对话。
孟子关于心性修养的学说受到宋钘等人的深刻影响，而孟子与
告子关于人性的辩论，是孟子思想中最为精采的部分。孟子以
捍卫儒学，排斥道家和墨家两大异端为己任，其雄辩的才华应
当与他游历稷下有关。齐国稷下学宫的设立，推动了战国时期
养士、尊士的风气。孟子周游各国，虽说都没能实现自己的抱
负，精神上一直处于困乏的状态，但生活方面的资源却颇为丰
厚。我们在《孟子》书中没有看到孟子有困乏窘迫之时❶，不
像孔子有被人包围、追杀，或绝粮于陈、蔡之间，或被人形容
为丧家之狗的落魄经历。弟子彭更曾经问孟子："几十辆车跟
着您，几百号人随着您，从一个国家吃到另一个国家，你不觉
得过分吗？"孟子却说："如果这样做不合乎道理，就是一篮
子饭食也不能接受；如果合乎道理的话，像舜那样从尧的手上
接收了整个天下，也不为过分，你还觉得过分吗？"❷他对诸
侯、贵族的态度也比较倨傲。他对弟子们说："和诸侯们说话，
要藐视他，不要将他看成高高在上的人。他的宫殿又高又宽，
我如果得志才不稀罕这样；他的佳肴满席杂陈，妻妾成群上百，
我如果得志才不稀罕这样；他们成天饮酒作乐，驰骋游猎，千
乘相拥，我如果得志才不稀罕这样。他们喜欢的，都不是我所

---

❶ 只有东汉人应劭的《风俗通义·穷通篇》中说孟子曾受困于邹、薛之间，没有粮食吃。但
从《孟子》书中可见其在邹见过邹穆公，在薛又接受过邑主人的馈赠，因此东汉人的说法
不可信。

❷《孟子·滕文公下》4章。

❶ But in the "Failure and Success" chapter of the *Comprehensive Deliberations on Customs* of the
Eastern Han scholar Ying Shao, it mentions that Mencius was in distress between Zou and Xue
with nothing to eat. But, from Mencius we know that he saw Duke Mu of Zou, and while in Xue
he received a gift from a local mayor. Therefore, the stories from Eastern Han men are not
reliable.

❷ *Mencius*, "Duke Wen of Teng," Ⅱ 4.

the ancients, so why should I be afraid of them?" ❶ This is the mental attitude of one wandering scholar who was venerated by each state and treated royally during the Warring States Period.

Approximately during the 34th year of the reign of King Wei of Qi (about 323 B.C.), King Yan of Song wanted to implement a humane government, so Mencius set forth with glee. His disciple Wanzhang asked him doubtfully, saying, "What would happened if a tiny state like Song were to implement an administration along the lines of the kingly way and provoked the ire of large states such as Qi or Chu, what should it do?" Mencius replied confidently, "All that is necessary is that it implements an administration based on the royal way and all within the four seas would look up to it in longing; athough Qi and Chu are large, what would there be to fear?" ❷ Of course, Mencius was unable to achieve his ambitions in Song; he urged the grandee Dai Yingzhi to reduce taxes, and to void the tariff toll in order to attract more people of the state. Dai Yingzhi's answered, saying that he would first reduce a part, then he would see what would happened the following year. An angry Mencius satirized him saying, "Someone stole chickens from his neighbor every day; another person admonished him that this was not the behavior of a gentleman. The first then responded, saying fine, he would first reduce his stealing, and merely steal one chicken per month; he would stop stealing the following year." ❸ He felt that worthies in the employ of the king of Song were too few, and the government would not make any improvements; therefore he accepted a gift of money and then returned to his homeland of the state of Zou.

Not long afterwards, Duke Ping of Lu came to power and wanted to employ Mencius' disciple Yuezheng Ke in his service. After Mencius heard about this he was so delighted that he could not sleep ❹; he then travelled to the state of Lu. But the favorite minister of the duke Zang Cang slandered him, spreading malicious rumors about him. So the duke lost all interest in visiting Mencius. At this time, Duke Ding of Teng died, and Duke Wen of Teng inherited his position; he sent a delegate to inquire about the proper burial rituals from Mencius. So Mencius went to the state of Teng where Duke Wen of Teng inquired several times about various political matters from Mencius. ❺ Even though Duke Wen of Teng was the state leader who most venerated Mencius, Teng was a smaller state than Zou, and the duke was a very timid and cowardly leader, and quite sickly. It was impossible for Mencius to accomplish anything in this state. Therefore, the 70-year-old Mencius left again, and went

追求的，我的理想都符合古人的礼制，我为什么要怕他们？"❶
这是战国时代游士受到各国尊宠礼遇而造成的精神状态。

大概在齐威王三十四年前后（约公元前323年），宋王偃想
要推行仁政，孟子欣然前往。弟子万章有些疑惑地问他："像
宋国这样的小国要推行王道政治，如果招惹齐、楚等大国的讨
厌该怎么办？"孟子自信地说："只要推行王道政治，四海之
内都会翘首以盼，齐楚虽大，有什么可怕的？"❷当然，孟子
在宋国也未能得志，他劝宋国大夫戴盈之减轻税收，免除关税，
吸引民众。戴盈之回答说先减一部分，明年再看吧！气得孟子
讥讽他说："有个人天天偷他邻居的鸡，有人告诫他这不是君
子做的事，他却说，好吧，我先少偷一些，一个月偷一只，明
年不再偷了。"❸他感到宋王周围的贤人太少，政治不会有所
改善，于是接受了宋王馈赠的礼金后回到了家乡邹国。

不久，鲁平公即位，想要起用孟子的弟子乐正克。孟子听
说之后，高兴得睡不着觉❹，便来到了鲁国。但是平公的宠臣
臧仓进谗言，说了孟子的坏话，鲁平公就打消了拜访孟子的念
头。这时，滕定公薨，滕文公嗣位，让人来向孟子请教丧礼。
接着孟子到了滕国，滕文公多次向他咨询政治。❺尽管滕文公
是最尊重孟子的国君，但滕国是一个比邹国还要小的国家，滕
文公也是个瞻前顾后，十分懦弱甚至多病的人，孟子在这里也
无法大有作为，于是70岁左右的孟子又去魏国这样的大国寻找

❶《孟子·尽心下》34章。
❷《孟子·滕文公下》5章。
❸《孟子·滕文公下》8章。
❹《孟子·告子下》13章。
❺《孟子·滕文公上》2章、3章。

❶ Mencius, "Jinxin," Ⅱ 34.
❷ Mencius, "Duke Wen of Teng," Ⅱ 5.
❸ Mencius, "Duke Wen of Teng," Ⅱ 8.
❹ Mencius, "Gaozi," Ⅱ 13.
❺ Mencius, "Duke Wen of Teng," Ⅰ 2, 3.

to the large state of Wei to seek for an opportunity ❶. At this time, King Hui of Liang, who ruled Wei, was already advanced in years and facing death. Wei was frequently defeated by Qi, Qin, and Chu, and this once strong stage had become completely discredited; on top of this the heir to the throne was of poor stuff. Mencius came at a bad time.

In 320 B.C., King Wei of Qi passed away, the next year King Xuan of Qi assumed the throne, and Mencius once again went to Qi and was appointed to be a high official. Approximately the third year of the reign of King Xuan (318 B.C.), Duke Wen of Teng died, and Mencius represented Qi at the state funeral in Teng ❷. During the 5th year of the reign of King Xuan (about 315 B.C.), a rebellion broke out in the state of Yan. The great minister of Qi, Shen Tong, privately inquired of Mencius whether it was permissible to invade Yan; Mencius said that it was ❸. After Qi captured the capital of Yan, King Xuan of Qi once again asked Mencius whether it was permissible to absorb the state of Yan; Mencius replied that if he were to absorb Yan, the people of Yan would be overjoyed, so go ahead and absorb it. At this time, the feudal princes plotted to combine forces and invade Qi to restore Yan. King Xuan asked Mencius once again; Mencius said, "The lord of the state of Yan tyrannizes the people; the people of the state think that you great king came to save them from calamity, so they brought drink and food to welcome your troops. But you instead kill their fathers and brothers, and plunder their sons and younger brothers, destroy their ancestral temples, and pillage their possessions. This is such cruel behavior. All of the people in the world originally feared the powerful state of Qi, and now Qi has grown even larger, but it is just as tyrannical and amoral as ever. Naturally it will cause unease among the feudal princes and bring about warfare. Please immediately order the release of prisoners, return your plunder, and consult with the people of Yan about a new lord, then you should pull back your troops." ❹King Xuan would not listen, so naturally the people of Yan rose up in rebellion, and the Qi troops were forced to retreat. King Xuan said, "I treated Mencius shamefully." A greatly disappointed Mencius proposed to return home on the basis of old age. Even though King Xuan personally visited him to detain him, and sent underlings to inform Mencius that the king would build a dwelling, and lavishly support Mencius and his disciples, Mencius still refused him.

机会❶。此时的梁惠王已经老暮垂死，魏国屡被齐、秦、楚击败，强大的魏国威风扫地，加之嗣君资质不佳，孟子来得不是时候。

公元前320年，齐威王去世，次年齐宣王即位，孟子再次来到齐国并被宣王尊聘为卿。大约在宣王三年（公元前318年）左右，滕文公薨，孟子代表齐国去滕国吊丧❷。宣王五年（约公元前315年）燕国发生内乱，齐国大臣沈同私下询问孟子可否讨伐燕国，孟子说可以❸。齐攻下燕国都城后，齐宣王又问孟子可否吞并燕国，孟子说如果您吞并燕国，燕国的老百姓十分高兴，那就吞并吧。这时，诸侯们谋求联合伐齐，恢复燕国，宣王再问孟子，孟子说："燕国君主残虐人民，燕国百姓以为大王您是来拯救他们于水火之中的，所以带着酒食来迎接您的军队。可是您却杀害他们的父兄，掳掠他们的子弟，毁坏他们的宗庙，抢劫他们的文物。这是何等的暴行！天下人本来就害怕强大的齐国，现在齐国的土地扩大了，还是如此的残暴无道，自然会引起诸侯们的不安，招致了战争。请您赶快下令释放俘虏，归还文物，与燕人商量立个新君，然后撤兵。"❹宣王不听，燕人果然奋起反抗，齐军被迫撤回。宣王说"我愧对孟子！"大失所望的孟子提出告老回乡，尽管宣王亲自来挽留他，又托人向孟子表示：想为孟子建造宫室，厚养孟子和他的弟子。还是被孟子拒绝了。

❶《史记·魏世家》载孟子与稷下大夫邹衍、淳于髡都去了魏国。
❷《孟子·公孙丑下》6章。
❸《孟子·公孙丑下》8章。
❹《孟子·梁惠王下》10章、11章。

❶ The "Hereditary House of Wei," *Historian's Records*, records that Mencius went to Wei with the grandees from Jixia Zou Yan and Chunyu Kun.
❷ *Mencius*, "Gongsun Chou," Ⅱ 6.
❸ *Mencius*, "Gongsun Chou," Ⅱ 8.
❹ *Mencius*, "King Hui of Liang," Ⅱ 10,11.

Looking at the entirety of Mencius' life, his time in Qi during his travels among the various states was the longest. Qi was also the strongest of all the states which he visited. His aspirations were very great, and naturally sought out the larger stage for his activities. Therefore, the second time that he left Qi he was hopeless. While departing from Qi, he stayed for three nights in the Qi county of Zhou, but he did not wait for the envoy dispatched by King Xuan to call him back❶. Mencius then directly departed the state and returned home. A disciple Chong Yu asked him en route back home, "You master do not seem too happy, but you all along have guided us by the words 'A gentleman never complains about Heaven, nor does he blame others.' " At this time, Mencius was at the end of his heroic task, and so said with emotion❷,

At that time and at this time, throughout history every five hundred years, a king will appear and also some important sages and worthies. It has been more than 700 years since the Zhou Dynasty was founded. As far as the number of years go, it has already been five hundred; as for the trend of the times, it is precisely the time that this king and these sages and worthies should appear. Heaven above most likely does not want to grant peace to the world below! If we want peace in the world below, in today's world nobody can achieve it, but I! If I did not come out then who would come out? So what is there to be unhappy about?

After returning home, he never went out again to serve in office, but composed his book with his disciple Wanzhang and others and lectured until his death of old age. The concluding words of the book *Mencius* are what Mencius said that was of profound significance. It records❸,

From Yao and Shun up to Tang of Shang it was five hundred plus years; Yu the Great and Gaoyao personally saw Yao and Shun and learned the Great Way. Tang of Shang learned the Way after hearing about it. From Tang of Shang up to King Wen of Zhou was also five hundred plus years. Yi Yin and Lai Zhu personally saw Tang of Shang and learned the Great Way. King Wen of Zhou learned the Great Way after hearing about it. From King Wen of Zhou until Confucius was more than five hundred years; Taigong Wang and Sanyi Sheng personally saw King Wen of Zhou and learned the Great Way. Confucius learned the Great Way after hearing it. From Confucius to the present day is only one hundred plus years. Being so near to the time of the

纵观孟子的一生，在齐国的游历时间最久。齐国也是他游历的国家中最为强大的。他的抱负很大，自然要寻求更为广阔的天地。所以第二次离开齐国时，他确实有些绝望。离开国都后，他特地在昼这个地方住了三个晚上，但没有等到宣王派来召回他的使者❶。孟子这才出境回乡。弟子充虞在途中问他："老师您看起来不太高兴。可是您从前教导我说：'君子是从不抱怨上天，也不责怪别人的'。"孟子此时英雄末路，不禁感叹道❷：

> 彼一时，此一时啊！历史上每过五百年一定会有王者兴起，还要出现一些重要的圣贤人物。从周代以来，已经有七百多年了，论年数，已过了五百年；论时势，正是这些王者圣贤出现的时候。上天大概是不想让天下太平了啊！如果想让天下太平，当今之世，舍我其谁？我不出来还有谁能出来呢？我有什么不快乐的呢？

回乡之后，他再也没有出仕，与弟子万章等人著书立说，直至终老。《孟子》一书的结束语是孟子说的一段意味深长的话❸：

> 从尧舜到商汤，经历了五百多年，大禹、皋陶是亲身见到尧、舜而知晓大道的；商汤是听说后知晓大道的。从商汤到周文王，也经历了五百多年，伊尹、莱朱是亲身见到商汤而知晓大道的；周文王是听说后知晓大道的。从周文王到孔子，又经历了五百多年，太公望、散宜生是亲身见到周文王而知晓大道的，孔子是听说后知晓大

❶《孟子·公孙丑下》12章。
❷《孟子·公孙丑下》13章。
❸《孟子·尽心下》38章。

❶ *Mencius*, "Gongsun Chou," II 12.
❷ *Mencius*, "Gongsun Chou," II 13.
❸ *Mencius*, "Jinxin," II 38.

sages, and being so near to the homeland of the sages, it is surprising that no one has succeeded them. It is probable that no one will ever succeed them!"

The tradition of transmission of the Great Way through Yao, Shun, Yu, Tang, King Wen, King Wu, the Duke of Zhou was first put forth by Confucius. In Chinese philosophic thought this transmission was called the "legitimate succession." In the last chapter of the *Analects*, "Yao yue," Confucius talked of the words spoken by Yao when he yielded the throne to Shun and when Shun yielded the throne to Yu, as well as the political speeches of Tang of Shang and King Wu of Zhou; finally he expounded on his own political ideals. Although Confucius self-consciously felt that the legitimate succession after the time of King Wen fell upon his own shoulders, he was highly disappointed and depressed. He sighed saying, "I have aged too severely, and for a long time now I have not dreamed of the Duke of Zhou." ❶Mencius was the very one to stride out and self-consciously succeed Confucius in shouldering the burden of expounding this legitimate succession. In this regard, he surpassed Confucius' disciples. Sima Qian said, "After Mencius mastered the knowledge of the Great Way, he went to see the Kings of Qi and Liang, but they did not agree with Mencius' doctrine, thinking that his theories were too impractical and unrealistic. At that time the state of Qin relied on Shang Yang and his teachings about enriching the state and strengthening the army. The states of Wei and Chu, one after the other, relied on Wu Qi to conquer or weaken enemy states. Kings Wei and Xuan of Qi relied on men such as Sunzi and Tian Ji, which caused the feudal princes to face east and to submit to Qi. The world at this time was pursuing diplomatic policies of either allying with or against Qin; men skilled in warfare were regarded as sages and worthies. But Mencius boldly proclaimed the moral and political teachings of Yao and Shun, Xia, Shang, and Zhou; so those rulers whom he was trying to persuade would not agree with him." ❷Such men as Shang Yang, Wu Qi, Sunzi, and Tian Ji were advocates of the rule of law, opposed traditional legalism and promoted conspiracies, and were skilled in the strategies of utilizing armies. Warring States military advisors ridiculed the moral teachings of the Confucians as being only fit to refine the moral nature and cultivate the body, but useless as techniques for making any military or political gains ❸. Therefore, the great Confucian master of the late Warring States Period Xunzi abandoned Confucian teachings based on the central core morality of humaneness and righteousness and constructed a new type of theory based on ritual teachings in order to accommodate the coming educational system of a unified nation. He

道的。从孔子到当今，只有一百多年，离圣人生活的时代如此短暂，距圣人的家乡如此接近，竟然没有继承他的人啊！大概永远也没有继承他的人了！

尧、舜、禹、汤、文王、武王、周公这个大道流行的传统，最早是孔子提出来的，中国哲学中称之为"道统"。《论语》最后一篇《尧曰》中，孔子讲了尧传位给舜，舜传位给禹时讲的话以及商汤和周武王的政治宣言，最后阐明了孔子自己的政治理想。孔子虽然自觉地认为周文王以后的道统担当在他的身上，但也有强烈的失落与焦虑感，叹息道："我衰老得太厉害了，好长时间没有再梦见周公了！" ❶ 孟子恰恰是继孔子之后自觉地站出来承担并发明了这个道统的人，在这一点上，他超过了孔子的弟子们。司马迁说："孟子通晓了大道之后，去见齐王、梁王，但他们都不赞同孟子的道理，认为他的学说过于迂阔，不切实际。当时秦国重用商鞅，国富兵强；魏国、楚国先后重用吴起，战胜并削弱了敌国；齐威王和宣王重用孙子、田忌这样的人，使得诸侯面朝东方，顺服了齐国。这时的天下都在追求连横合纵的外交战略，以能打仗的人为圣贤，可是孟子大谈尧、舜和夏、商、周的道德和政治，所以和他游说的国君不合拍啊！" ❷ 商鞅、吴起、孙子、田忌这些人都是主张法治、反对传统的法家或是崇尚阴谋、精于战略的兵家，战国时的谋士们讥讽儒家的仁义道德只能修身养性，决非进取之术❸。战国晚期的儒家大师荀子便放弃了以仁义为核心的儒学，建构了一种新的礼教学说，以适应即将到来的统一国家的政教制度。他

---

❶《论语·述而第七》5章。
❷《史记·孟荀列传》。
❸《战国策》卷二十九《燕策一》。

❶ *Analects,* "Shu'er," 7.5.
❷ *Historian's Records,* "Biographies of Mencius and Xunzi."
❸ *The Records of the Warring States,* "Yan" vol. 1.

criticized Mencius from the standpoint of Confucianism and his intellectual ancestors Zisi, et al. for praising the Way of Yao and Shun all the live-long day. Actually he did not grasp the truth of Confucianism. He also criticized the Confucianism of Zisi and Mencius based on the effort to gain great learning and cultivate skills, their knowledge both broad and eclectic, their ancient traditions divorced from reality, their advocacy of "Five Phases" thought, their vague and eccentric teachings that were hard to understand or implement❶.

Actually, the theories of great thinkers mostly are unable to fit with reality. Through investigating history, through participating or observing the age in which they lived, and through personal participation and experience, they ponder fundamental questions of humanity; they supply spiritual resources and the ability to make value judgements for later generations. They are unable to clothe or feed people, but store up spiritual resources that cannot be exhausted. Some people may feel that Mencius was a failure in terms of his actual accomplishments, but Confucianism from Confucius on combined theory with practice as equally important; they cannot be separated. It is different from the contemplative type of philosopher or the religious prophet with a practical bent. Having a philosophy that is not practical will realistically suffer many setbacks, and is something that is anticipated. The reason that they still strive to put their teachings into practice or to proselytize their teachings is precisely because this fulfils their missions and individual accomplishments. Mr. Feng Youlan said that Confucians feel that the original condition and strength of the existence of all things in the universe is called "order" (ming). For all our activities to be successful they must coordinate with these requirements. But this kind of coordination, seen in the overall scheme, is outside of the scope which we can control. Therefore what we are able to do does not go beyond wholeheartedly doing our best to do what we know we should without worrying about success or failure. Acting in this manner is to "know the order." To know the order is an important prerequisite for being what the Confucians describe as a gentleman. Knowing the order also means to recognize the inevitability of the existence of the world. In this way, one will not be entangled with external success or failure. If we can accomplish this, to a certain degree we will never suffer failure. Because, if we do our utmost to perform our duty, this effort itself fulfils our moral duty. This has nothing to do with the external concerns of success or failure❷.

从儒家的立场批判孟子和他的先师子思等人成天称颂尧舜之道，其实并不知道其中的真谛。他还指责子思、孟子代表的儒家才高志大，见闻又多又杂，根据古代的传说闭门造车，鼓吹什么'五行'学说，说得怪僻隐晦，令人难以理解和实行❶。

其实，大思想家的学说大多不能切合实际，他们通过研究历史，通过参与或观察自己所处的时代，通过自己的实践和体验来思索人类的根本问题，为后人提供精神资源和价值判断能力。他们无法让人们衣食无忧，却为人类储藏了取用不尽的精神资源。人们可能还会认为，孟子是一个行动上的失败者。但是儒家学派从孔子开始就将思想与实践看得同样重要，二者不可分割，这与沉思型的哲学家和出世的宗教先知不太一样。自己的学说不切实际，在现实中遭受挫折，也是他们意料中的事。他们之所以还去实践、宣传，因为这正是他们的使命和成就自我的途径。冯友兰先生说，儒家认为整个宇宙的一切存在的条件和力量叫做"命"，我们的活动，要取得成功，总是需要这些条件的配合。但是这种配合，整个地看来，却在我们能控制的范围之外。所以我们能够做的，莫过于一心一意地尽力去做我们知道是我们应该做的事，而不计较成败。这样做，就是"知命"。要做儒家所说的君子，知命是一个重要的条件。知命也就是承认世界本来存在的必然性，这样，对于外在的成败也就无所萦怀。如果我们做到这一点，在某种意义上，我们也就永不失败。因为，如果我们尽应尽的义务，那么，通过我们尽义务的这种行动，此项义务也就在道德上算是尽到了，这与我们行动的外在成败并不相干❷。

❶《荀子》卷三《非十二子》。
❷ 冯友兰《中国哲学简史》第四章，北京，北京大学出版社，1996，第40页。

❶ *Xunzi*, vol. 3, "Against the Twelve Philosophers."
❷ Feng Youlan, *A Short History of Chinese Philosophy* (Beijing: Beijing University Press, 1996), chapter 4, p. 40.

The book of *Mencius*, this record of Mencius' conversations, is the medium containing his spiritual legacy. The *Historian's Records*, "Biographies of Mencius and Xunzi," records that Mencius and his disciple Wanzhang et al. composed "*Mencius* in seven chapters;" this includes "King Hui of Liang," "Gongsun Chou," "Duke Wen of Teng," "Lilou," "Wanzhang," "Gaozi," and "Jinxin." Each chapter is divided into two parts, I and II. And each chapter is further divided into verses, in all 260 verses with 35,226 characters. Notwithstanding some adjacent chapters or verses developing around a common question, no chapter has a clear theme. So the first line of each chapter supplies several words to serve as chapter title. This is a practice of works dating back to high antiquity. The *Analects* and the *Book of Poetry* both follow this practice. Those in the book engaging in dialogue with Mencius include feudal princes, high officials, and scholars. Of course, the majority are his disciples, such as Gongsun Chou, Wanzhang, Yuezhengzi, Gongduzi, Chen Zhen, Chong Yu, Xianqiu Meng, Cheng Dai, Peng Geng, Wuluzi, Tao Ying, Xu Bi, Meng Zhongzi, et al. Although scholars of later generations hold different views regarding the process of composition of this book, most agree that the book was jointly compiled by Mencius and his disciples; some wording possibly derived from the emendations of disciples or students of disciples.

The transmission of the book *Mencius* is due to the merit of Han Dynasty editorial work. Starting during the 3rd year of Emperor Cheng of the Western Han (approximately 26 B.C.), father and son Liu Xiang and Liu Xin presided over a twenty-year project of editing the ancient books in the royal library. Because anciently, books and other records were written on bamboo strips, after a long period of time, the strings that bound the strips together into books would break, therefore the strips would break or fall out. In addition to this, often these books were single chapters that circulated independently, not like our modern books, which are printed after being composed and checked; instead they circulated chapter by chapter after composition by being privately copied. The wording would develop errors, lacunae, or interpolations through the process of copying. Therefore, copies of *Mencius* possibly included different numbers of chapters, and the language of various copies would have differences. Some editions would even contain more than seven chapters because someone added a chapter or two, or erroneously incorporated somebody else's work into their own copy. Later on, these errors were transmitted down the ages and were difficult to detect. These different phenomena have been verified by recent archeological finds. For example, the

　　《孟子》这本谈话录体裁的书是孟子精神遗产的载体。《史记·孟荀列传》记载孟子与弟子万章等作"《孟子》七篇"。即《梁惠王》、《公孙丑》、《滕文公》、《离娄》、《万章》、《告子》、《尽心》，每篇各分上下两部分，篇中文字再分为章，全书共260章，35 226字。尽管一些相邻的章节围绕一个问题展开，但每篇都没有一个很明确的主题，只是在每篇的首句中选择几个字做题目。这是中国上古时代典籍题篇的一种方式，《诗经》、《论语》也是如此。书中与孟子对话的人有诸侯、士大夫、学者，当然大多数是他的学生，比如公孙丑、万章、乐正子、公都子、陈臻、充虞、咸丘蒙、陈代、彭更、屋庐子、桃应、徐辟、孟仲子等。尽管后世学者对这本书的编纂过程有不同的看法，但大多认为这本书由他本人与弟子们共同编纂，有些文字可能出自弟子或再传弟子的修订。

　　《孟子》一书的流传要归功于汉代人的整理。西汉成帝河平三年（公元前26年）开始，刘向、刘歆父子主持了一次长达20年之久的皇家图书馆的古籍整理工作。由于中国上古时代的典籍是书写在竹简上的，时间长了，编联竹简的绳子会散断，因而造成脱简断篇的现象。此外，这些典籍往往是单篇独行的，并不像我们现在的书，在文字编定后再付诸印刷，而是写好一篇就在外面传抄一篇，文字也会在长期的传抄过程中发生讹变、

silk manuscript versions of the *Laozi* and the *Commentary on the Book of Changes* from the Han dynasty tomb at Mawangdui in Changsha, Hunan, and the *Art of War: Sunzi's Military Methods* from the Han tomb at Yinqueshan, Shandong, and the bamboo strip version of the *Laozi* from the Chu tomb at Guodian, Jingzhou, Hubei, all exhibit many differences from the received texts we have today. When Liu Xiang and his son were editing each book, they first searched for various editions, and on this foundation they selected a good copy in the royal library as the base text. Then they compared other versions such as editions contained in other government offices or privately owned copies as well as versions that circulated among the people to compare and collate, to determine the title of the book, contents, and wording. Then they would assign others the task of using bamboo strips or silk scrolls to transcribe a new version, called a "definitive edition." For each definitive version they would compose a "Bibliographical Introduction" that would record the book title, names of chapters, the various copies used in the work of collation, the life of the author, content of the book and its academic value, etc. Lastly, this "Bibliographical Introduction" would itself be copied, and compiled with others into a "Separate Register" for the convenience of readers. The language of the "Separate Register" has largely been lost, but the names of books and their chapter names, and other data were incorporated by the Eastern Han historian Ban Gu into the "Monograph on Bibliography" chapter of his *History of the Han*. While determining the table of contents of each book, Liu Xiang and his son characterized the chapters actually composed by the author as "inner chapters" or "the central book." Chapters which had been added later or erroneously incorporated, or passages appended to the end of the work were called "outer chapters," "the outer book," or "miscellaneous chapters." The "Monograph on Bibliography" recorded a *Mencius* in eleven chapters; the Eastern Han literatus Ying Shao's *Comprehensive Deliberations on Customs*, "Chapter on Failure and Success," mentions that Mencius and his disciple Wanzhang, et al. "compiled a central book and outer book in eleven chapters in all," demonstrating that four of these chapters were so-called "outer chapters." The Eastern Han scholar Zhao Qi said, "The additional four outer chapters were 'Nature is Good,' 'Debating over Texts,' 'Explanations of the Classic of Filial Piety,' and 'Enacting Government.' But the contents are recondite and crude, simplistic and open, quite different from the contents of the 'inner chapters.' I am afraid that they were imitations by men of a later age attributed as the words of Mencius❶." Because the outer chapters did not circulate widely, they gradually became lost.

脱漏或增加。所以，古代《孟子》的抄本可能篇数不等，不同抄本的文字也有出入。甚至还会有七篇以上的抄本，这是因为有人增造篇章，或者误将别人的著作编入自己的抄本，后来以讹传讹，难以辨别。这些现象也被当代考古发现所证实，比如湖南长沙马王堆汉墓中出土的帛书《老子》、《易传》；山东银雀山汉墓出土的《孙子兵法》；湖北荆州郭店楚墓出土的竹简《老子》，都与我们的传世文本出入其多。刘向父子整理每一部书时，都在广搜抄本的基础上，以皇家收藏的好抄本做底本，再用政府部门或私人藏本以及民间流传的抄本进行校勘，确定书的名称、篇目、文字，再让人用竹简或丝帛誊写出一个新的抄本，称为"定本"。他们为每一部书的定本撰写一个《书录》，记录书名、篇名、用于校勘的抄本、作者的生平、书的主要内容和学术价值等内容。最后将所有定本的《书录》单独抄出，编成一部《别录》，方便读者查阅。《别录》的文字大多散佚，但书名、篇目等被东汉史学家班固录入《汉书》的《艺文志》。刘向父子确定书的篇目时，将作者撰写的文字称为"内篇"或"中书"，将后人增造或误收的篇目、文字附在书的后面，称为"外篇"、"外书"或"杂篇"。《艺文志》中著录《孟子》十一篇，东汉人应劭《风俗通义·穷通篇》中说孟子与弟子万章等人"撰写了中书、外书共十一篇"，说明十一篇中有四篇属于外篇。东汉赵岐说："又有外书四篇是《性善》、《辩文》、《说孝经》、《为政》，内容僻陋浅显，与内篇差别很大，恐怕是后世之人模仿并托名于孟子的文字❶。"由于外篇流传不广，逐渐散失了。

---

❶《孟子章句题辞》。

❶ *Chapters and Verses of Mencius*, "Introduction."

The earliest version of the seven-chapter edition that we still use today is the one edited and annotated by the Eastern Han scholar Zhao Qi known as the *Chapters and Verses of Mencius*." Chapters and verses" is a type of commentary on the classics developed during the Eastern Han Dynasty by government officials. In addition to explaining the words in each sentence of a classical text, this genre would also summarize the language of each chapter, and provide an evaluation or elaboration. During the reign of the Western Han Emperor Wen (179 B.C.-157 B.C.), he restored the system of 70 erudites that derived from the Qin Dynasty. Such Confucian classics as the *Book of Poetry*, and *Book of History*, and such commentaries or commentarial records on the classics as the *Analects*, *Classic of Filial Piety*, *Erya* dictionary, etc. as well as such philosophical works as *Mencius* and *Laozi*, all had the office of erudites established to study them. But by the 5th year of the Jianyuan reign period of Emperor Wu (136 B.C.), the court adopted the cultural policy of "Solely venerating Confucian arts, dismissing the Hundred Philosophical Schools." The court only established five erudites for the five classics of the *Book of Poetry*, *Book of History*, *Rites*, *Book of Changes*, and *Spring and Autumn Annals*, and abolished the study of the commentaries, commentarial records, and philosophical schools mentioned above. The Five Classics are political and religious statutes inherited by Confucius from ancient sage kings. Because the *Analects*, *Classic of Filial Piety*, and *Erya* were produced by the disciples of Confucius, they were ranked as elementary and intermediary textbooks. The *Mencius* was ranked among the biographical studies or philosophical schools. The *History of the Han*, "Monograph on Bibliography," ranked *Mencius* among Confucian works. But in Han period literature, sometimes the *Mencius* was regarded as a commentarial record❶. The court abolished the other offices of erudites. All in all, during the Han Dynasty court scholars attempted to utilize the classical studies of the Confucians to construct an external system of culture and education, and follow the line advocated by Xunzi; they did not have any interest in the internal thought of Mencius in expounding and elaborating Confucianism. But some scholars among the people greatly esteemed Mencius. For example, Yang Xiong, a classicist and literatus from the later period of the Western Han, felt that Mencius did not belong among the various philosophers because he completely inherited the thought of Confucius, and felt that the relationship between Confucius and Xunzi was that of adherents of the same school belonging to different sects within it ❷. During the Eastern Han period, conflict between great officials on the one hand and royal in-laws and eunuchs on the other hand intensified. Confucians were

我们现在看到的《孟子》七篇最早的版本，是东汉人赵岐整理、注解的《孟子章句》。所谓"章句"，是汉朝官方经学的注解体例，除了对经书中每一句的文字作出解释之外，还要对每一章的文字作出概括、评述或发挥。西汉文帝时（公元前179—157年）恢复了秦朝的七十博士制度。《诗经》、《尚书》等儒家经书、《论语》、《孝经》、《尔雅》等解释经书的传记以及《孟子》、《老子》等诸子都被立为博士。可是到了汉武帝建元五年（公元前136），朝廷遵循"独尊儒术，罢黜百家"的文化政策，只立《诗》、《书》、《礼》、《易》、《春秋》五经博士，撤销了传记诸子。五经是孔子继承的古代圣王的政教宪章，《论语》、《孝经》、《尔雅》因出自孔子弟子之手，被列为初级和中级教育的教科书，《孟子》则归入传记或诸子之列❶，撤销了博士。总的来说，汉代是要利用儒家的经学建构外在统一的文教制度，走的是荀子的路线，对孟子阐释和发明的儒学内在思想并不感兴趣。但是一些民间的学者却对孟子推崇有加。比如西汉后期的经学家和文学家扬雄就认为：孟子不属于诸子，因为他完全继承了孔子的思想，而荀子与孔子关系就是同门异户了❷。东汉时期，士大夫与外戚、宦官的矛盾加深，儒者不能推行其政治理想，转向自我的道德坚守，崇尚气节，加之此

---

❶《汉书·艺文志》列《孟子》为儒家，但汉代文献中有时也称《孟子》为《传》，见《汉书·楚元王传》、《后汉书·梁冀传》、《说文解字》等。
❷ 扬雄《法言》卷十八《君子》。

❶ See *History of Han*, "Biography of King Yuan of Chu," *History of Later Han*, "Biography of Liang Ji," the dictionary *Explaining Simple Graphs and Analyzing Compound Characters*, etc.
❷ Yang Xiong, *Model Sayings*, 18, "Gentleman."

unable to achieve their political aims, so they shifted toward maintaining their own moral selves and upholding their characters. In addition to this, at this time classical scholarship among officials had declined, and intellectual circles returned to pre-Qin philosophers for resources. Therefore, Mencius' advocating nurturing one's flood-like and righteous *qi*, and emphasizing elevating one's own moral thinking was profoundly accepted. The earliest annotated edition of the *Mencius* that is mentioned in historical sources is the *Chapters and Verses of Mencius* compiled by Cheng Zeng❶. Liu Tao, an opponent in the national academy of the exclusive political power of the eunuchs, also compiled a work entitled *Restoring Meng Ke*. Although the works of Cheng and Liu are no longer extant, from the titles of the works we know that the former work esteemed the *Mencius* as a classic, and the later sought to restore the theories of Mencius. At the end of the Eastern Han period, two annotated versions of the *Mencius* appeared, one was Gao You's *Mencius with Annotations*, no longer extant today; the second was Zhao Qi's *Chapters and Verses of Mencius*.

Zhao Qi was born in the household of an important official; when he grew up and became an official himself he had great ambition. He was upright and honest; but because he offended a relative of a powerful eunuch, his entire family was arrested and executed. Fortunately, he escaped and fled, and took refuge along the Yangtze River, the Huai River, Mt. Tai, and the seashore. Later he concealed his identity and sold biscuits in a market in Beihai. One day a famous scholar, over twenty-year old Sun Song, saw him in the market and felt that he had the look of an unusual man. He then ordered him to ascend his chariot; after lowering the curtains, he said, "As soon as I saw you I could tell that you, sir, are not a seller of biscuits. If you are not avoiding a feud with an enemy then you are fleeing the law. I am Sun Song of Beihai; I possess a household with a hundred members and thus I am well able to support you sir." Zhao Qi had heard of the fine reputation of Sun Song, so told him the truth about himself. Sun Song took him home, ascended the hall and announced him to his mother with the following words, "Today your son visited the market and found a friend who is now my soul mate!" Thereupon Zhao Qi lived for several years in a secret room in Sun Song's home; he stayed until the power of the eunuchs collapsed and a state-wide amnesty was announced, only then did he dare emerge and accept a summons to office. In old age he often represented as emissary of the pitiable last emperor of the Han Dynasty to mediate during war with such warlords and adventurists as Cao Cao, Yuan Shao, and Liu Biao, begging for monetary support for the court. He died at over ninety years of age

时官方经学衰落，思想界纷纷回到先秦诸子中去寻求资源，于是孟子主张培养浩然正气，提升自我道德的思想受到了重视。史书上记载最早的《孟子》注本是程曾撰写的《孟子章句》[1]。反对宦官专政的太学生领袖刘陶也撰写过《复孟轲》。程、刘之文虽已不存，但从著作题目上便可知前者将《孟子》推崇为经书，后者要求恢复孟子的学说。东汉末期，有两部《孟子》的注本，一是高诱的《孟子注》，今已不存；二是赵岐的《孟子章句》。

赵岐出身于士大夫之家，出来做官时，志向远大，正直廉洁，因为得罪了宦官的亲戚，全家遭到搜捕杀戮。赵岐侥幸逃脱，在长江、淮河、泰山和海滨一带流亡避难，后来隐名埋姓，在北海市场上卖饼为生。一天，20多岁的名士孙嵩在市场上见到赵岐，觉得此人气度不凡，便命他上车，放下帷幕说："先生一看就不是个卖饼的人，没有怨仇在身，便是亡命之徒。我是北海孙嵩，拥有百口之家，能够养活先生。"赵岐从前也听说过孙嵩的美名，于是以实情相告。孙嵩将赵岐带回家，上堂禀报母亲说："孩儿今天出游，得到一位生死之交的好朋友！"于是赵岐便在孙嵩家的密室里安居了几年，直到宦官势力垮台，天下大赦，才敢出来应聘做官。他在年暮之际还经常代表汉朝最后一位可怜的天子到曹操、袁绍、刘表这些军阀和野心家那里调停战争、乞讨朝廷的开支。90多岁时，老死在军阀刘表的

---

[1] 《后汉书》卷七十九《儒林传》。

[1] *History of Later Han*, vol. 79, "Biographies of Confucians."

in the territory of warlord Liu Biao❶. The events of his life can be read in the famous ancient Chinese vernacular novel *Romance of the Three Kingdoms*. The *Chapters and Verses of Mencius* was composed during his period of exile and distress, and was his spiritual support. In the *Chapters and Verses of Mencius*, "Introduction," he wrote, "At age 40 when I knew the mandate of Heaven, I suffered a great calamity, and lived in exile for more than ten years. I was both mentally and physically exhausted, and my hair and beard turned white, my spirits were confused and disordered. But I still studied diligently to review the old and learn the new, and hoped to be able to compose a work to clarify the Way, to restore my spirits and to forget illness and old age. Among Confucians only the thought of Mencius is grand and broad, yet subtle and profound. His work is worthy of editing and annotating!"

During the mid-Tang period, Han Yu and thinkers faced the country being carved up by military governors and the loss of the political stability characteristic of the high Tang era. He felt that government classicists were unable to make Confucian thought influential in mundane society, and was unable to deflect the control over world affairs and the human mind exerted by the two religions of Buddhism and Taoism. Nor was it able to enlarge the great way of the great Confucians. Thereupon, Han Yu composed a work *Tracing the Origin of the Way*, declaring that humaneness and virture constituted the Confucian way. The legitimate succession of this way was transmitted from Yao to Shun, from Shun to Yu, from Yu to Tang, from Tang to King Wen, King Wu, and the Duke of Zhou, and from them to Confucius, and finally from Confucius to Mencius. After Mencius died, no one transmitted it to later ages. Han Yu's declaration signified a shift from constructing external models of the age of classical scholarship to constructing the internal spiritual world of the age of New Confucianism. During the Dazhongxiangfu reign periods of the Song Dynasty (1008-1016), the Song emperor Zhenzong ordered Sun Shi to edit and establish the text of Zhao Qi's *Chapters and Verses of Mencius*. During the Northern Song Dynasty, Fan Zhongyan, Ouyang Xiu, Wang Anshi as well as Neo-Confucians Zhou Dunyi, Zhang Zai, Cheng Hao, Cheng Yi, et al., all venerated Mencius. In the 6th year of the Yuanfeng reign period (1083), Emperor Shenzong issued an edict to posthumously honor Mencius as the Duke of the State of Zou. The next year, the spirit tablet of Mencius was placed within Confucian temples. In the 5th year of the Zhenghe reign period of Emperor Huizong (1115), the court recognized a temple to Mencius in Zou County, and issued an edict to offer sacrifices to him. During the Southern Song Dynasty, the *Orthodox Interpretation of Mencius*, a work that originated

领地上❶。他的事迹，可以在中国古代著名的白话小说《三国演义》里读到。《孟子章句》正是他在流亡困厄之中的著作，是他的精神支柱。他在《孟子章句·题辞》中说："我40多岁知天命的时候，遭受大难，流亡十多年，心力交瘁，须发皆白，精神散乱。但我一直勤勉学习，温故知新，希望能著书明道，调养精神，忘却老病。儒家当中，只有孟子的思想宏大开阔而又微妙精深，值得我去整理解释啊！"

唐代中期，韩愈等思想家面对藩镇割据，唐朝盛世不再的政治局面，认识到官方的经学不能使儒家思想影响世俗社会，不能抵抗佛、道二教对世道人心的控制，不能发扬光大儒家之道。于是韩愈写了《原道》，声称遵循仁义就是儒家的道，这个道统从尧传到舜，从舜传到禹，从禹传到汤，从汤传到文王、武王、周公，从文王、武王、周公传到孔子，由孔子传到孟子，孟子死了，便没有人传下去了。韩愈的声明标志着从建构外部范式的古典经学时代转入建构精神世界的新儒学时代。北宋大中祥符年间（公元1008—1016），宋真宗命孙奭校定赵岐的《孟子章句》。北宋的范仲淹、欧阳修、王安石，以及理学家周敦颐、张载、程颢、程颐等都推尊孟子。元丰六年（公元1083），宋神宗敕封孟子为邹国公。次年，孟子的牌位被供入孔庙。宋徽宗政和五年（公元1115），朝廷承认邹县的孟庙，下诏祭祀。

---

❶《后汉书》卷六十四《赵岐传》。

❶ *History of the Later Han Dynasty*, vol. 64, "Biography of Zhao Qi."

from among the people that was falsely attributed to Sun Shi, was accorded official status among the canon of works on the classics.

However, Song Confucians were not happy with Zhao Qi's *Chapters and Verses of Mencius*, because of its classical manner of explanation that emphasized glosses on words and explanations of sentences; this made it impossible to profoundly expound Mencius' thought and teachings on self-cultivation. The Southern Song Neo-Confucian Zhu Xi criticized Zhao Qi's *Chapters and Verses of Mencius* for its clumsiness and lack of clarity. ❶ Another Southern Song Neo-Confucian Lu Jiuyuan also criticized *Chapters and Verses of Mencius* for its sketchy treatment. ❷ Therefore, Zhu Xi selected from 12 Song Dynasty commentators on Mencius to compile his *Collected Commentaries on Mencius* in seven chapters. This work, along with Zhu Xi's *Chapters and Verses of the Great Learning*, *Chapters and Verses of the Doctrine of the Mean*, and *Collected Commentaries on the Analects* were all grouped by later scholars into the collection the *Four Books*, which formed a new canon relative to the *Five Classics*. The wording of this new canon was concise and easy to transmit; it further clarified the legitimate transmission of the Confucian way. In the 1ˢᵗ year of the Chunyou reign period of Emperor Lizong of the Southern Song (1241) the court issued an edict to praise and award Zhu Xi, declaring him to be the successor to Mencius. This line of legitimate succession was accepted by the major Confucians of this dynasty, who transmitted it to later generations. Ever since, both the *Analects* and *Mencius* were regarded as classics. In the 2ⁿᵈ year of the Huangqing reign period of Emperor Renzong of Yuan Dynasty (1313), the *Four Books* of Zhu Xi were established as the official textbook in the examination system. These books continued to be so used during the Ming and Qing dynasties, forming the core of the new classical studies. In the 1ˢᵗ year of the Zhishun reign period of Emperor Wenzong of the Yuan Dynasty (1333), the court conferred on Mencius the posthumous title of the "Second Sagely Duke from the State of Zou." At this point, the positions of Mencius and his work became established within the Chinese academic value system.

南宋时，一本由民间儒生撰写并伪称孙奭所作的《孟子正义》被立为官方经学的经典。

　　不过，宋儒对赵岐《章句》并不满意，因为这是经学式的解释，注重文字训诂和文句讲解，不能深入发抉孟子的思想和修养功夫。南宋理学家朱熹批评赵岐的《章句》粗拙而不明白❶，另一位南宋理学家陆九渊也批评《章句》文义疏略❷。于是朱熹采掇宋代十二位儒者对《孟子》的理解，撰成《孟子集注》七卷，与他的《大学章句》、《中庸章句》、《论语集注》一道被后人并称为《四书》，成为相对于"五经"的新经典系统，这个新经典系统文字简练，易于传播并且昭示了儒家的道统。南宋理宗淳佑元年（公元1241），朝廷下诏褒奖朱熹，宣称孟子之后，道统被本朝大儒们实践、继承了下去。自此《孟子》与《论语》并列为经书。元仁宗皇庆二年（公元1313）将朱熹的《四书》定为科举考试的教科书，沿用至明、清两代，成为新的经学。元文宗至顺元年（公元1333），朝廷封孟子为"邹国亚圣公"。至此，孟子及其著作的地位在中国学术与政治的价值系统中皆被确立。

---

❶ 朱熹《朱子语类》卷五十一。
❷ 《陆九渊集》卷三十四。

❶ Zhu Xi, *Classified Sayings of Zhuzi*, vol. 51.
❷ *Anthology of Lu Jiuyuan*, vol. 34.

孔子画像
Portaits of Confucius

孟子画像
Portait of Mencius

二　良知——人性的起点

Chapter Ⅱ　Conscience: The Point of Departure for Discussing Human Nature

Between Confucius and his disciples, they did not mention human nature very much; his explanation of human nature was ordinary yet profound. He only said eight words, "By nature men are close, but by practice they are far apart." ❶ The meaning is people's natures are similar, but what they learn in life is different, therefore the differences among men are very distant. He further said, "Heaven has created virtue in me." ❷ The meaning is that "It was Heaven which placed fine virtue within me." The previous line was the commencement of Xunzi's emphasis on altering thought on human nature; the last line was the commencement of Mencius' emphasis on expanding thought on human nature.

When Duke Wen of Teng was the heir apparent, one time he visited the state of Chu. While passing through Song, he made it a point to call on Mencius. Mencius lectured to him on the principle that human nature was good; every time he opened his mouth he mentioned matters pertaining to Yao and Shun. The lofty doctrine that Mencius explained made this crown prince Duke Wen of Teng feel that it was too lofty to attain, so he pondered over it all the way home. When he returned home from Chu, he once again called on Mencius, wishing to ask whether there was any shortcut available. It seems that Mencius had some sort of premonition when he said to him "Does the heir apparent doubt my words? Actually, there is only one great way that must be followed. Once a brave knight in the state of Qi was discussing his own bravery with Duke Jing of Qi. He said that when facing a powerful enemy, he thought to himself, 'He is a hero, but so am I, so why should I fear him?' Confucius' disciple Yan Hui said, whatever type of man Shun was, I am such a man. A man of service should be like Shun. Zengzi's disciple Gongming Yi said that King Wen was his teacher, would the Duke of Zhou deceive me? Your state of Teng although rather small, but all told added up to fifty *li* square, and could be managed well to become a large state. It says in the *Book of History* that if one uses medicine and it does not make one dizzy or dazzled, then it cannot cure illness. So do not be afraid that you cannot succeed!" ❸

The reason that Mencius felt that the way that he taught was the only one to follow was because he went to the starting point of the Great Way. Each one possesses the same human nature, therefore, each one possesses the same starting point. Mencius thought that, Yao and Shun becoming sages was the ideal development deriving out of human nature. Fine virtue within internal human nature is our natural resource; as long as one commences from the starting point of human nature, then one is able to unify the family and proceed to ordering the state and then the world. This commencement point is not

孔子和弟子之间不过多地讨论人性，但他对人性见解平常而深刻。他只说了八个字"性相近也，习相远也"。❶意思是：人性是相近的，但后天的学习不同，所以人与人的差距很远。他还说"天生德于予"。❷意思是：天将美德生给我。前面一句话开启了荀子重视改造人性的思想，后面一句话开启了孟子重视扩充人性的思想。

滕文公还在做太子的时候，有一次出访楚国，经过宋国时，特地拜见了孟子。孟子对他讲了人性本来是善良的道理，开口闭口都在说尧舜的事。孟子说的大道理让滕文公这个小国的储君感到高不可攀，琢磨了一路，从楚国返回时，又去拜访孟子，想问问有何捷径可行。孟子好像有预感似的，见面就说："太子怀疑我的话吗？其实能够遵循的大道只此一条。齐国有个勇士和齐景公谈论自己的勇气，他说我面对强敌，心想： 他是个男子汉，我也是个男子汉，我为什么要惧怕他呢？孔子的弟子颜回说，舜是什么样的人，我也是什么样的人，有作为的人就应该像舜那样。曾子的弟子公明仪说，文王，是我的老师；周公难道会欺骗我？你们滕国虽说小了一些，但拼拼凑凑也有五十里见方，还是能治理成一个好国家的。《尚书》中说： 如果用药不能让人头晕目眩，就治不好病。你不要怕做不到啊！"❸

孟子之所以认为自己讲的道理是唯一可行的，是因为他回到了大道的起点，这个起点就是人性。每一个人都具备同样的人性，因此每个人都具备同样的起点。孟子认为，尧舜成为圣人就是人性发展的理想过程，内在于人性中的美德就是我们的

---

❶《论语·阳货第十七》2章。
❷《论语·述而第七》23章。
❸《孟子·滕文公上》1章。

❶ *Analects*, "Yang Huo," 17.2.
❷ *Analects*, "Shu'er," 7.23.
❸ *Mencius*, "Duke Wen of Teng," Ⅰ1.

different for sages or commoners. Once someone asked Mencius, "Are all men able to become a Yao or a Shun?" Mencius answered with no hesitation at all, "Of course!" ❶ Nor were there any cultural or ethnic differences. Mencius said, "Shun was a man of the Eastern barbarian people, King Wen was a man of the Western barbarian people; they lived in places separated by a thousand *li*, and in time separated by a thousand years. But they were both able to become sages, and rule the Chinese people, and accomplish exactly the same thing, because the way to becoming a sage is the same" ❷ Therefore, Mencius expounded the "theory that human nature is good" as the starting point for his own thought. This starting point included two contents: First, human nature is equal; the reason that this equality is able to be established is because human nature is endowed by Heaven. Two, the most important component of this human nature endowed by Heaven is the moral endowment.

The character for "nature" (*xing*) evolved from the one for "birth" (*sheng*). This character for "birth" can be understood as reproduction, to be born, life, or inborn. Therefore, when we say "a matter of life and death," the word *xing* signifies human life. When we say, "The rivers and mountains are easily changed, but original nature is difficult to shift," *xing* means that quality endowed by Heaven and its original essence; it is inborn or a natural product. This range of meanings finds general agreement among pre-Qin philosophers. The first sentence in the Confucian classic *Doctrine of the Mean* says, "What Heaven above determined is our natures." ❸ Gaozi said, "The inborn, original essence is nature." ❹ Xunzi also said, "The thing which is born in us with life is nature." ❺ The Taoist Zhuangzi said, "The operation of the Heavenly way was chaotic and confused, lacking form. All things received the Heavenly way and obtained life; this then is 'virtue.' Before life took on material form, chaotic and confused *qi* had already started to divide and circulate with no gaps. This formed the inherent prerequisites for life, which is known as 'order.' When this division and activity of the *qi* quieted down, stopped and built up, then all things were given birth and all manner of physical forms and

资源，只有从人性这个起点出发，才能修身齐家进而治国平天下。这个起点没有凡人与圣人的分别，有人问过孟子："人人都能成为尧舜吗？"孟子毫不犹豫地回答道："当然！"❶也没有文化与种族的分别，孟子说："舜是东夷人，文王是西夷人，他们生活的地方相距千里，时代相差千年，但他们得以成为圣人，统治华夏，所作所为竟然完全一样，因为成就圣人的道路是一样的❷。"因此，孟子发明了"性善论"作为自己思想的起点，这个起点包括两个内涵：第一，人性平等，这种平等性之所以能够成立，是因为天赋人性。第二，天赋人性中最重要的是道德禀赋。

"性"字是从"生"字演化而来的，"生"可以理解为生殖、出生、生命、天生，因此当我们说"性命攸关"时，性就是人的生命；当我们说"江山易改，本性难移"时，性就是人的天赋和本质，是天生的或自然的产物。这个范畴，先秦诸子大都认同。儒家经典《中庸》第一句说："上天命定给我们的就是性。"❸告子说："天生的本质就是性。"❹荀子也说"生下来就是这样的东西便是性"❺。道家的庄子说："天道的运行，混沌无形。万物禀承天道而获得生命，这便是'德'。当生命还不具备形质时，混沌之气已开始分化，周流而无间隙，形成了生命的先天条件，这便是'命'。当气的分化运动静止停滞，

---

❶《孟子·告子下》2章。
❷《孟子·离娄下》1章。
❸《礼记·中庸》："天命之谓性，诣性之谓道，修道之谓教。"
❹《孟子·告子上》3章。
❺《荀子·正名》："生之所以然者谓之性。"

❶ *Mencius*, "Gaozi," II 2.
❷ *Mencius*, "Lilou," II 1.
❸ *Record of Rites*, "Doctrine of the Mean" literally puts it, "What Heaven orders is called nature, fulfilling nature is called the way, cultivating the way is called teaching."
❹ *Mencius*, "Gaozi," I 3.
❺ Or, as it literally says in *Xunzi*, "Rectification of Names," "The reason life is the way it is called nature."

properties were endowed. This then was 'physical form.' The physical forms of all things received different types of qi, different types of qualities and principles of growth. This then was ' nature.' " ❶

We can see from the words of Zhuangzi that nature is not only such natural endowments as the physical form, qi, and spirit bequeathed by Heaven to man and all things, it is also the direction and energy bequeathed by Heaven to complete the process of life. As such, human nature and the nature of things are similar to the seeds of life; it is necessary to adhere to their internal principles of growth. Therefore, regardless of whether it is a matter of fulfilling human nature or the nature of things, one important thing is to follow the principles included in something's original nature as it grows. Creating fine external conditions causes its internal growing power to become exhausted. On this point pre-Qin philosophers were in agreement. The second sentence of the *Doctrine of the Mean* says, "Following the development of nature is the way of man; making human nature preserve the direction of development that it should possess is transformative education." Taoists feel that "The original nature of water is clarity; if mud or sand gets mixed in, then of course it turns turbid. Since birth men possess a relatively large supply of vital energy; fame and fortune and the desire for material goods tempt them each day, causing them to forget themselves in the face of benefit; it is injurious to life and nature, and will not permit one to be long-lived. External things are used to nurture and protect our lives; we cannot get things backwards and use our natures to nurture external things! " ❷

However, because of different understandings of Heaven, the content of what Heaven endows to human nature was itself different. In the tradition of rites and music inherited by Confucians from the Western Zhou, Heaven is not purely natural existence, but instead is an abstract thing for men with volition, feelings, and morality. It not only endows mankind with natural life, it also endows mankind with moral and cognitive powers. The *Commentary of Mr. Zuo*, which records aristocratic thought during the Spring and Autumn Period, said that heaven has the six kinds of qi or vapors: clouds and sunshine, wind and rain, night and day. Man has six kinds of volitions as good and evil, joy and anger, sorrow and happiness. Earth has the five phases of metal, wood, water, fire and earth. Man has the social relations of lord and minister, one above and one below, and husband and wife, one inside and one outside. When the rites are carried out, man harmonizes with the nature of heaven and earth; this causes human nature to be long-lived. In order to deflect criticism by Taoists, Confucians during the Warring States Period strove to verify the fact

便生成了万物，赋予万物各种体态、条理，这便是'形'。万物的形体中禀承的各种气，各有不同的质地和生长法则，这便是'性'。" ❶

从庄子的话中可见：性不仅是上天赋予人和万物的形体、气质、精神等自然资质，还是上天赋予人和万物完成生命过程的方向和能力，如此，人性和物性如同有生命的种子，必然要遵循其内在的法则生长。因此，实现人性也好，实现物性也好，重要的一条就是顺应其本性中包含的生长法则，创造良好的外部条件，使其内在的生长能力得以竭尽。这一点，先秦诸子的意见也是一致的。《中庸》第二句说："依循性的发展就是人道，使人性保持其应有的发展方向就是教化。"道家认为："水的本性是清净的，搅进了泥沙，当然混浊。人生来具有相当大的生命力，名利、物欲天天来诱惑他，使他见利忘身，伤生害性，不能长寿。外物是用来养护我们的性命的，不能反过来用我们的性命来养护外物！" ❷

但是，由于对天的理解并不统一，因而天赋予人性的内涵也就不一样了。儒家继承的西周礼乐教化传统中，天不完全是纯粹的自然存在，而是有意志，有情感，有道德的，是人的抽象物。它不仅赋予人类自然生命，还赋予人类道德和认知能力。记载了春秋时期贵族思想的《左传》中说：天有阴阳、风雨、晦明六气，人有好恶、喜怒、哀乐六志；地有金、木、水、火、土五行，人有君臣上下、夫妇内外的伦理。奉行礼，与天地之性相和谐，可使人性得以长养。战国的儒家为了应付道家的批判，努力证明天道和人性中具备道德。比如《易传》中说：

---

❶《庄子·天地》。
❷《吕氏春秋》卷一《本生》。

❶ *Zhuangzi*, "Heaven and Earth."
❷ *The Spring and Autumn Annals of Mr. Lü*, vol. 1, "Tracing the Root of Nature."

that both the Way of Heaven and human nature possessed the element of morality. For instance, the *Commentary on the Book of Changes* said, "That Heaven gives birth to all things is the greatest virtue." ❶ "One element of Lunar (*yin*) and one of Solar (*yang*) together form the Way; the Way transforms and nurtures all things, this then is goodness. All things are born by receiving the Way, this then is nature. When those with humaneness see the Way, they are called humane; when those with wisdom see the Way, they are called wise." ❷

Yet Warring States Period Taoists felt instead that the Way of Heaven was nature and had no volition, therefore it only created man's natural life and could not endow mankind with morality. Morality and all forms of culture are products acquired after birth. Not only did human nature not contain morality, but it was precisely this morality that caused mankind to lose their Heavenly endowed natures. Only casting it off would allow man to return to the Great Way. Zhuangzi borrowed Laozi's oral teachings to admonish Confucius, saying, "How can it be true that humaneness and righteousness are the original natures of mankind? Actually, Heaven and Earth in the beginning possessed their own laws, the sun and moon possessed their own luminescence, the stars and asterisms possessed their own order, the birds and beasts from the beginning multiplied, trees and shrubs from the beginning grew and matured. Please follow in response to the Great Way and that is sufficient. Why target humaneness and righteousness? It is like beating gongs and striking drums to set out to find a lost child. This is how you disorder the original nature of man!" ❸

Mencius was completely opposed to cataloguing human nature as a part of the natural essence of humanity; his debate with Gaozi started with this issue. Gaozi was a thinker who partook of Taoism, Confucianism, and Mohism. He said, "The original nature of man is like a tree such as a willow, and humaneness and righteousness are like utensils such as a cup or tray. Originally, man's nature had no humaneness or righteousness; it was necessary to be straightened and changed before it was able to become humane and righteous, just like one uses willow wood to fashion a cup or tray." Mencius refuted him, saying, "Please may I enquire, do you follow the original nature of the willow to fashion the cup or tray?" Or do you have to destroy the original nature of the willow to fashion them? If the later is the case, then does this mean that one must destroy man's original nature to accord with humaneness and righteousness? What will lead to destroying the humaneness and righteousness in the world is certainly your theory!" ❹ Taoists also

"天生育万物就是最大的美德。" ❶ "一阴一阳构成道，道化育万物，这就是善，万物禀承大道而生，这就是性。仁爱的人看见道，称之为仁，有智慧的人看见道，称之为智。" ❷

而战国时代的道家则认为，天道是自然的，没有意志的，因此只生成人的自然生命，不可能赋予人类道德。道德和一切文化都是人类后天的产物，不仅人性当中不具备道德，而且正是这些道德使得人类丧失了天性，只有摒弃它们才能使人回归大道。庄子借老子的口教训孔子说："仁义难道是人的本性吗？其实天地本来就有规律，日月本来就有光明，星辰本来就有序列，禽兽本来就会成群，树木本来就会成长。请你顺应大道就行了，何必标举仁义，好像敲锣打鼓去找丢失的孩子？你这是在扰乱人的本性！" ❸

孟子十分反对将人性归之为人的自然本质，他与告子就此展开辩论。告子是一个兼采道家、儒家和墨家的思想家，他说："人的本性就好像是杞柳这样的树木，仁义就好像杯盘器皿。人性之中本来没有仁义，一定要经过矫揉改变之后才顺从仁义，就好像用杞柳来制作杯盘一样。"孟子反驳道："请问您是顺着杞柳的本性来制作杯盘呢？还是毁坏杞柳的本性来制作杯盘呢？如果是后者，那也要毁伤人的本性才能使之顺从仁义吗？率领天下人祸害仁义的，一定是您的学说了！" ❹道家也承认，

---

❶《周易·系辞下》："天地之大德曰生"。
❷《周易·系辞下》："一阴一阳之谓道，继之者善也，成之者性也。仁者见之谓之仁，知者见之谓之知"。
❸《庄子·天道》。
❹《孟子·告子上》1章。

---

❶ *Book of Changes*, "Great Commentary," Ⅱ "The great virtue of Heaven and Earth is called life."
❷ It literally says in the *Commentary on the Book of Changes*, "What we call one element of *yin* and one of *yang* is the Way, the one who receives it is good; what completes it is nature; when the humane one sees it, call him humane; when the wise one sees it, call him wise."
❸ *Zhuangzi*, "The Way of Heaven."
❹ *Mencius*, "Gaozi," Ⅰ 1.

recognized that human nature was the same as the nature of things, and they were not necessarily just inert objects; they included internal physiology and the potential for growth. Therefore, Mencius pursued this line of questioning concerning this doctrine, querying that since one cannot violate the internal physiology of something to develop its nature, then if morality is not inherent within man's physiology, then there is no basis for morality to exist. Gaozi again said, "The natural endowment bequeathed by Heaven is what is called nature." Mencius asked, "You state that the natural endowment bequeathed by Heaven is what is called nature, does this mean that we can regard all white colored things as what are called white?" Gaozi replied, saying, "This is precisely so." Mencius then said, "Is the white of white feathers the white of white snow, the white of snow the same thing as the white of white jade?" Gaozi said, "This is precisely so." Mencius said further, "Then is the nature of a dog like the nature of an ox, and is the nature of an ox the same as the nature of a man?" From the standpoint of logic, Mencius used the device of playing tricks with concepts to set up a trap for Gaozi. But Gaozi could not escape the trap, and was unable to respond. This is because Gaozi was a person, his moral consciousness and status identity made it impossible for him to be constrained by the bounds of logic and regard human nature as equivalent to the nature of an ox. The nature that Mencius was expounding was not merely the natural essence of man, neither was the development of human nature not merely adhering to inherent and natural principles of physiology; within the growth process of human nature there were also a moral endowment and a potential role for morality. Human nature possessed a moral quality; this was precisely the basis of what made a human a human, and that special quality which distinguished human nature from the nature of other things. What Mencius described as human nature was very close to what the *Doctrine of the Mean* meant by "moral nature."

Although the character for nature (*xing*) developed out of the character for life (*sheng*), their difference lies in the presence or absence of the "heart" element as a radical. *Xing* is a phonetic compound, with the *sheng* character indicating the sound; the "heart" element expresses the meaning. In Chinese philosophy, the "heart" character usually does not represent the heart but indicates the mind, the intellect and thought. Therefore, the *xing* character reveals to us its most simple concept: *xing* is the life recognized by the mind, and life that is controlled by the mind and perhaps life that possess intelligence. The relationship between the mind and nature was probably a topic opened up for debate at the Jixia Academy during the reign of King Wei

人的本性与物性一样，不完全是静固的物质，其中包含着内在生理和生长的潜力，因而孟子追问了这样的道理：既然不能违背杞柳的生理来发挥其物性，那么，道德如果不内在于人的生理，道德就没有存在根据。告子又说："天生的资质就是所谓的性。"孟子问："你说天生的资质就是所谓的性，是否可以认为一切白色的东西都叫做白吗？"告子回答："正是这样。"孟子便说："白色羽毛的白犹如白雪的白，白雪的白犹如白玉的白吗？"告子回答："正是这样。"孟子又说："那么，狗的性犹如牛的性，牛的性犹如人的性吗？"从逻辑学上看，孟子用偷换概念的方法给告子设了个圈套，但告子竟然钻不出来，哑口无言。因为告子是一个人，他的道德意识和身份认同意识决定他无论如何不会拘泥于逻辑，将人性等同于牛性。孟子阐述的性，不仅仅是人的自然本质，人性的发展也不仅仅是遵循其中的自然生理，人性的生长过程中，还有道德禀赋和道德潜能的作用。人性具有道德性，这正是人之所以为人的根据，是人性区别于其他物性的特殊性。孟子说的人性，与《中庸》里的"德性"很接近。

"性"字虽然是从"生"字演化而来的，但它们的区别就在于有没有"心"字旁。"性"是个形声字，"生"是表达字音的声旁，"心"才是表达字意的形旁。中国哲学里的"心"多不表示心脏，而是喻指头脑、意识和思想。所以，"性"字向我们透露出一个最简单的概念："性"是被心所认识、被心所主宰或者是具有智性的生命。心和性的关系，大概在齐威王时

of Qi. These debates involved the internal structure of human nature, which made the understanding of pre-Qin philosophers concerning human nature even more profound.

In the *Guanzi*, a text that belongs to works from the Jixia school, are two essays with the style of Taoism which are associated with the school of Song Xing, the "Art of the Mind" and the "Working on the Inner. " They regard the mind as the controller of all sensory organs; when sensory organs make contact with external things, this creates feelings and desires which disturb the tranquility and knowledge of the mind, causing it to be unable to control the sense organs or human nature. Therein lies the need to reduce desires. The mind is not only able to control the sensory organs of the body, furthermore "there is a mind within the mind," and "the mind can be used to conceal the mind." In other words, the mind possesses the power to be self-aware.

The literature associated with other Confucian schools also preserves similar viewpoints. For example, the *Record of Rites*, "Record of Music" says, "Men all have blood, *qi*, and wisdom which constitute their natural, original natures. But such feelings as joy and anger, sorrow and happiness are not the normal state; different feelings are produced following from the reaction of sensory organs as they make contact with external things." At this time, the different choices made by the mind are manifested." Among the bamboo strips from Chu discovered at Guodian in Hubei during the decade of the 90's of the twentieth century was one Confucian work called *Nature Emerges from the Order*. It contains the follow passages, "All men possess similar human natures, but none of their minds has a set aim. They will be moved by contact with external things, they will be pleased and attracted, and can be controlled and set at ease only after training." "The human natures of all men within the world are the same, but all men apply their minds in different ways; this is the role of education." Therefore, the thinkers of many Confucian schools produced a paradox, that is, that human nature is the mixed blend of nature and morality. It is the foundation possessed in common by all men, but the completion of human nature depends on the role of control played by the mind and spirit; yet the movements of the mind and spirit are controlled by external things; therefore, aspirations that accord with morality completely or partially rely on external training. If this is true, there are two bases for morality.

For example, Gaozi felt that human nature was such desires as food and sex, with nothing inherently good or evil about them, and that human morality was dependent upon acquired education. But he also felt that humaneness was internal and that righteousness was external. He said that I love my own

期的稷下学派中已经开展了讨论，这些讨论涉及到人性的内部结构，深化了先秦诸子对人性的认识。

属于稷下学派文献的《管子》中，有属于宋钘学派的《心术》、《内业》两篇道家风格的文章，其中认为心是一切感官的统率，感官与外物接触，产生了情感和欲望，搅扰了心的宁静和智识，使之无法统率感官，控制人性，因此需要寡欲。心不仅能控制身体感官，而且"心之中又有心"，"心可以用来藏心"，也就是说，心还具备自我认识的能力。

其他儒家学派的文献也有近似的观点。比如《礼记·乐记》说："人都有血气心智构成的自然本性，但喜怒哀乐等情感是没有常态的，随着感官对外物的反应而发出不同的情感，此时，心的不同的选择便显现了出来。"20世纪90年代湖北郭店出土的战国楚简中，有一篇儒家文献叫《性自命出》，其中说："人虽然具备相同的人性，可是每个人的心都没有一定的志向。会被外物触动，会被愉悦吸引，受过训练才能自制，安定下来。""四海之内的人性都一样，但人人的用心都不一样，这是教育的作用。"因此，许多儒家学派的思想家产生了一个悖论，即人性是自然与道德的混合体，这是每个人都具备的基础，可是人性的完成有待于心灵的宰制作用，而心灵的活动是受外物控制的，所以，符合道德的心志完全或部分地依赖于外在的训练。如果是这样话，道德就有了两个根据。

比如告子认为人性就是饮食男女的欲望，其中没有善也没有不善，人的道德完全取决于后天的教育。但他又认为仁是内在的，义是外在的。他说我爱自己的弟弟，却不爱秦国人的弟

brother, but do not love a brother from the state of Qin; this is due to the fact that when I see my own brother sentiments of gladness are naturally produced. Therefore, humane love is part of one's internal, original nature. But in the case of a man from Qin, as long as he is older than me, I need to respect him, because being older in age is an objective reality, and the mind of respecting the aged is formed by training in ritual education, not because my mind harbors the emotion of respect for him. Therefore, righteousness is external. This explains why Gaozi regarded the mind and nature as two very different things.

Mencius refuted him, saying, "If age is an external relationship, then respecting the elderly does not emerge from one's inner mind or original nature. Well then, is there not the slightest difference in the feelings between seeing an elderly horse and an elderly person? If there is a difference, then is the righteousness that you observe external to age or is it internal to respecting elderly persons? Just as you said that food and sex are man's original nature, you like to eat the roast meat from your own home, and also like to eat the roast meat from a man of Qin, then is roast meat external, or can it be that the pleasure you get from the roast meat you like to eat is also external and not something internal to your original nature?" ❶

Such moral abilities as humaneness and righteousness are internal, are self-sufficient, and also internal to the human mind. Mencius certainly did not deny the place of darkness within human nature, but because the potential for self-awareness existed in the mind, once the human mind became self-aware, it was like lighting a lamp, all the darkness within human nature was illuminated. At this time human nature was completely good. Perhaps someone would say, if we agree with Mencius' point of view, and regard the original moral nature as the characteristic that makes man what he is, then this type of human nature just exists within the human mind, and nature and the mind form one entity, because the mind is able to be self-aware and demonstrate this type of human nature. Modern Chinese philosopher Mou Zongsan used eight words to provide a precise summary of Mencius' theory of the mind and nature: "Humaneness and righteousness are internal, and nature is manifested in the mind." ❷

Since Mencius felt that the mind and nature were one single entity, and emphasized the basis of morality within the human mind, he profoundly expounded the internal condition of morality. Gongduzi once asked Mencius, "Gaozi said, human nature was originally neither good nor evil; someone also said, human nature can be good and also cannot be good, for instance at the time of Kings Wen and Wu of Zhou every one tended towards goodness; but at

弟，是因为我看到自己的弟弟就自然产生了高兴的心情，所以仁爱是内在的本性。而即便是秦国人，只要他比我年长，我就要尊敬他，因为年长是一个客观外在的事实，尊敬长者之心是礼教训练形成的，不是因为我心里对他有敬重之情，所以义是外在的。这说明告子将心与性看成两个事物。

孟子反驳他说："如果年长是一种外在的关系，因而尊敬老者不出于你的内心或本性，那么你见到一匹老马和见到一位老者时的心情是否毫无区别呢？如果有区别，那么你遵守的义，是外在于老者呢，还是内在于尊敬老者的人呢？正如你说饮食是人的本性，你喜欢吃自己家的烤肉，也喜欢吃秦国人的烤肉。请问烤肉是外在的，难道你喜欢吃烤肉的嗜好也是外在的而不内在于你的本性吗？"❶

仁、义等道德能力都是内在、自足的，而且内在于人心。孟子并不否认人性中有黑暗的地方，但由于自觉的潜能就存在于心中，所以，人心一旦自觉，就像点燃了一盏明灯，人性中所有的黑暗都被照亮，此时，人性就是全善的。或者说，如果我们认同孟子的观点，将人的道德本性看成是人之所以为人的特性，那么这种人性只存在于人心之中，性心一体，因为只有心能够自觉、自证这种人性。中国现代哲学家牟宗三用八个字对孟子的心性论作了精到的概括："仁义内在，性由心显。"❷

既然孟子认为心性一体，而且强调道德根据内在于人心，所以他深入阐述了道德的内在状态。公都子问孟子："告子说，

---

❶《孟子·告子上》4章。
❷ 刘述先《孟子心性论的再反思》，[美] 江文思、安乐哲编《孟子心性之学》，梁溪译，北京，社会科学文献出版社，2005，第194页。

❶ Mencius, "Gaozi," Ⅰ4.
❷ Liu Shuxian, "More Reflections on Mencius's Theory of Mind and Nature," in Mencius xinxing zhi xue (Mencius' Learning of Mental-Nature), Liang Xi trans. Jiang Wensi (James Behuniak Jr.) and An Lezhe (Roger T. Ames), eds. (Beijing: Social Sciences Academic Press, 2005), p. 194.

the time of Kings You and Li of Zhou, everyone was cruel and harsh. Still another said, the natures of some people were good, and the natures of some people were not good. Among the people of Yao some were as ignorant and obstinate as Shun's younger brother. Yet such an evil person as Gusou (Shun's father) had such a good son as Shun. Zhou was so brutal and became king, but he had such worthy and fine relatives as Weizi Qi and Prince Bigan. Yet master, you say that 'human nature is originally good.' Well are they all wrong in what they say?" Mencius said, "According to the original nature of men, they should all be able to accomplish the fine virtue of goodness. This is what I said about the doctrine of man's nature being originally good. As for those men who are not good, we cannot blame their natural endowment or heavenly quality. The heart of compassion and pity is had by all; the heart of shame and humbleness is had by all; the heart of respect and yielding is had by all; the heart of right and wrong and good and evil is had by all. The heart of compassion is none other than humaneness; the heart of shame is none other than righteousness; the heart of respect is none other than ritual courtesy; the heart of right and wrong, good and evil is precisely wisdom. Humaneness, righteousness, ritual courtesy and wisdom are not external things received from the outside but are something that I originally possessed. It is just that I did not pursue them well enough, that's all. Therefore we say, 'Pursue it and you will get it, abandon it and you will lose it.' The differences among men are sometimes double or five times, and sometimes countless in their degree; this is precisely because they have not fully developed their original natures and natural endowments. The *Book of Poetry* sings that "Heaven bore the common people, with substance and principle. The people hold to moral principles, fine is their moral integrity." ❶ Confucius said, "The author of this poem is someone who understood the Great Way! With things we get rules and models; the people abide by these rule and models and therefore like fine moral character." ❷ Since humaneness and righteousness are internal in the human heart, therefore we cannot discuss human behavior in terms of good and evil merely based on the phenomena that we perceive; men should do good; as for one's evil actions done in real life, they are unrelated to one's natural endowment; this is Mencius' explanation of nature being good.

Mencius further called the heart of compassion, the heart of shame, the heart of respect, and the heart of right and wrong as the "four seeds," that is, humaneness, righteousness, ritual courtesy, and wisdom, four sprouts of the moral nature. First of all is the heart of compassion, because it starts first from the loving and sympathetic hearts of humaneness. Mencius said, "All men have

人性本来没有善与不善。也有人说，人性可以为善，也可以不为善，比如文王、武王时，人人都向善；幽王、厉王时，人人都暴戾。还有人说，有的人性善，有的人性不善。尧的人民中也有像舜的弟弟这样愚顽的人；瞽叟（舜的父亲）这样的坏人，却有舜这样的好儿子。纣如此残暴，而且做了君主，却有微子启、王子比干这样的贤良。而夫子您却说'人性本善'，那么他们都说错了吗？"孟子说："依照人的本性，它应该可以成就善的美德，这就是我所说的人性本来就是善的道理。至于那些不善的人，并不能归罪于他的禀赋和天资。恻隐同情之心，人人都有；羞恶廉耻之心，人人都有；恭敬辞让之心，人人都有，是非好恶之心，人人都有。恻隐之心就是仁，羞恶之心就是义，恭敬之心就是礼，是非好恶之心就是智。仁义礼智不是从外面接受的东西，而是我本来就有的，只不过没有好好去追求罢了。所以说，'追求便会得到，舍弃便会失去。'人和人之间相差一倍、五倍甚至无数倍，就是因为没有充分发挥本性和资质。《诗经》唱道：'天生烝民，有物有则。民之秉彝，好是懿德。'❶孔子说：'这首诗的作者，是个明白大道的人啊！有事物，便有法则；百姓遵循天赐的法则，所以喜欢美好的品德。'"❷仁义既然内在于人心，所以我们就不可以仅仅根据看到的现象讨论人的善恶行为，人应该为善，至于他在现实生活中为恶，与人的禀赋无关，这就是孟子说的性善。

孟子又将恻隐之心、羞恶之心、恭敬之心和是非之心，称之为"四端"，即仁、义、礼、智四种德性的萌芽。这里的恻隐之心是首要的，因为这是肇始于仁的爱心与同情心。孟子说：

❶《诗经·大雅·烝民》。
❷《孟子·告子上》6章。

❶ *The Book of Poetry*, "Greater Elegentiae," "The Common People."
❷ *Mencius*, "Gaozi," I 6.

sympathetic hearts. The ancient sage kings, due to possessing this kind of heart, all implemented humane government that was sympathetic to the people. Why do all men possess this heart? As an example, when all people see a small child about to fall into a well, they will all produce a heart of shock and compassion. The reason for producing this kind of feeling is not to please the parents of the child, nor is it to gain social prestige, even less is it out of loathing for the cry of the child, but it is because of instinct. Therefore, one could not be human without the heart of compassion, one could not be human without the heart of shame, one could not be human without the heart of yielding, and one could not be human without the heart of right from wrong. The heart of compassion is the sprout of humaneness, the heart of shame is the sprout of righteousness, the heart of yielding is the sprout of the heart of ritual courtesy, the heart of right and wrong is the sprout of wisdom. The human heart possesses these four kinds of sprouts, just like the body has four limbs. From birth man has these sprouts of fine virtue, but those who claim that they are unable to use them violate and abandon themselves; those who think that their lord is unable to administer a humane government are those who abandon their lords. Everyone possesses these 'four seeds;' if they knew to strive to enlarge them, then it would be like fire that was just kindled, in the end it will shine light on the whole world; it would also be like a spring of water flowing out, in the end it will became a great current. If one is able to enlarge these seeds, then it would be sufficient to stabilize all-under-heaven. But if they are not able to be enlarged, then even being filial to one's parents would not be able to be done!" ❶ Mencius described the condition of the seeds after they are enlarged: "The original nature of the gentleman is for the roots of humaneness, righteousness, ritual courtesy and wisdom to be planted in their hearts; this makes for a peaceful and smooth appearance, a glow appears on the countenance and shoulders, and even as far as the four limbs. With every move of the body one can understand him without his speaking." ❷

The four seeds can also be collectively called "the heart of humaneness and righteousness," or "heart of goodness." Mencius said, "A mountain was covered with the luxurious growth of grasses and trees; every day men hacked away at it with axes, and let cows and sheep graze on it; it soon became bare. Later everyone thought that this mountain had never grown any grass or trees; was this indeed the original nature of the mountain? Men are this way, do they indeed lack the heart of humaneness and righteousness? The reason they have lost their heart of goodness is like men on the mountain hacking away and herding livestock!" ❸ The heart of goodness is the psychological instinct of

"人人都有怜悯之心。古代的圣王因为有这样的心，才推行怜悯人民的仁政。为什么人人都有此心呢？譬如人人看到小孩要跌入井中，都会产生惊骇恻隐之心，之所以产生这样的心情，并不是要讨好孩子的父母，也不是要博取社会声誉，更不是厌恶小孩的哭声，而是发自本能。所以，没有恻隐之心就不是人，没有羞恶之心就不是人，没有辞让之心就不是人，没有是非之心就不是人。恻隐之心是仁的萌芽，羞恶之心是义的萌芽，辞让之心是礼的萌芽，是非之心是智的萌芽。人的心中有这四种萌芽，就好像身体有了四肢。生来就有这四种美德的萌芽，却自称能力不行的人是自暴自弃的人；认为他的君主不能推行仁政的人，就是背弃君主的人。每个具有这'四端'的人，如果都知道去努力扩充它们，就会像火刚被点燃，终究会光明普照；就会像泉水涌出，终究会汇成巨流。如果能扩充它们，便足以安定天下；如果不能扩充，连孝养父母都做不到！" ❶孟子描绘了四端被扩充后的状态："君子的本性，仁义礼智根植在他的心中，他的神采清和润泽，焕发于他的面容、肩背，乃至于四肢。举手投足之间，可以不言而喻。" ❷

四端也可以统称为"仁义之心"或者"良心"。孟子说："一座草木茂盛的山，天天用斧子砍伐，再放牛羊去吃，变得光秃秃的，人们都以为这座山不生草木，这难道是山的本性吗？人也是这样，难道人没有仁义之心吗？他之所以丧失了良心，也像人们在山上砍伐放牧一样啊！" ❸良心是人的心理本

❶《孟子·公孙丑上》6章。
❷《孟子·尽心上》21章。
❸《孟子·告子上》8章。

❶ *Mencius*, "Gongsun Chou," Ⅰ6.
❷ *Mencius*, "Jinxin," Ⅰ21.
❸ *Mencius*, "Gaozi," Ⅰ8.

man and innate intelligence; Mencius attributed them both to man's moral endowment, and called it the power of goodness or knowledge of the good: "All instinct that man knows but not through learning is the power of goodness; all principle that is understood without thought is knowledge of the good. No child of two or three but loves his parents, and after growing up none but respects and reverences their older brothers. Loving parents is indeed humaneness, respecting and reverencing older brothers is indeed righteousness. There are no other reasons for this, because these two are universal virtues." ❶ It is not true that Mencius did not understand the principle that man possessed a natural, original nature; but he stressed even more that each individual possessed the temperament of goodness. In other words, since "men hold this heart in common," that is, all share the same feelings, then it must be true that "the heart holds this principle in common," that is, all think the same way. He said, "The mouths of men are all addicted to the same flavors; the ears all interpret sounds in the same way; the eyes have the same aesthetic reaction to the same pleasing sights; why is it only men's heart that lack this commonality?" And what are the common points in the hearts of men? It is reason, it is righteousness! The sages were those who arrived before us at the points in the heart that are common to all men. Therefore, righteousness and reason are able to please our hearts, just like oxen, sheep, pigs, and dogs are able to satisfy our food addictions." ❷ He even enlarged the meaning of mind to be the "big entity." Gongduzi asked him, "All men are similar, then why are some great men with moral conduct, while some men are petty men with no shame?" Mencius said, "Those who know how to satisfy the most important organ, sometimes called the 'big entity,' will become great men; those who only know how to satisfy the secondary organs, sometimes called 'minor entities,' will become petty men." Gongduzi inquired further, " They are all similar in being men, so why do some men satisfy the great entity while others satisfy the small entities?" Mencius said, "The organs such as the eyes and ears cannot think, therefore are often deceived by external things. External things are murky and deceiving, causing the eyes to blur and ears to mishear. The function of the mind is to ponder, with pondering comes perception and the reception of internal virtue; without pondering nothing at all can be gained. This is an exclusive endowment given to us by Heaven, we should first nurture and protect this large entity, then the minor entities will not be deceived. This is the way to become a great man." ❸ Mencius felt that the distinction between

能和天生的智性，孟子全部归之于人的道德禀赋，还称之为良能和良知："凡是人不学就会的本能，就是良能；用不着思考就明白的道理，就是良知。两三岁的孩子没有不亲爱父母的，长大后没有不恭敬兄长的。亲爱父母就是仁，恭敬兄长就是义，这没有其他的缘故，因为这是两个普遍的美德。"❶孟子并非不明白人具有自然本性的道理，但他更强调人人都具有善的心性，也就是说，既然"人同此心"，那么就应该"心同此理"。他说："人的口对于美味都有共同的嗜好，耳对于音乐都有共同的听觉，眼睛对于美色都有共同的美感，为什么惟独人心没有共同处呢？人心共同的地方是什么呢？是理，是义啊！那些圣人就是先于我们得到人心共同之处的人。所以，义理能够愉悦我的心，就像牛羊猪狗能满足我的嗜好一样。"❷他甚至将心放大为人的"大体"。公都子问他："同样都是人，为什么有的人是有道德的大人，有的人是无耻的小人呢？"孟子说："知道去满足自身的重要器官或者叫作'大体'的人就会成为大人，只知道去满足自身的次要器官或者叫作'小体'的人就成为小人。"公都子又问："同样是人，为什么有人去满足大体，有人去满足小体呢？"孟子曰："眼和耳这些器官不会思考，所以常被外物蒙蔽。外物扑朔迷离，使得眼花耳乱。心的功能是思考，一旦思考就能觉察、获得内在于其中的美德，不思考则一无所获。这是上天专门赐予我们人的禀赋，我们应该先养护这样的大体，那么小体就不可能迷失。这样就能成为一个大人。"❸孟子认为，人与禽兽的区别就在于这一点点微小之处，

---

❶《孟子·尽心上》15章。
❷《孟子·告子上》7章。
❸《孟子·告子上》15章。

❶ *Mencius*,"Jinxin," Ⅰ15.
❷ *Mencius*,"Gaozi," Ⅰ7.
❸ *Mencius*,"Gaozi," Ⅰ15.

men and birds and beasts was in this very small point; mediocre men cast it off, and great men preserve it. ❶

Mencius criticized other thinkers who did not know what human nature was. He felt that discussions concerning human nature in the world only treat a kind of "cause;" that is, standards and practices determined by men. They regard the humaneness, righteousness, ritual courtesy and wisdom that are inherent in internal human nature as belonging to external moral categories. These external, manmade moral categories are all for the purpose of changing the function of human nature. These other thinkers did not realize that human nature is self-sufficient and completely good; they did not know that men incline towards moral behavior precisely because that is where the significance of being human lies. There are still others who detest knowledge, feeling that knowledge destroys the human nature endowed by Heaven. However, if human knowledge is similar to that used by Yu the Great to control the floods, then how could this make men detest knowledge? Yu the Great drained off the flood waters by merely taking advantage of the given circumstances, and following what was natural. If human knowledge is also similar to this, operating in accordance to man's original nature, then it is a kind of great wisdom. Heaven is so lofty, the stars as so distant, but as long as one knows the principles of their motion, a thousand years of calendrical calculations are able to be projected. ❷ Mencius said, "Shun understood the principles of things and the original nature of mankind. He only acted in accordance with humaneness and righteousness, but was not implementing humaneness and righteousness." ❸ Modern Chinese philosopher Liang Shuming reached a penetrating understanding of this; he said, "Sense is not something objective, if one mandates a sensible path and orders other to follow it, that would be enacting humaneness and righteousness, but often it would be inappropriate, and not worth following. The world perhaps blames Confucius and Mencius for the teachings of the 'Three Cardinal Relationship and Five Constant Virtues'— precisely teachings based on humaneness and righteousness. But this means they do not understand Confucius or Mencius." ❹

To coerce action to apply morality to change human nature is to regard mind and nature as two things, or is a continuous demand for thinking of the gain that results from morality, such as what was advocated by Gaozi or Mohists. Yet opposing the wisdom inherent in the natural, original nature of

平庸的人丢弃了，君子保存了。 ❶

孟子批评其他思想家并不知道人性究竟是什么。他认为：天下人谈论的人性，只不过是在谈一种'故'，也就是人为规定的准则和习惯。他们将内在于人性的仁义礼智当成了外在的道德规范。这些外在的、人为的道德规范，都是以改善人性的功利主义为出发点的。他们不知道人性是自足的、全善的，不知道人趋向于道德，正是人之所以为人的意义所在。还有些人讨厌智识，认为智识穿凿破坏了人的天性。但是，如果人的智识像大禹治水那样，怎么会令人讨厌呢？大禹疏通水，只是因势利导，顺其自然，如果人的智识也像这样顺应人的本性，那就是一种大智慧了。天如此之高，星辰如此之远，只要知道它们的运行法则，上千年的历法都能推算出来。 ❷孟子说："舜明了事物的情理和人类的本性，他只是顺着仁义前行，而不是推行仁义。" ❸中国现代哲学家梁漱溟对此有透彻的理解，他说："情理原不在于客观，若规定一条情理而要人们践行之，那便是行仁义了，往往不适当，不足取。世或以'三纲五常'的教训——那正是以仁义为教——归咎孔孟，固非能知孔孟者。" ❹

强行用道德改变人性，是将心性当作两个事物，或是一味讲求道德功利主义的思想，如告子或墨家的主张；而反对人类

❶《孟子·离娄下》19章。
❷《孟子·离娄下》26章。
❸《孟子·离娄下》19章。
❹ 梁漱溟《人心与人生》第18章，上海，学林出版社，1984，第227页。

❶ *Mencius*, "Lilou," Ⅱ19.
❷ *Mencius*, "Lilou," Ⅱ26.
❸ *Mencius*, "Lilou," Ⅱ19.
❹ Liang Shuming, *Human Mind and Human Life* (Shanghai: Academia Press, 1984), chapter 18, p. 227.

mankind should be the fundamental interpretation of Taoists❶. Since human nature for Mencius is both morality and wisdom, it is also endowed by Heaven and something natural; the power of goodness and knowledge of the good follow the course of man's life and naturally sprout and grow. Human nature is regulated by morality, just like human nature is regarded as being regulated by nature. Mencius clearly differentiated between two kinds of categories for human nature. He said, ❷

> The response of the mouth to fine flavors, the response of the eyes to beautiful sights, the response of the ears to music, the response of the nose to fragrant scents, and the response of the fours limbs to comfort— all are part of human nature bestowed by Heaven. But whether they are able to satisfy depends completely on the dispositions of fate. Therefore, the gentleman does not regard these as Heavenly-endowed nature, nor does he intentionally pursue them. The humane love shared by father and son, the duty between lord and minister, the ritual ceremony between host and guest, the wisdom possessed by the worthy, and the Way of Heaven observed by the sage—whether they can be achieved all depends on fate. But these qualities are all precisely part of the moral nature that is bequeathed to us by Heaven. Therefore, the gentleman does not let them be disposed of by fate, rather he strives to achieve them himself.

The majority of modern men who have received a scientific and rational education perhaps will lean more towards the Taoists' or Xunzi's viewpoints, and feel that neither morality nor culture are endowments of Heaven, but are the results of an acquired education. In our view, Mencius thought on "human nature is originally good" seems to contravene the presuppositions of common-sense theories. However, if we return to the age of Mencius, then we will discover that the chaotic age of the Warring States was pervaded with violence, destruction of morality, and pursuit of profit at the expense of righteousness, so many thinkers lost faith in morality and human nature. Perhaps they demanded a return to nature, or attempted to use force to correct human nature; only Mencius refined the commonplace concept of human nature into a metaphor for morality, and elevated man from an entity of nature into an entity of morality, and from this led humanity to an endless effort at self-renewal. This was due to his complete faith in the Heavenly-endowed nature of man to have

自然本性中具有智识，应该是道家的观念❶。孟子的人性既是道德和智识，也是天赋和自然，这些良能、良知随着人的生命过程自然地萌生、成长。人性是由道德规定的，正如认为人性是由自然规定的一样。孟子明确地区分了两种不同的人性范畴，他说❷：

> 口对于美味，眼对于美色，耳对于音乐，鼻对于芬芳，四肢对于舒适，这些都是人的天性，但能否满足，全听命运的安排，所以君子不将这些当作天性，不作刻意的追求。父子之间的仁爱，君臣之间的道义，宾主之间的礼仪，贤者具有的智慧，圣人体察的天道，能否实现也取决于命运，但这正是天赋予我们的德性，所以君子不把这些委托给命运去安排，而是努力去实现。

大多数接受过科学与理性教育的现代人可能会更多地同意道家或荀子的观点，认为道德与文化决不是人的天赋，而是后天教育的结果。在我们看来，孟子"性本善"的思想似乎是一种违背常识的理论预设。但是如果我们回到孟子的时代，就会发现，在那个暴力横行，道德沦丧，见利忘义的战国乱世，有那么多的思想家对道德和人性丧失了信心，或者要求回归自然，或者企求用强力矫正人性，只有孟子将人性从一个常识概念提炼成了一个道德喻体，将人从一个自然主体升华为一个道德主

---

❶ 本段的解释及前段关于"故"的解释参考了裘锡圭《由郭店简〈性自命出〉的"室性者故也"说到〈孟子〉的"天下之言性也"章》。裘锡圭《中国出土文献十讲》，上海，复旦大学出版社，2004，第269页至273页。

❷《孟子·尽心下》24章。

❶ The interpretation of this section, and the interpretation of the previous section concerning "cause" refer to Qiu Xigui, "'Mencius' Explanations on Nature in the World' as viewed from the passage 'What houses nature is order' from the Guodian bamboo work *Nature Emerges from Order*," in *Ten Lectures on Ancient Works Excavated in China* (Shanghai: Fudan University Press, 2004), pp. 269-273.

❷ *Mencius*, "Jinxin," Ⅱ 24.

this type of ability, and belief in the human mind being able to blend human nature with the Way of Heaven and to achieve transcendence. Mencius' theories were very inspirational, and manifested the compassion and faith in humanity of a great thinker.

体，从而引导人们不断地自我更新，因为他完全相信人类天生就有这样的能力，相信人的心能将人性与天道合而为一，实现超越，正是这一点，孟子的学说带有极大的感召力，彰显了一个伟大的思想家对人类的同情与信心。

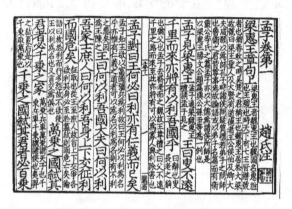

东汉赵岐注《孟子章句》

Eastern Han Zhao Qi's *Chapters and Verses of Mencius*

南宋朱熹《孟子章句集注》

Southern Song Zhu Xi's *Collected Commentaries on Mencius*

三　仁义礼智——道德体系

Chapter III　Humaneness, Righteousness, Ritual Courtesy, and Wisdom: The Moral System

The theory of Mencius' "Four Seeds" revealed that the source of morality was in the human mind and nature; but among the "Four Seeds," humaneness, righteousness, ritual courtesy, and wisdom form a moral system produced after deep and careful thought. Ever since Confucius, Confucians strove to expound the spirit of the traditional culture of ritual and music in order to reconstruct the collapsed sentiments of the times. It wasn't until Mencius promoted this type of moral system that the order and boundaries of Confucian morality were clearly manifested.

Before Confucius, many different moral categories appeared in the education based on the rites and music of the aristocracy. Such sources that narrated the history of the Spring and Autumn Period as the *Commentary of Mr. Zuo*, and *Conversations of the States*, frequently cited such moral categories as the "Five Teachings," and "Six Virtues" ; in fact there are more than ten kinds. For instance, respect, loyalty, faith, humaneness, righteousness, wisdom, bravery, ritual courtesy, filial piety, kindness, yielding, compassion, chastity, correctness, and the like. Among these moral virtues, humaneness, righteousness, ritual courtesy, and wisdom already appeared, but they were merely several moral behaviors among many, nor was the position of humaneness prominent. The relationship between humaneness, righteousness, ritual courtesy, and wisdom had not yet been established. Moreover, the number of moral categories demonstrates even clearer that morality was manifested in the external scope of ritual education, and had not been transformed into a self-aware moral spirit. Within the pre-Confucian moral system based on rites and music, filial piety was at the highest-level of morality, and was the respect and love for parents inherent within humanity. Because the rites and music were erected on the order of the patriarchal system of clan society and culture, ancestral worship became the common belief of families, the state, and the world; filial piety rose to become the political ideology of maintaining the Son of Heaven as the grand patriarch of the world. The fine virtue of Kings Wen, Wu, and Cheng celebrated in song in the *Book of Poetry* was always filial piety. Because in a society based on clans with shared blood ties, the position of lord and minister, father and son was equivalent. On the foundation of filial piety, other extended virtues emerged such as being kind to one's brothers, being loyal to one's lord, and being faithful to one's friends; of course in addition there appeared the virtues of kindness and benevolence on the part of elders and lords towards sons and grandsons and subjects. As one kind of fine virtue, humaneness was linked to filial piety; humaneness was a synonym of love. Aristocrats of the Spring and Autumn

　　孟子的"四端"之说揭示了道德根源于人的心性，而"四端"中的"仁义礼智"又是一个经过深思熟虑的道德体系。从孔子以来，儒家就努力阐释传统礼乐文化精神，以求重建崩溃了的世道人心，直到孟子提出这样一个道德体系，儒家的道德的秩序和境界才得以清晰地显现。

　　在孔子之前，贵族的礼乐教育中就出现了许多道德名目。在《左传》、《国语》等叙述春秋历史的文献中，动辄列举出"五教"、"六德"之类的德目，甚至多至十几种，比如敬、忠、信、仁、义、智、勇、礼、孝、惠、让、慈、贞、正等等，在这些道德中，仁、义、礼、智都已出现，但它们只是众多德行之一，仁的地位并不突出，仁、义、礼、智的关系也没有建立。而且道德名目如此繁多，说明道德更多地表现为外在礼教规范，没有转化为自觉的道德精神。在孔子以前的礼乐文化体系中，孝是最高级的道德，是人类天生对父母的敬爱。由于礼乐是建立在宗法血缘秩序上的氏族社会文化，因此祖先崇拜成了家、国、天下的共同信仰，孝上升为维护天子作为天下大宗的政治意识形态。《诗经》中歌颂的文王、武王、成王的美德都是孝。由于在血缘氏族社会中，君臣与父子的身份是一致的。在孝的基础上，生发出对兄长的悌，对君主的忠，对朋友的信，当然还有长辈和君主对子孙和臣民的慈爱与恩惠。仁作为一种美德也与孝相关。仁是爱的同义词。春秋时代的贵族们认为，作为

Period felt that as ordinary men, loving one's own parents and brothers was being humane; but as rulers, planning for the welfare of the state and the people was also being humane❶ . Confucius and his disciples regarded humaneness in the same manner. He said, "If the lord and nobility were able to treat their relatives with true feelings, then the common folk would respond by creating the fine virtue of humaneness." ❷ His student You Ruo also said, "Filial piety and brotherly kindness are the root of humaneness." ❸ But Confucius' understanding of humaneness surpassed that of earlier men, and hence established it as the foundation of his ethics.

To Confucius, the humaneness that existed in the heart was extended from blood relatives outward as love to all humanity, and this type of humaneness and love was not limited to the love and care that derived from sentiment or the charity that derived from welfare. Instead, it was a kind of moral aid. His disciple Fan Chi asked him what humaneness was. Confucius said, "Loving others." He also asked what wisdom was. Confucius said, "Knowing mankind." Fan Chi did not understand, so Confucius said further, "Recommending and promoting upright men to lead the non upright can make them upright." ❹ He said to his disciple, "What is humaneness? When one wants to improve himself, he wants to help others improve themselves at the same time. When one wants to complete a task, he also wants to help others complete their tasks." ❺ He further said to his disciple Zhonggong, "The humane person does not force what he does not like on others." ❻ He further said, "The humane person is not only able to love others, he is also able to loathe others." ❼ Confucius even felt that the humane were able to embody many types of moral conduct. He said that the respectful would not encounter disgrace, and that the tolerant would be embraced, the sincere would be trusted by others, the diligent would be able to complete affairs, and the kind would be able to lead others; those who are able to enact these five types of fine virtues

一般的人，爱自己的父母兄弟就是仁；作为统治者，为国家和人民谋取福利就是仁❶。孔子和他的弟子也是如此看待仁的。他说："君子贵族们能以真情对待他的亲人，民众就会感发出仁爱的美德。"❷他的学生有若也说："孝和悌是仁的根本。"❸但是孔子对仁的理解超越了前人，并以此奠定了他的伦理学基础。

孔子心中的仁是由血亲之爱推及到全人类的爱，而这种仁爱又不止于情感上的爱护或是福利上的施予，而是道德上的帮助。他的弟子樊迟问他，什么是仁，孔子说："爱人。"又问什么是智，孔子说："知人。"樊迟没能明白，孔子又说："推举正直的人，来领导不正直的人，可以让他们变得正直起来。"❹他对弟子子贡说："仁是什么呢？自己想要成就自己，同时也要帮助别人成就自己；自己想要干成事业，也要帮助别人干成事业。"❺又对弟子仲弓说："仁者不把自己不喜欢的事强加给别人。"❻他还说："仁者不仅能够爱别人，还能够厌恶别人。"❼孔子甚至认为仁能够包涵很多德行。他说恭敬就不会遭到侮辱，宽容就会受到拥护，诚信就会得到别人的托付，勤敏就能干成事业，慈惠就能领导别人，能处处履践这五种美

---

❶《国语·晋语一》。
❷《论语·泰伯第八》2章。
❸《论语·学而第一》2章。
❹《论语·颜渊第十二》22章。
❺《论语·雍也第六》30章。
❻《论语·颜渊第十二》2章。
❼《论语·里仁第四》3章。

❶ *Conversations of the States*, " Conversations of Jin," 1.
❷ *Analects*, "Taibo," 8.2.
❸ *Analects*, "Xue'er," 1.2.
❹ *Analects*, "Yan Yuan," 12.22.
❺ *Analects*, "Yong Ye," 6.30.
❻ *Analects*, "Yan Yuan," 12.2.
❼ *Analects*, "Inward Virtue," 4.3.

then are the humane. ❶

Therefore, Confucius extended humaneness to be the ideal of human life and the standard of conduct, even regarding it as more important than life itself. His disciple Yan Hui asked him what humaneness was. He responded, "Overcome one's selfish desires and restore one's words and actions to conform with the rites, this is therefore humaneness. If one day this is done, then the people of the world would agree that you are humane. Achieving humaneness depends completely on oneself to be achieved, how could it be dependent on others?" He even said, "Men of lofty ideals and humaneness will not drag out a dishonorable existence and injure humaneness, they are willing to sacrifice their lives to complete their humaneness." ❷

Now we are in a good position to perceive the line of Mencius' thinking. Out of all the different types of virtuous conduct, he selected humaneness, righteousness, ritual courtesy, and wisdom, and systematically expounded the contents and relationships of these four. "The basic essence of humaneness is to serve one's father and mother; the basic essence of righteousness is to follow one's older brothers and elders; the basic essence of wisdom is to understand the principles of humaneness and righteousness and be steadfast in upholding them; the basic essence of ritual courtesy is to be restrained and refined in how one enacts humaneness and righteousness. And the basic essence of happiness is to take joy in humaneness and righteousness; therefore happiness is created. Once happiness is created then it cannot be stopped, since it cannot be stopped then imperceptibly the hand will start to move and the feet to dance." ❸ . From this we may observe that humaneness and righteousness are the most fundamental components in Mencius' moral system, and wisdom and ritual courtesy are the self-awareness and practice of humaneness and righteousness, as well as the means through which to enter the moral realm of happiness. Mencius went a step further and internalized them as the human heart, that is, the sphere of actions of ritual, righteousness and objective reason are roots that produce the heart of respect and yielding and the heart of good and evil. Even though humaneness, righteousness, ritual courtesy, and wisdom are manifested as the hearts of compassion, shame, respect, and right and wrong, these four types of mentalities all can be summed up in one heart, the heart or mind of goodness or as it is sometimes called, the "heart of humaneness and righteousness." Historical sources antedating Mencius and the Confucian classics all lack the phenomenon of the two words "humaneness and righteousness" occurring together. Yet in *Mencius*, the phrase "humaneness and righteousness" has already formed a fundamental sphere on its own, and is the

德就是仁。❶

所以，孔子将仁推作人生的理想和行为准则，甚至比生命还重要。他的弟子颜回问他什么是仁，他说："克制自己的私欲，让自己的言行复归于礼，这就是仁。一旦做到这样，天下的人都会称许你的仁。实现仁，全靠自己去做，难道还要依赖别人吗？"他甚至说："志士仁人，不会苟且偷生而损害仁，只有牺牲生命来成全仁。"❷

至此，我们可以看出孟子的思想路径。他在众多的德行中选择了仁义礼智，系统地论述了四者的内涵与关系："仁的实质是侍奉父母；义的实质是顺从兄长；智的实质是明白仁义的道理并坚守下去，礼的实质是对仁义进行节制文饰。而乐的实质就是喜欢仁义，于是快乐便产生了。快乐一旦产生便无法中止，无法中止便不知不觉地手舞足蹈了起来。"❸由此可见，仁与义是孟子道德体系中最基础的构成，智与礼是对仁义的自觉与履践并由此进入快乐的道德境界。孟子进一步将它们完全内化为人心，即便是礼、义这样的行为规范和客观事理也是恭敬辞让之心和羞恶之心产生的根源。仁义礼智尽管体现为恻隐之心、羞恶之心、恭敬之心和是非之心，但这四种心态皆统于一心，这个心可以称作"良心"，或者叫"仁义之心"。孟子以前的历史文献和儒家经典里都没有"仁义"二字并称的现象，而在《孟子》中，"仁义"已经成了一个基本范畴，是他的学

❶《论语·阳货第十七》6章。
❷《论语·卫灵公第十五》9章。
❸《孟子·离娄上》27章。

❶ *Analects*, "Yang Huo," 17.6.
❷ *Analects*, "Duke Ling of Wey," 15.9.
❸ *Mencius*, "Lilou," Ⅰ27.

core of his theory. Mencius compared humaneness to a house where one dwells in peace, and compared righteousness to the correct path. If one cannot intuit this, then it is like leaving the home vacant with no one dwelling in it, or like abandoning the correct path. Abandoning the self is a very tragic thing.❶ He said that humaneness was man's heart, and righteousness was man's path. Abandoning the correct path and refusing to travel it, losing the heart and not seeking it, truly are tragic. Some people will seek after a chicken or a dog if it runs away, yet if they lose their own hearts they do not know enough to go to seek them. The path of learning is none other than to seek for one's lost heart.❷

Mencius was the same as Confucius, he held humaneness in the highest esteem. He also felt that humaneness was the love that was an extension of the intimate feelings shared between father and son, and was different from general love. He said, "The gentleman has protective love towards things but does not extend the virtue of humaneness; he extends the virtue of humaneness to the people but does not have close love. Because a gentleman possesses feelings of close love towards his relatives, therefore he is able to have feelings of humane love towards the people. Because he has feelings of humane love, he therefore has the feelings of protective love towards things." ❸ Therefore, humaneness is a kind of root planted in the human heart, and is true morality based on the natural feelings of the closeness of humanity. This type of morality is the fundamental ethics of humanity, and is the most universal kind of love. Therefore, Mencius took a step further in asserting, "Humaneness, so called, is to be human. When humanity is combined with humaneness, this is the Way." ❹ The humaneness of Confucius is both a personal internal virtue as well as a standard of behavior and ideal for living. Yet when Mencius proposed the principles of humanity and righteousness, he regarded humaneness an even more fundamental virtue, and assigned the standard of behavior to the category of righteousness. Humaneness cannot bear bad things, and righteousness cannot perform bad things. Humaneness is self-expressed, and righteousness is self-regulated. He said, "Men all have things that they cannot bear, and take this kind of sympathetic love and extend it to things that they do not love; this then is humaneness. Men all face things that they are willing to do, so they take this kind of internal principle and extend it to things that they are not willing to do; this then is righteousness. When men are able to expand the heart that cannot bear to harm others, humaneness can be used without depletion; when men are able to expand the heart that is not willing to bore a hole in a wall to steal and plunder, righteousness then can be used without depletion. When men

说核心。孟子将仁比作人安居的家室，将义比作人正确的道路，如果不能自觉到这一点，就好像空着家室不居住，舍弃正道不去走，遗弃自我，实在是很悲哀的事。❶他说仁就是人的心，义就是人的路。舍弃正道不走，遗失了心不知去寻找，真是可悲啊。有的人，鸡犬跑了都知道去找，而自己的心丢了却不知道去找。学问之道没有别的，就是找回丢失了的心。❷

　　孟子与孔子一样，对仁推崇备至。他也认为仁是由父子亲情推广出的爱，与一般的爱不同。他说："君子对于事物，爱护它们但不施加仁德；对于人民，施加仁德但不亲爱。君子因为对亲人有亲爱之情，所以能够对人民有仁爱之情；因为对人民有仁爱之情，所以对事物有爱护之情。"❸所以，仁是一种根植于人心，以人类的自然亲情为基础的真实道德，这样的道德才是人类的基本伦理，也是最普遍的爱。所以孟子进一步断言："所谓仁，就是人。人与仁合起来，就是道。"❹孔子的仁既是一个人的内在德性，又是人的行动准则与人生理想，而孟子提出仁义，则将仁看成更加基本的德性，而将人的行动准则归之于义。仁是不忍，义是不为；仁是自发的，义是自律的。他说："人都有不忍心的事，将这种爱怜之心推及到他不爱的事情上就是仁；人都有不愿做的事，将这种内心的原则推及到他愿意做的事上就是义。人能够扩充不忍害人的心，仁就使用不尽；能扩充不愿穿墙打洞偷盗行窃的心，义就使用不尽。人

❶《孟子·离娄上》10章。
❷《孟子·告子上》11章。
❸《孟子·尽心上》45章。
❹《孟子·尽心下》16章。

❶ *Mencius*, "Lilou," Ⅰ10.
❷ *Mencius*, "Gaozi," Ⅰ11.
❸ *Mencius*, "Jinxin," Ⅰ45.
❹ *Mencius*, "Jinxin," Ⅱ16.

are able to expand their words and actions without being slighted by others, then there is no place that does not meet with righteousness. A scholar, upon seeing a wealthy and noble man, cannot casually strike up a conversation with him, yet does so anyway of his own volition; this act is to entice him with words in order to facilitate his own gain. Upon seeing a worthy and fine man, he instead does not know that he should converse with him, this is to use silence to keep away from morality." ❶ In his work *Collected Commentaries on Mencius*, Zhu Xi explained in a profound manner Mencius' viewpoint on humaneness and righteousness, "Humaneness is the moral character of the heart, the root of love. Righteousness is the constraint of the heart, the rationale of things." ❷

Righteousness is manifested as the heart of shame, and can be called a type of ability to be aware of shame. Confucius once admonished his disciples, saying that as scholars they must maintain the heart of shame in all their conduct. ❸ Mencius also said, "Men cannot do without the sense of shame; if one lacks shame in the face of humiliation, then one truly has no shame!" Righteousness is the highest form of moral discipline; it is even more important than trustworthiness. Mencius said, "Not every sentence of the words spoken by sages with morality has to be kept, not everything done has to have good results, but all must be based on the principle of righteousness." ❹ He solemnly declared ❺,

Fish is what I like to eat, bear palm is also what I like to eat. But if I cannot have them both, I would discard the fish and choose the bear palm. Life is what I like, righteousness is also what I like. If I cannot have them both then of course, I would discard life and select righteousness. Because there is something that I yearn for more than life, therefore I cannot drag out a dishonorable existence; because there is something that is more fearful than death, therefore I cannot evade disaster. If existence is the greatest thing sought in human life, if death is the greatest disaster in human life, then in order to exist or to avoid death, then there should be nothing that I would not do. However, there are some who are not willing to continue to exist, and are not willing to avoid death. From this we can see that there are some things more valuable than life in this world, and there are some things more hateful than death. This type of heart of righteousness is not something only possessed by the sages and worthies, but is possessed in common by all men. It is just that the sages and

能够扩充自己不被别人轻蔑的言行，就没有一处不合乎义。一个士人，见到富贵的人，不可以与他随便交谈却主动与他交谈，这是用语言来引诱他，以便自己获取利益；见到贤良的人，却不知道与他交谈，这是用沉默来远离道德，以便自己获取利益，这就是穿墙打洞偷盗行窃的人。"❶朱熹在他的著作《孟子集注》中深刻地解释了孟子的仁义观念："仁是心的品德，爱的根据。义是心的制约，事的情理。"❷

义体现为羞恶之心，也可以说是一种能够自我察觉羞耻的能力。孔子就曾告诫过他的弟子说，作为一个士，在自己的行为中要保持羞耻之心。❸孟子也说："人不可以没有羞耻感，没有羞耻的耻，真是无耻了啊！"义是最高的道德纪律，甚至比诚信还重要。孟子说："有道德的圣人们，说出来的话不必句句守信用，做事情不必都有结果，一切都以义作为原则。"❹他郑重地说❺：

> 鱼是我喜爱吃的，熊掌也是我喜爱吃的；二者不能都吃到，当然舍弃鱼而选择熊掌。生命是我喜爱的，义也是我喜爱的；二者不能一起得到，当然舍弃生命而选择义。因为有比生命更令我向往的东西，所以我不苟且偷生；因为有比死亡更令我恐惧的东西，所以我不逃避灾祸。如果活着是人生最大的追求，如果死亡是人生最大的祸患，那么为了活着或逃避死亡就可以无所不为。

---

❶《孟子·尽心下》31章。
❷ 朱熹《孟子集注》卷一。《四书章句集注》，北京，中华书局，1983，第201页。
❸《论语·子路第十三》20章。
❹《孟子·离娄下》11章。
❺《孟子·告子上》10章。

❶ Mencius, "Jinxin," II 31.
❷ Zhu Xi, *Collected Commentaries on Mencius*, in *Collected Commentaries on the Chapters and Verses of the Four Books* (Beijing: Zhonghua Book Company, 1983), vol. 1, p. 201.
❸ *Analects*, "Zilu," 13.20.
❹ *Mencius*, "Lilou," II 11.
❺ *Mencius*, "Gaozi," I 10.

worthies are able to keep it. A basket of rice, a pot of soup, and one can keep on existing after consuming them, but without eating them one would die of hunger. But if we were to change the rice to dog meat and have others eat it, not even those starving on the roadway would accept it; if we threw it on the ground for others to eat, not even beggars would deign to glance at it. If one were to accept with alacrity a high office with high pay without asking whether it would be commensurate with ritual propriety, let me ask, what benefit does a high office and high pay hold for me? Would I get to live in a beautiful palace, have a host of wives, and let my poor relatives and friends thank me for my charity? Things that in the past one was willing to die in order to avoid doing, nowadays are accepted and enjoyed and for their vain glory. Can this be the way it should be? This is simply crazy!

Regarding righteousness with the same importance as Confucius regarded humaneness, Mencius felt that righteousness was more precious than life. To complete humaneness and select righteousness was the highest goal of moral accomplishment for Confucianism. Over the course of Chinese history, at the juncture when the country and people faced their greatest crisis, to sacrifice one's life for the sake of humaneness and to select martyrdom for a righteous cause spurred to action many men of humaneness and great ambition.

In addition to combining "humaneness and righteousness" together, he also combined "ritual courtesy and righteousness." "Ritual courtesy and righteousness" are ancient concepts; during the Spring and Autumn Period they were used to indicate external ritual ceremonies and moral principles. Mencius not only interpreted righteousness as human self-discipline, he also interpreted ritual courtesy as the heart of respect and yielding, and considered it to be a supplement to the heart of humane love and compassion. The heart of respect and yielding actually is a type of love, manifested as concern and veneration between individuals. It is mankind's moral foundation for not being willing to compete with or kill each other, not at all rigid ritual requirements. Ritual courtesy and righteousness seem to be external, but both are based in the human heart; therefore Mencius said, "Rites that do not accord with ritual courtesy, and righteousness which is not in accord with righteousness— the sagely and the worthy do not observe them." ❶ He also was opposed to those who went against human nature, who clung to ritual practice at all cost. The sophist Chunyu Kun posed a difficult question to Mencius, asking him, "Men and women are not permitted to give or accept things directly from each other, is this part of the ritual system?" Mencius said, "Yes." Chunyu Kun asked

不过，有些人不愿意这样活下去，不愿意这样躲避死亡，由此可见世上有比生命更可贵的东西，有比死亡更可恶的东西。这种道义之心并不仅仅是圣贤才有，而是人人都有，只是圣贤能够不丧失它罢了。一筐饭，一盆汤，吃了便能活下去，不吃就要饿死。可是象唤狗一样让人来吃，饥饿的路人也不会接受；扔在地上给人吃，就是乞丐也不屑一顾。有人不问是否符合礼义，欣然接受了高官厚禄。请问高官厚禄对于我有什么益处呢？是为了居住华丽的宫室，妻妾成群，让贫穷的亲友感激我的施舍吗？过去宁愿去死都不愿意接受的事，今天却为了这些享受和虚荣而接受了，这难道是应该的吗？这简直就是丧心病狂！

与孔子看重仁一样，孟子认为义比生命还珍贵。成仁取义，是儒家道德实践的极端方法。在中国历史上，当国家与民族出现危难之际，杀身成仁，舍生取义，激励了许多仁人志士。

孟子除了将"仁义"并称之外，还将"礼义"并称。"礼义"是很古老的概念，春秋时代就用来指称外在的礼仪与道德原则。孟子既将义解释为人的自律，又将礼解释为恭敬辞让之心，作为对仁爱恻隐之心的补充。恭敬辞让之心其实也是一种爱，体现为人类之间的关爱与尊敬，是人类不愿意互相争夺、互相残杀的道德基础，并非缰死的礼法规范。礼义看似外在，但根据皆在人心，所以孟子说："不符合礼的礼，不符合义的义，圣贤们是不去遵守的。"❶他也反对人们违背人性，死守礼法。辩士淳于髡出了个难题问他："男女之间不能直接赠予或接受东西，这是礼制吗？"孟子说："是。"淳于髡又问：

---

❶《孟子·离娄下》6章。

❶ *Mencius*, "Lilou," Ⅱ 6.

further, "If your sister-in-law fell into a well of water, would you extend your hand to pull her out?" Mencius said, "If one's sister-in-law fell into a well and one did not extend one's hand to pull her out, this would simply be a case of acting like a ruthless wolf or jackal. Men and women not making contact, this is ritual practice; a sister-in-law drowning in water, and lending a helping hand, this is to be accommodating!" ❶ Mencius especially opposed rulers utilizing ritual practice to oppress the people. One time King Xuan of Qi said to him, "Ritual practice prescribes that a minister who has quit his post must wear mourning clothes for a lord whom he used to serve. May I enquire what the basis of this is?" Mencius said, "A ruler who is able to receive admonition from a minister, and dispense kindness towards the people, this kind of minister leaving his now non-essential post lets others escort him out of the state. He sends somebody ahead of time to the place he is headed towards to make preparations. If he does not return within three years of leaving, then the land and housing that had been given him are forfeited. This is called 'the rites of three.' When this type of ruler passes away, those ministers who have left his service will wear mourning clothes. The conditions at present are different now. Rulers do not accept admonition from their ministers, and treat the people harshly. A minister leaving his post under such circumstances would have the ruler send his minions after him to arrest him, or would send them to where the minister has settled to browbeat him. As soon as he left his post, his land and housing were confiscated. This is called being a personal enemy. Why should one treat an enemy well by wearing mourning clothes? " ❷

"Wise" in the scope of Confucianism indicates wisdom, knowledge, and recognition. Confucius said, "The wise are not deluded, the humane do not worry the brave do not fear." ❸ In the *Doctrine of the Mean*, it says, "Wisdom, humaneness, and bravery are three types of the greatest form of fine virtue." Confucius also said that wisdom meant to know others, therefore the wisdom of Confucians meant to an even greater degree moral wisdom with regard to others. Yet Mencius took an additional step in explaining wisdom as the heart of good and evil, becoming a kind of ability to make moral judgments, and was to a certain degree cleverness or intelligence. King Xuan of Qi would not accept Mencius' words, and after attacking and occupying the state of Yan he enacted a tyrannical regime, provoking the resistance of the people of Yan. King Xuan said, "I am treating Mencius shabbily." His great minister Chen Jia made excuses for the king, saying, "You great king should not blame yourself. Think about it, comparing you with the Duke of Zhou, who could have more humane love and wisdom?" King Xuan of Qi said, "Good grief, how could you

"如果嫂子掉进水里，伸手拉她吗？"孟子说："嫂子掉进水里都不伸手去拉她，这简直就是豺狼。男女不相接触，这是礼法；嫂子溺水，援手相救，这是变通！"❶孟子还特别反对统治者利用礼法来压迫臣民。有一次齐宣王对他说："礼法中规定：已经离职的臣子也要为过去侍奉过的君主穿孝服。请问凭什么应该这样呢？"孟子说："能够接受臣下的进谏，对人民施予恩惠。臣下因故离开，让人护送他出境，事先派人到臣下要去的地方作好安排。离开三年还不回来，才收回赐给他的田地房舍。这叫做'三有礼'。象这样的君主薨亡了，那些离职的臣子会为他穿孝服的。如今的情况就不同了，不接受臣下的进谏，对人民严酷，臣下因故离开，君主便派人拘捕他，又让人到他去的地方扼制他，人一走便没收他的土地房舍。这叫做仇敌。对待仇敌，哪有为他穿孝服的道理！"❷

智在儒家的范畴中指的是智慧、知识、认识，孔子说："智者不疑惑，仁者不忧虑，勇者不恐惧。"❸《中庸》里面说："智、仁、勇，是天下三种最大的美德。"孔子还说智就是知人，所以儒家的智更多地指关于人和道德的智慧，而孟子进一步将智解释为是非之心，成为一种道德判断能力和发挥仁爱的能力，并非一般意义上的聪明或心智。齐宣王不听孟子的话，攻占燕国后施行暴政，引发了燕国人的反抗。宣王说："我要愧对孟子了。"他的大臣陈贾却为国君开脱，说："大王不要自责，想想看，您与周公比，谁更有仁爱和智识呢？"齐宣王说："啊

❶《孟子·离娄上》17章。
❷《孟子·离娄下》3章。
❸《论语·子罕第九》29章。

❶ *Mencius*, "Lilou," Ⅰ 17.
❷ *Mencius*, "Lilou," Ⅱ 3.
❸ *Analects*, "Zihan," 9.29.

say something like this? How can I be compared with the Duke of Zhou?"
Chen Jia said, "The Duke of Zhou let his elder brother Guanshu oversee the
Yin people, but Guanshu led the Yin people in rebellion. If Duke of Zhou was
able to anticipate Guanshu's actions yet granted him permission go anyway,
thus letting him fall into unrighteousness, he would not have been humane. If
Zhou Gong was not able to anticipate this result, then he would have been
unwise. In such matters the Duke of Zhou was unable to be either humane or
wise, so how much less with regard to you? I will go and ask Mencius about it,
and see what he has to say." Thereupon Chen Jia went to visit Mencius, and
asked him, "What type of man was the Duke of Zhou?" Mencius said, "An
ancient sage." Chen Jia asked further, "He let Guanshu oversee the Yin people,
yet Guanshu instead led the Yin people in rebellion. Did this really happen?"
Mencius said, "Yes." Chen Jia asked again, "Did the Duke of Zhou anticipate
that Guanshu would rebel, yet on purpose let him go oversee them?" Mencius
said, "The Duke of Zhou did not anticipate that he would rebel." Chen Jiao
asked a final question, "It sounds as if even sages would make mistakes,
right?" Mencius refuted him, saying, "The Duke of Zhou was a younger
brother, Guanshu was his elder brother; could a younger brother suspect his
elder brother? Wasn't this mistake of the Duke of Zhou a reasonable thing?
How much more so for ancient gentlemen who correct their mistakes; modern
gentlemen make mistakes then compound them. Ancient gentleman made
mistakes, such as with regard to eclipses of the sun or moon; this is something
visible to the people. But when they rectified their mistakes, this was also
visible to the people. Modern gentlemen not only make mistakes, but do not
stop at compounding them but also brazenly look for excuses with no sense of
shame!" ❶ To Mencius, the error was Guanshu's, not the Duke of Zhou's. The
Duke of Zhou was heartfelt in his use of humaneness to treat others, herein lay
his great wisdom.

An even more elevated moral realm than humaneness and ritual courtesy
was sageliness; sageliness was another kind of great wisdom. It says in one
Confucian classic, "Sageliness is a flower that has grown out of wisdom." ❷ It
is of the highest grade, and permeates great wisdom ❸. Mencius also said,
"Between fathers and sons is humane love; between lords and subjects is the
righteousness of the Way; between hosts and guests is ritual ceremony; what
the worthy possesses is wisdom; and what the sage perceives is the Way of
Heaven." This explains that from the starting point of humaneness, it can be

呀，你这是说的什么话？我怎能与周公比？"陈贾说："周公
让自己的哥哥管叔去监视殷人，而管叔却率领殷人反叛。倘若
周公能够预见管叔会这样做却让他去监视殷人，陷哥哥于不义，
那是不仁；倘若周公不能预见到这样的结果，那是不智。仁而
且智，这样的事连周公都做不到，何况您呢？我先去问问孟子，
看他怎样说。"于是陈贾来见孟子，问道："周公是一个怎样的
人？"孟子说："古代的圣人。"陈贾又问："他让管叔去监视
殷人，管叔却率领殷人反叛，请问有这回事吗？"孟子说：
"有。"陈贾再问："周公是预知他会反叛，却有意让他去监视
殷人吗？"孟子说："周公事先不知道。"陈贾最后问道："如
此说来，圣人也是会有过错的啦？"孟子反驳道："周公是弟
弟，管叔是哥哥，弟弟难道还会怀疑哥哥吗？周公犯这样的错
误，不是很合乎情理吗？何况古代的君子有过错就改正，现在
的君子，有了过错竟然将错就错。古代君子犯错误，好像日蚀、
月蚀，老百姓都能看见；他改正错误时，老百姓们也能看得见。
现在的君子们，岂止将错就错，还厚颜无耻地寻找借口！"❶
在孟子看来，本来错在管叔，不在周公。周公由衷地以仁待人，
这正是周公的大智。

比仁义礼智更高的道德境界是圣。圣是一种更大的智慧。
儒家经典里说："圣是智开出的花"❷，是上等的、通贯广大
的智❸。孟子也说"父子之间是仁爱，君臣之间是道义，宾主
之间是礼仪，贤者具有的是智慧，圣人体察的是天道"。这说

---

❶《孟子·公孙丑下》9章。
❷《大戴礼记·四代》："圣，知之华也。"
❸《尚书·洪范》孔安国传："于事无不通谓之圣。"

❶ Mencius, "Gongsun Chou," II 9.
❷ The Record of Rites of Master Dai, "Four Generations." Or, as it literally says, "Sageliness is the flower of wisdom."
❸ The Book of History, "Great Plan," Commentary of Kong Anguo says, "There is a kind of sageliness that permeates all things."

extended to the rituals of lord and subject, host and guest, and a righteous society, and elevate it to become the moral realm of a worthy person, even to becoming the universal realm of the sage. Sageliness is a very hard realm to attain. Confucius once sighed, saying, "I have never seen a sage, but if I could see a gentleman then I would be satisfied." ❶ Zigong once asked Confucius, "If someone's virtue influenced the people, and his charity extended to all of life, what kind of man would this be, can we term him a humane man?" Confucius said, "Why limit him to being humane? He would certainly be a sage. Even Yao or Shun would be hard pressed to accomplish this much." ❷ One of Mencius' disciples once asked him whether he had attained to the realm of a sage; Mencius told him, "Before, Zigong asked Confucius, ' Master, should you be considered a sage person?' Confucius said, 'As for sageliness, it is something that I cannot reach, I just study without tiring, teach others unceasingly, and that is it.' Zigong said, ' To learn without tiring is wisdom; to teach others unceasingly is humaneness. To be humane as well as wise—master, you are already a sage!' Confucius did not boast of being a sage person, so what is this question of yours?" ❸

In 1973, a Western Han dynasty tomb at Mawangdui near Changsha, Hunan, yielded a silk manuscript called "The Five Phases;" it expounded the contents and relationships of the five virtues of humaneness, righteousness, ritual courtesy and sageliness. It is considered by modern scholarly circles be a Confucian text that was influenced by Mencian theory. Possibly it was the "Five Phases" theory of the school of Mencius and Zisi as attacked by Xunzi ❹. It considers that humaneness and righteousness are the roots of ritual courtesy and wisdom, that the four virtuous acts of humaneness, righteousness, ritual courtesy, and wisdom together constitute humaneness, and that the five virtuous acts of humaneness, righteousness, ritual courtesy, wisdom, and sageliness together constitute virtue. Goodness is the human way, virtue is Heaven's way, but the path from the human way to Heaven's way is wisdom. Later Confucians in the Han also adopted the approach of coordinating the Five Virtues with the Five Phases, that is, coordinating the Confucian virtues of humaneness, righteousness, ritual courtesy, and faithfulness with the wood, metal, fire, water, and earth of the Yinyang specialists; they then explained morality in terms of material bodies that circulated among mankind and the universe. All in all, the set of "humaneness, righteousness, ritual courtesy, and

明由仁这个起点，可以推及到君臣宾主的礼、义社会，再上升成为一个贤人的道德境界直至圣人的宇宙境界。圣是一个非常难以达到的境界。孔子曾感叹说："圣人我见不到了，我能见到君子就满足了。"❶子贡问孔子："如果有人泽被于民，普济众生，这样的人是什么人，可以说他是个仁人吗？"孔子说："岂止是仁啊，一定是圣人了！就是尧和舜，也许都难以做到啊！"❷孟子的弟子也曾问过孟子是否达到了圣人的境地，孟子告诉他："从前子贡问孔子说：'老师您算得上是圣人了吗？'孔子说：'圣，我是达不到的，我只不过学而不厌，诲人不倦罢了。'子贡说：'学而不厌，是智；诲人不倦，是仁。仁而且智，老师您已经是圣人了！'孔子都不自居为圣人，你问的是什么话呢？"❸

公元1973年，在湖南长沙马王堆西汉墓中出土了一种叫做《五行》的帛书，其中阐论仁、义、礼、智、圣五种德行的内涵与关系，被学界认为是受到孟子学说影响的儒家文献，很可能就是被荀子攻击的子思、孟子学派的"五行"学说❹。其中认为仁义是礼智的根源，仁义礼智四行构成善，仁义礼智圣五行构成德。善是人道，德是天道。而由人道通往天道的途径是智。后来汉儒又采用了五德配五行的方法，即用儒家的仁义礼智信分别配合阴阳家的木金火水土，将道德解释为周流于人体和宇宙万物之中的物质实体。总之，"仁、义、礼、智"是中

❶《论语·述而第七》26章。
❷《论语·雍也第六》29章。
❸《孟子·公孙丑上》2章。
❹ 参见庞朴《〈五行篇〉评述》，庞朴《稂莠集——中国文化与哲学论集》，上海，上海人民出版社，1988，第427页至449页。

❶ *Analects*, "Shu'er," 7.26.
❷ *Analects*, "Yongye," 6.29.
❸ *Mencius*, "Gongsun Chou," Ⅰ 2.
❹ See Pang Pu, "*Five Phases*, Evaluated and Expounded," in *The Langyou Collection: Chinese Culture and Philosophical Disquisitions* (Shanghai: Shanghai People's Publishing House, 1988), pp. 427-449.

wisdom" is the most influential moral system in traditional Chinese culture.

Zhu Xi once evaluated Mencius' "nature is good theory" as follows: "Humaneness, righteousness, ritual courtesy, and wisdom are principles that have not been released. Compassion, shame, yielding, right and wrong have all been externally released. So compassion is similar to peach-kernals (*taoren*) and apricot kernals (*xingren*) sprouting into tender shoots. The Four Seeds that Mencius invented is a doctrine that Confucius never invented. All that people know is that Mencius refuted the school of Yang Zhu and attacked the school of Mohism, but they do not realize that, with regard to the heart of humaneness and righteousness, he had such as great discovery. Criticizing heresies was the merit of defending the frontier, and inventing the Four Seeds was the merit of stabilizing the country." ❶

国传统文化中最有影响的道德体系。

朱熹曾经如此评价孟子的性善说："仁义礼智是尚未发出来的道理，恻隐羞恶辞让是非是已经发出来的端倪。如同桃仁、杏仁是仁，萌发出来的嫩芽是恻隐。孟子发明四端，是孔子没有发明过的道理。人们只知道孟子拒斥杨朱学派和抨击墨家学派，却不知道他在仁义之心方面有如此大的发明。批判异端是捍卫边境的功劳，发明四端才是安定社稷的功劳。"❶

---

❶ 朱熹《朱子语类》一一九。

---

❶ Zhu Xi, *Classified Sayings of Zhu Xi*, 119.

深受孟子思想影响的中国艺术，这是宋代山水画，遵从儒家道德境界
Chinese Art deeply influenced by the thought of Mencius
The picture of Mountains and Rivers of Song Dynasty following the
Confucian moral realm

四　我善养吾浩然之气——道德与精神的修养

Chapter Ⅳ　I am Good at Nurturing My Flood-like Qi:
Moral and Spiritual Self-Cultivation

In the viewpoint of Mencius, the practice of morality, fundamentally speaking, was definitely never a process of external training or obedience but was rather a matter of how to perceive internal morality and maintain moral action. Furthermore, one should enact humaneness and righteousness in a self-aware and willing manner to advance towards an entirely spontaneous and natural enactment of humaneness and righteousness. If one is forced to be moral, his moral conduct actually is of no consequence. Ancient Chinese philosophy called the highest realms of spirit and cultivation the "union of Heaven and man." Mencius regarded that being able to completely give free rein to one's heart of goodness, one's knowledge of goodness, and one's power of goodness and other moral dispositions would enable one to completely master the self, and to realize Heaven's order, and thereby reach the realm where one becomes fused as one with the universe. This is completely different from the Taoist effort to transcend morality and return to nature, thereby achieving the freedom of fusing with the universe. In the same way, Confucians were not wise men who sought to avoid the world or engage in esoteric speculation; therefore, their Heaven and man fusion was not a mysterious journey or experience, but was rather part of daily life at home, social activity and self-reflection.

It is hard to use words to truly experience the moral realm; if one must of necessity vocalize it, then the best word would be happiness. Confucius claimed that he was so happy that he forgot his sorrows, and even did not realize the passing of time❶. He also said that a life based on simple fare included an element of happiness, because those satisfied with a life of poverty enjoyed moral happiness; in the eyes of those who would not do anything to enjoy wealth and honor, these things were like passing clouds❷. A conscious-free gentleman all day long is composed and at ease in mind, but a petty man all day long frets and is ill at ease❸. Confucius' disciples were also this way. For instance Yan Hui, the one with the best moral cultivation, was praised by Confucius as follows: "Yan Hui is truly worthy and virtuous! He makes do with one bowl of rice, one gourd of water, and lives in a slum; others could not stand such straits. Yet Yan Hui did not alter his happiness; he truly is worthy and virtuous." ❹ Mencius not only experienced this type of happiness, but also was able to analyze it. Mencius said :

　　在孟子看来，道德的实践从根本上说，决不是外在训练与服从的过程，而是如何在内心察觉道德，保持道德行为，并从自觉自愿地履践仁义进展到自然而然地履践仁义。如果一个人只是迫不得已去服从道德，他的道德行为其实是毫无意义的。中国古代哲学将最高的精神与修养境界叫做"天人合一"。孟子认为能够完全地发挥出良心、良知、良能等道德本性，就能完全把握自我，知道天命，从而达到与宇宙融为一体的境界。这和道家通过超越道德，回归自然从而与宇宙融合的自由境界完全不同。同样，儒家也不是避世或玄想式的哲人，所以他们的天人合一境界不是神秘的经历或经验，而是日常的家居生活、社会活动和自我反省。

　　真正体验到的道德境界很难用语言表达，如果一定要说出来，那就是快乐。孔子声称自己快乐得忘记了忧愁，甚至不觉得岁月的流逝❶。又说粗茶淡饭的生活包含着快乐，因为甘于清贫生活的人享受的是道德上的快乐，那些不择手段图谋到的富贵享乐，在他们的眼里好像浮云一般❷。问心无愧的君子，成天胸怀坦荡；心里有鬼的小人，成天忧愁不安❸。孔子的弟子们也是这样，比如，道德修养最好的颜渊，孔子称赞他："颜回真是有贤德啊！一筐饭、一瓢水，住在贫民窟里，别人都不能忍受这样的困苦，颜回却不改变他的快乐，颜回真是有贤德啊！"❹孟子不仅体验了这样的快乐，并且能够分析这样的快乐。他说：

---

❶《论语·述而第七》19章。
❷《论语·述而第七》16章。
❸《论语·述而第七》37章。
❹《论语·雍也第六》11章。

---

❶ *Analects*, "Shu'er," 7.19.
❷ *Analects*, "Shu'er," 7.16.
❸ *Analects*, "Shu'er," 7.37.
❹ *Analects*, "Yongye," 6.11.

A gentleman enjoys three kinds of happiness, but the happiness of a lord ruling the world is not one of them. Parents still alive and brothers safe with no calamities, these exemplify the first type of happiness. Being able to lift up one's head with no shame before Heaven, lowering the head with no shame before men, these exemplify the second type of happiness. Gaining splendid talent from around the world and educating them, these exemplify the third type of happiness. A gentleman possesses these three kinds of happiness, but the happiness of a lord ruling the world is not one of them! ❶

These three types of happiness actually are moral realms; the case of parents and brothers being safe is precisely the realm of filial piety and brotherly kindness. Above, not being ashamed before Heaven, and below, not being ashamed before men, is precisely the realm of Heaven and man fused as one. Nurturing splendid talent in the world is precisely what Confucius said about "the self wanting to complete the self, and at the same time wanting to help others complete themselves" which is the realm of humane love. Mencius declared that man could feel the realm of "all things being replete in me;" that is, to discover that the principles that underlie all things are all replete in one's own self. In such a realm, one can return to his own person and master the true nature of morality, and feel the greatest happiness. Only by feeling in one's own body this moral truth will one be able to know that other persons' bodies also are replete with this kind of truth, and thereby strive to extend oneself to others, to achieve humane virtue; there will never be a more convenient path to this goal. ❷

The realm of happiness described by Mencius is not a kind of spiritual fantasy, because there is still another experience, that of the difficult process of moral cultivation; to Mencius, this is the training of the mind. Similar to how we refer to training the body in Kungfu as "martial arts," or "boxing arts," the training of the mind is also called the "art of the mind." Cheng Hao, a Neo-Confucian philosopher of the Northern Song Dynasty, said, "In discussing the art of the mind, no one can compare with Mencius." ❸

Confucius had already recognized the educational method of enlightening the human mind. He said, "I will not try to enlighten anyone until he is perplexed and resentful, and will not try to enlighten him before he wants to

　　君子有三种快乐，而君临天下的快乐并不在其中。
父母健在，兄弟无灾，这是第一种快乐；仰头对得起天，
低头对得起人，这是第二种快乐；得天下英才而教育，
这是第三种快乐。君子有此三乐，但君临天下的快乐并
不在其中！❶

　　这三种快乐其实都是道德境界，父母兄弟无恙，正是孝悌
的境界；上不愧对天，下不愧对人，正是天人合一的境界；培
养天下的英才，正是孔子所说的"自己想要成就自己，同时也
要帮助别人成就自己"的仁爱境界。孟子声称人可以感受到一
种"万物皆备于我"的境界，也就是发现万事万物的道理无一
不具备于我的身上。在这样的境界中，他可以返回自身，把
握到道德的真实性，感觉到最大的快乐。在自己身上体验到
这样的道德真实性，才知道别人身上也一定具备这样的真实
性，因而勉力地推己及人，实现仁德，再也没有比这更便捷
的途径了。❷

　　孟子描述的快乐境界决不是一种精神幻觉，因为他还有另
一种体验，即道德修炼的艰辛过程，在孟子看来，就是心的锻
炼。像我们谈论身体的修炼功夫如"武术"、"拳术"一样，心
的修炼功夫也叫"心术"。北宋理学家程颢说，"讨论心术，没
有人比得上孟子。"❸

　　孔子就已认识到启发人心的教育方法，他说："不到他困
惑愤懑时不去开导他，不到他想说却说不出来时不去启发

---

❶《孟子·尽心上》20章。
❷《孟子·尽心上》4章。
❸ 明陈士元《孟子杂记》引程颢曰："论心术无如孟子。"

❶ *Mencius*, "Jinxin," Ⅰ 20.
❷ *Mencius*, "Jinxin," Ⅰ 4.
❸ Chen Shiyuan of the Ming Dynasty, in his *Miscellaneous records on Mencius*, quoted Cheng Hao saying, "In discussing the art of the mind there is nobody like Mencius."

express himself but cannot." ❶ Mencius also felt that the human mind could be self-enlightened in the midst of difficulties; this is an important method for being able to achieve this type of enlightenment of the mind and spirit. He cited the growth experiences of some ancient sages and worthies to discuss this principle: ❷

The Great Shun grew out of being a peasant, legend has it that from the hard labor of building walls he was promoted. Jiao Ge was employed out of his experience of selling fish and salt. Guan Zhong was released by a prison warden. Sun Shu'ao was discovered on a distant seashore. Baili Xi was bought from a slave market. Therefore, when Heaven above wanted to confer a great mission on someone, it would first test his resolve through trials, labor his person, starve him and deprive his body of water, make him loose all with nothing going his way. In this way, it can shock his mind and spirit, make him determined in disposition, and increase his abilities. Men often commit errors before they are able to produce an attitude of wanting to correct themselves. It is only through suffering internal difficulties and after the thoughts are blocked by problems that one will rouse oneself to accomplish something. It is only after the internal emotions become expressed in the countenance and one cries out loud that others will be able to understand you. The reason a state is able to exist is the same; when internally a state lacks the rule of law and ministers who are able to aid in government, and externally faces no strong enemies or invasions, this type of state will often be destroyed or perish. From all of this was can discern a common principle: one survives in the midst of difficulty; one perishes amid ease and happiness.

He further said, "A man with morality, wisdom, skill, and talent often thereby faces difficulties. Solitary servants or sons born from minor concubines have lives that are full of worry from day to day, and are constantly anxious, therefore they are able to understand the ways of the world." ❸ If one lives in an environment of ease and indulgence, then one's disposition and mind will be lost just like chickens or dogs which run off; only by living in a hostile, ill at ease environment will the mind become self-aware, become enlightened, and be able to utilize the knowledge of goodness and the power of goodness. This then is the so-called art of "arousing the mind to produce an enduring nature."

他。"❶孟子也认为，人心在困境中能够自我发作，这是启发心灵自觉能力的重要手段。他列举了一些古代圣贤的成长经历来谈论这个道理❷：

> 大舜是从农夫成长起来的，传说是从筑墙的苦役中被提拔的，胶鬲是从经营鱼盐的商贩中被起用的，管仲是从狱吏手中释放出来的，孙叔敖是从边远的海滨被发现的，百里奚是从奴隶市场上买出来的。因此，上天要把重大的使命降临到这个人的身上，一定让他心志困苦，筋骨劳累，身体饥饿，一无所有，事事皆不如愿，这样就可以震撼他的心灵，坚韧他的性情，增强他的能力。人经常有过错，才会生发出改正的心愿；内心困苦，思虑困塞，才会发愤有为；内心的情感表露于面容，呐喊出声音，才能被人理解。一个国家生存的道理也是如此，国内缺少有法度、能辅佐的大臣；国外没有强敌与外患，这样的国家往往会灭亡。由此可以明白一个真理：生于忧患，死于安乐。

他还说："有道德、智慧、技术、才华的人，往往因为他有苦难。孤立的臣子、小妾生的孩子，他们日日操心，时时忧虑，所以能通晓人情世故。"❸人的心性如果处在安逸放纵的境界中，心就会象鸡犬那样跑失，只有处于忧患不安的环境中，心才会自我警觉，启动并运用他的良知、良能。这便是所谓的"动心忍性"之术。

---

❶《论语·述而第七》8章。
❷《孟子·告子下》15章。
❸《孟子·尽心上》18章。

---

❶ *Analects*, " Shu'er," 7.8.
❷ *Mencius*, " Gaozi," Ⅱ15.
❸ *Mencius*, " Jinxin," Ⅰ18.

Confucians in general all considered that the mind and nature have to experience the training of external ritual and music before being able to be correct and proper, and come under the control of the self. Xunzi said, "Man's blood, mind, and thoughts are able to flow freely and without obstruction through the tempering of ritual, otherwise they will be sluggish and confused, wild and arrogant." ❶ To Xunzi, the mind is like a basin of water; whether it is level and still, clear and bright depends completely on its external condition ❷. The *Record of Rites* also considers that indulging in pleasures and other behavior that does not comport with ritual propriety do not make contact with the mind and spirit, idle and evil dispositions do not exist in the body; the organs of the ears, eyes, nose, mouth, and mind are the only things that can feel sensations, and only human beings are able to follow righteousness in their conduct ❸. Mencius' art of the mind was not striving to perform an external activity that exerted force to change the mind; his method could be training through the rites and music, and it could occur in a bad environment, or in a state of clear self-consciousness. But the goal was all along to develop an internal ability to enlighten the human mind, thus causing the human mind to illuminate itself and shine within. Mencius called this condition "consciousness." He said to his disciples, Yi Yin originally was a hermit in the wilds cultivating his own morality. The reason that he came out to accept Tang's recruitment was that he suddenly felt that "Heaven above bore and nurtured humanity designing to let those who first became enlightened enlighten those destined for later enlightenment. I am one among humanity who was first enlightened, so I must let others become aware of the way of goodness of Yao and Shun. If I do not set out to enlighten them, who would do so?" ❹

Mencius gained a deep awareness concerning human psychology; he said, "Confucius once said, 'Handle it, it exists, abandon it, you will lose it.

　　儒家一般都认为，心性经过外在礼乐的训练才能中规中矩，自我克制。荀子说："人的血气、心意、思虑，通过礼来调治就能通畅和顺，不然就会悖乱狂傲。"❶在荀子看来，心如一盘水，它是否平静、是否清明全部取决于外在的条件❷。《礼记》中也认为，淫乐与非礼的事不与心灵接触，怠惰与邪恶的情绪不存在于身体，耳目鼻口心等感官才能具有感知能力，人才能顺着道义去行事❸。孟子的心术并非谋求外力来改变心的活动方式，他的方法可以是礼乐的训练，可以是恶劣的环境，也可以是清醒的自我意识，但其目的皆在于启发出人心的内在能力，使得人心自明内照。这种状态，孟子称之为"知觉"。他对弟子说，伊尹本来是一个隐居田野，独善其身的人，他之所以出来接受汤的聘用，因为他突然感到："上天生育了人类，就是要让先知先觉的人启迪后知后觉的人。我就是人类当中的先知先觉，我要让人们觉悟到尧舜的善道。我不去启发他们，谁去启发他们呢？"❹

　　孟子对人的心理活动有着深刻的体验，他说："孔子曾经

---

❶《荀子·修身》："凡用血气、志意、知虑，由礼则治通，不由礼则勃乱提僈。"
❷《荀子·解蔽》："故人心譬如盘水，正错而勿动，则湛浊在下而清明在上，则足以见须眉而察理矣。微风过之，湛浊动乎下，清明乱於上，则不可以得大形之正也。"
❸《礼记·乐记》："淫乐慝礼不接心术，惰慢邪僻之气不设于身体，使耳目鼻口心知其百体，皆由顺正以行其义。"
❹《孟子·万章上》7章。

❶ *Xunzi*, " Self-Cultivation." As it is put literally, " In everything which needs the blood and the vital breathe *qi*, the will and mind, knowledge and consideration, if tempered by ritual then they will be function smoothly; but if not tempered by ritual, then they will be sluggish, confused, and arrogant."
❷ *Xunzi*, " Resolving Perplexities." As Xunzi put it, " Therefore the human mind is like a basin of water, if upright and still it is turbid below but clear above; this makes it good enough to reflect the beard and eyebrows of a man, and to observe the water's principle. With a slight breeze passing by, the turbidity moves down below, and the clarity gets confused above, then one cannot
❸ grasp the correctness of its form."
As the *Record of Rites*, " Record of Music," puts it, " Indulging in pleasure and evil rites does not make contact with the art of the mind, indolent and deprave airs do not establish themselves in the body. That which causes the ears, eyes, nose, mouth, and mind to sense all things is that they all correctly follow justice."
❹ *Mencius*, " Wanzhang," Ⅰ7.

Coming and going at no set time, there is no telling where it goes.' What he was talking about was the human heart!" ❶ He also said, "Even an inferior way of chess playing, if one does not concentrate with his entire mind, cannot be mastered. Yi Qiu was a master at chess; if he were to teach two students, one would concentrate and listen to his teacher; the other one was absent-minded, musing about shooting swan-geese flying overhead in the sky. Although these two students were learning the same way, the latter was definitely not up to the former. Was this due to him not being as clever as the former? Of course not!" ❷ Therefore, although both possessed the same mind of goodness from birth, if one cannot firmly control it, then one will be swallowed up with things, and turn debauched.

To concentrate is the condition of preserving the original clarity of awareness of the internal mind and concentration. To summon the will is to produce correct thinking. Mencius also called this type of "art of the heart" the "unmovable heart." But the unmovable heart does not mean that one controls one's heart. Some people, in complying with the ritual practices of morality, do so blindly with one eye closed and their minds confused. Zhu Xi describes this type of cultivation method as "dim and unperceptive, and unconscionably unaware ❸." Mencius very much emphasized the mutual influence between the mind and spirit and the feelings of blood and *qi*, and emphasized the relationship between blood and *qi* and the psychological condition which they create. During the age of Mencius, Taoists in the Jixia Academy such as Song Xing and others possibly had already treated the problem of nourishing the *qi*. In the *Guanzi*, "Art of the Mind," it says, "With the four limbs in correct position, the blood and *qi* level and still, the mind and thoughts unified, the ears and eyes will not be deluded, and will be able to clearly sense things." It further says, "The vital essence, ghosts, spirit and *qi* dwell in the human heart, but come and go, present in all places, reaching all places. The reason some men cannot stay in a good spiritual condition is because of irritability. If the mind is able to be concentrated and be level and still, the way of life will naturally be set in one's body. For the one who obtains the way, the harmonious and fine *qi* in the body permeates the skin and the pores, and no rotten or putrid *qi* dwells in the breast." It also says, "*Qi* is something rife in the body; when correct, it is the standard for action. As for a gentleman, if the *qi* rife in his body is not fine and good, then his mind will not be at ease; his actions will not be upright, and the people will not obey him." Mencius profoundly understood this type of theory. He also considered that the roots of

说过：'操持住它，就存在；放弃它，就跑失。进进出出全无定时，不知它要去往何方。'说的就是人的心啊！"❶又说："即便是下棋这样的小道，如果不能一心一意也学不好。奕秋是个下棋高手，如果让他教两个学生，一个专心致志地听老师的话；另一个心不在焉，想着去射天上的鸿雁。这两个人虽然一道学习，但后者一定不如前者。是因为他不如前者聪明吗？当然不是了！"❷因此，人虽然天生具备良心，但是如果不能操持得住，便会沉溺于外物，自我放逸。

专心，就是保持内心原本的清醒和专注的状态；致志，就是产生出正确的思想。孟子也将这样的"心术"叫作"不动心"。但是不动心并不是强制住自己的心。有的人遵守道德礼法是盲目的，眼一闭，心一横，朱熹称这样的修养方法是"冥然无觉，悍然不顾"❸。孟子很注重人的心灵与血气情感的互相影响，注重心与气的关系及其造成的心理状态。在孟子的时代，稷下学宫里的道家人物宋钘等可能已经讨论养气的问题。《管子·心术》中说："四肢端正，血气平静，一心一意，耳目就不会迷惑，就能清楚地感知事物。"又说："人的精神灵气存在于人心，一来一往，无处不在，无处不至。之所以有人不能处于良好的精神状态，是因为急躁。心能专一平静，生命之道就自然定于其身。得道的人，他身体里的和美之气蒸泄于肌理与毛孔之间，胸中毫无腐败之气。"还说："气，是充斥于身体中的东西，正，是行为的准则。对于君子来说，充斥的气不美好，心

---

❶《孟子·告子下》8章。
❷《孟子·告子上》9章。
❸《孟子集注》卷三，《四书章句集注》，第231页。

---

❶ *Mencius*, "Gaozi," Ⅱ 8.
❷ *Mencius*, "Gaozi," Ⅰ 9.
❸ Zhu Xi, *Collected Commentaries on Mencius*, in *Collected Commentaries on the Chapters and Verses of the Four Books*, vol. 3, p. 231.

human blood, *qi*, and emotions lay in the human mind, and issued forth from the mind. But he explained that the kind of *qi* of life that exists in the mind and spirit was a moral *qi* that exists in the heart of goodness, and understood that the energy of life was a moral energy. He told his disciple Gongduzi that both day and night, the inner heart constantly produces the fine virtue of goodness, especially at night. When the mind and spirit of each man and his body are tranquil and still and in a condition of harmony, this type of psychological condition is called "night *qi*." So at daybreak, the *qi* within each man is equal parts good and evil. However, during the day, when they come in contact with things and are doing things, their mind of goodness often is imprisoned or lost. Day after day it is hard to maintain this type of "night *qi*." It is just like the grass or trees on a mountain, even though they grow each day, they cannot withstand the hacking and cutting of men or the grazing of oxen and sheep, so it is hard to preserve them. This makes them little different from birds and beasts ❶. Therefore, in order to preserve one's own mind of goodness, one needed a set of techniques for nurturing the *qi*. One time, he was discussing with his disciple Gongsun Chou how to avoid letting the heart be moved; it was a very brilliant dialogue ❷ :

Gongsun Chou asked, "If you master were to be the prime minister of Qi and were able to achieve your own political ideals, would you become the hegemon of the world or would your enact the royal way? Neither would be difficult to do. Reaching such a position you certainly would have to worry over something. In this case would you let your heart be moved?"

Mencius said, "I wouldn't, since reaching the age of forty I have not let my heart be moved."

"Speaking like this, you master are certainly much braver than that brave hero Meng Ben?"

"It isn't that difficult; Gaozi first reached the realm of not letting his mind be moved."

"Well, is there a method to not letting your mind be moved?"

"There is. Like when the brave hero Beigong You was nurturing his bravery, even when his skin was hurt he did not shirk, or when his eyes

就不安宁；行为不端正，民众就不服从你。"孟子对这样的理论有深刻的理解。他也认为人的血气情感根源于人心，从心中生发出来。但他将这种存在于心灵之中的生命之气阐发为存在于良心之中的道德之气，将生命的能量理解为道德能量。他告诉弟子公都子：人在白天和夜里，内心都时时发生出善良的美德，特别是在夜里，每个人的心灵与身体都处于平静、和谐的状态，这样的心理状态可叫做"夜气"。所以在天明之际，每个人内心的好恶都差不多。可是到了白天，当他与外物接触，有所作为，他的良心往往受到囚禁或亡失，日复一日，人就很难保持这种"夜气"，就像山上的草木，尽管天天都在长，但也经不住人们的砍伐和牛羊的啃食，难以保持，就与禽兽相差不远了❶。所以，要保持自己的良心，还有一套养气的功夫。一次，他与弟子公孙丑谈论如何不动心，这是一场精彩的对话❷：

公孙丑问道："老师如果担任齐国的卿相，能够实现自己的政治理想，将来称霸天下或推行王道，都不是困难的事。能到这样的地步，一定有所恐惧担忧，请问你是否会因此而动心呢？"

孟子说："不会的，我到四十岁就不动心了。"

"这么说来，老师比孟贲这样的勇士勇敢得多了。"

"这并不难，告子比我先达到不动心的境界。"

"那么，做到不动心有方法吗？"

"有的。像北宫黝这样的勇士在培养自己的勇气时，

---

❶《孟子·告子上》8章。
❷《孟子·公孙丑上》2章。本文对这段话的理解，参考了冯友兰《孟子浩然之气章解》一文，冯友兰《中国哲学史》下册，附录五。第423页至431页。

❶ Mencius, " Gaozi," I 8.
❷ Mencius, " Gongsun Chou," I 2. For the understanding of the present work on this passage, see Feng Youlan, " Explanation of Mencius' chapter on Flood-like Qi," in *History of Chinese Philosophy*, vol. 2, Appendix Five, pp. 423-431.

were pierced he did not give way. A little setback was viewed as being humiliated in public. He could not endure the attacks of commoners, nor could he endure the oppression of the lord of a state. Killing a lord of state was the same as killing a commoner; he never feared the feudal princes, but would repay an eye for an eye."

"The brave hero Meng Shishe had another technique for nurturing his bravery. He said, 'In my mind, there is no difference between a strong enemy and a weak enemy. If one first considers strength or weakness, large numbers or small numbers before sending out the troops, or first considers victory or defeat, gain or loss before joining in battle, this type of person would certainly be afraid of a strong enemy. So how could I be able to be ever victorious? I just concentrate on screwing up my own courage, and have no fears!'

The method Meng Shishe used to nurture his bravery was similar to that of Zengzi, and that of Beigong You was similar to Zixia. I do not know who among these two men was braver, but the method used by Meng Shishe was more simple and easy to implement. Before, Zengzi once said to Zixiang, 'Do you love bravery? I once heard Confucius say something about what great bravery was. If upon self-introspection one came to realize that he was in the wrong, even if the opponent was a commoner, he would not deceive him. If upon self-introspection one came to realize that he was in the right and his qi was steadfast, even in the face of a numerous force of men and horse, he would bravely march onward.' Compared to this, Meng Shishe's method of nurturing his bravery was to hold on to his bravery. His unmovable mind came from his steadfast qi, therefore it was not as simple and easy to implement as the method of Zengzi. Zengzi's bravery came from the judgment of his internal morality, so he was in the right and his qi was steadfast. "

Gongsun Chou further said, "Your student dares to ask, can I please hear the difference between your unmoved heart, master, and that of Gaozi?"

Mencius said, "Gaozi once said, 'Words cannot clearly describe true principles, so they should be abandoned. There is no need to seek whether there is any true principle within the mind. If the mind is ill at ease, then one should use true principles to control one's own ambitions, no need to seek help from whether your qi is steadfast or not.' I think that the first half of Gaozi's words are erroneous, but the second half make some sense. Why shouldn't one seek help from qi to control the

肌肤受创也不后退，眼睛被刺也不避让，稍有挫败，如同当众受辱。既不能忍受布衣平民的攻击，也不能忍受大国君主的压迫，杀一国君如杀一匹夫，从不惧怕诸侯，睚眦必报。

勇士孟施舍另有一套培养勇气的方法，他说：'在我心中，强敌与弱敌没有区别。如果先考虑众寡强弱再出兵，先考虑胜负得失再交锋，这样的人一定惧怕强敌。我哪能做到百战百胜？我只专注于鼓起自己的勇气，无所畏惧罢了！'

孟施舍培养勇气的方法很像曾子，而北宫黝很像子夏。我不知道这两个人谁更勇敢，但是孟施舍的方法更为简约易行。从前曾子曾经对子襄说：'您爱好勇敢吗？我曾经从孔子哪里听说过什么是大勇：如果反躬自省而自觉理亏，即便对手是个布衣匹夫，我也不去欺负他；如果反躬自问而理直气壮，即便面对千军万马，也勇往直前。'相比之下，孟施舍的养勇只是守持住一股勇气，他的不动心是由于气壮，所以还不如曾子的方法简约易行，曾子的勇气来自于内心的道德判断，理直而气壮。"

公孙丑又说："学生斗胆提问，老师您的不动心与告子的不动心，可以让我有所闻知？"

孟子说："告子曾经说过：'语言不能说清楚道理，就应当舍弃，不必求助于心里是否有理；于心有所不安，就应该用道理强制住自己的心志，不必求助于气势是否雄壮。'我认为告子的话，前半句是错的，后半句还算有些道理。为什么不求助于气就能强制住心呢？因为按照

mind without it? Because according to Gaozi's logic, the mind is the controller of the *qi* and *qi* is that part of the mind that fills the emotions of the body. The mind determines the *qi*; where the mind lodges, *qi* is always manifested along with it. Therefore Gaozi said, 'Maintain the mind, and do not let *qi* leak out.' "

Gongsun Chou broke in with a question, "Since Gaozi said, 'Where the mind lodges, *qi* is always manifested along with it.' Why did he then further say, ' Maintain the mind, and do not let *qi* leak out?' Why is that?"

Mencius said, "Because when the mind is concentrated and unified then it can control the emotions and the *qi*. But after the emotions and the *qi* are blended together, they will instead disturb the mind. It is like a person going all out using his strength to run straight ahead. The power of his *qi* is brimming; suddenly he trips and falls, the power of his *qi* will be affected, but whether it is brimming or diminished, his mind will either get firmer or weaker!"

"Master, then let me inquire, what are your own strengths?"

"I am able to understand the words of others, and I am good at nurturing my flood-like *qi*."

"What may I ask is the flood-like *qi*?"

Mencius said, "It is hard to explain clearly! This type of *qi* is the greatest, the strongest; used correctly to be nurtured and not harmed, it will fill the space between heaven and earth. This type of *qi*, when coordinated with righteousness and the Way, will circulate all around. Without them, the *qi* will erode and weaken. This type of *qi* comes from the thickening of righteousness that exists within the mind in a spontaneous way. It grows each day, but is not something that is produced by a sudden seizure of righteousness used to control the mind. As soon as something disturbs the peace of the mind, then it deteriorates and weakens. Therefore I say, Gaozi does not understand at all what the meaning of righteousness is, because he regards it as something external that is within the human mind. As for our internal righteousness, it must be nurtured, but do not have any pre-conceived requirements. Do not forget it in the mind, but do not intentionally force it to grow. Do not be like that man from Song! Once a man from Song was worried about the lack of growth among his rice sprouts, so he went out to tug at them. Tiring out, he returned home, saying, 'Today I am so tired! I helped my rice sprouts to grow!' His son rushed off to take a look at the field, but

告子的说法，心志是气的统帅，气是充满于身体里的情感意气。心志决定意气，心志所到之处，必有气随之显露。所以告子说：'把持住心志，不要泄气。'"

公孙丑插问道："告子既然说'心志所到之处，必有气随之显露。'为何又说'把持住心志，不要泄气。'这是为什么呢？"

孟子说："因为心志专一就会控制情感意气，但情感意气凝聚之后也会反过来撼动心志。比如一个人鼓足了劲向前跑，他的气势很旺盛；忽然跌了一跤，他的气势就会受挫，但无论是旺盛还是受挫，他的心志也随之变得坚定或软弱啊！"

"请问老师您的长处是什么呢？"

"我能知晓别人的言辞，我善于培养我的浩然之气。"

"请问什么是浩然之气？"

孟子说："这就很难说清楚了！那种气，最伟大，最刚强，用正直来培养而不伤害它，它就会充塞于天地之间。那种气，配合着义与道而周流；没有了它们，气就会败馁无力。那种气是由存在于内心之中的义集聚起来，自然而然，日久生成的，决非从外面袭夺一义来控制内心就能产生出来的。只要有一件事情做得于心不安，那种气就会败馁无力。所以我说，告子根本不懂什么是义，因为他把义看成了外在于人心的东西。对于我们内心的义，一定要养，但不要有所预期规定；心中不要忘记，但也不要刻意强求生长。不要像宋人那样啊！有个宋国人担心禾苗不能生长，便去将禾苗拔高一些。他疲惫地

all of the sprouts had died. Actually, in the world there are very few who do not engage in this type of activity of tugging at sprouts. Those who think that there is no benefit to nurturing rice shoots are those who certainly do not plant their fields, but those who intentionally demand that their rice shoots quickly grow are those who tug on shoots. Acting in this way, not only is of no benefit, instead it is also harmful."

"May I enquire what it means to understand others' words?"

Mencius said, "I am able to understand the defects of one sided words; I am able to understand the flaws in boastful words; I am able to understand the partiality of casual words; and I am able to understand the errors in vague words. These types of words which are not in keeping with righteousness, if produced in the human mind, they will endanger the government; if manifested in governmental practice they will harm governmental affairs. If another sage were to appear, he certainly should listen to what I have said!"

Nurturing the *qi* is a method of self-cultivation inseparable from the method of understanding words. Confucius once said, "If one does not understand the Mandate of Heaven, there is no way to become a gentleman. If one does not understand the rites, there is no way to be established in society; if one does not understand words and speech, there is no way to understand others." ❶ To understand words is to understand men, and to nurture the flood-like *qi*; then the mind will no longer be fearful or doubtful; from this one will have a profound mastery of human nature, righteousness and principles, and the Way of Heaven. Only then will one have the standard by which to evaluate other's words and minds.

Mencius' theory on nurturing the *qi* transcended mere training of the nature and mind, and caused them to comform with the moral sphere. It also transcended the scope of Zengzi's moral self-awareness. It is not the learning of the normal gentleman, instead it is the learning of how to become a sage or a great man. Feng Youlan said, "The bravery that Zengzi gained from maintaining righteousness, although great, still pertains to the relationship between men. The flood-like *qi* of Mencius gained by gathering righteousness is something that pertains to the relationship enjoyed between men and the cosmos." "This flood-like *qi* exists squarely in the middle of the cosmos. Although it is only limited to the average size of a full-grown man, in this realm it already has transcended limitations and has advanced to where there are no limits." ❷ Therefore, nurturing the flood-like *qi* is the process of the human spirit participating in the actions of the universe through developing

回到家说：'今天我太累了！我帮助禾苗生长了！'他的儿子赶到田里一看，禾苗全都枯死了。其实天下很少有人不干这种拔苗助长的事。那些认为培育禾苗没有益处的人固然是不种田的人，而刻意要求禾苗快快生长的，便是拔苗的人。这样做，不仅没有益处，反而还有害处。"

"请问什么是能够知晓别人的言辞呢？"

孟子说："片面的言辞我能知道它的蔽陋之处；夸大的言辞我能知道它的缺陷之处；随便的言辞我能知道它的偏离之处；隐晦的言辞我能知道它的理亏之处。这些不合乎义的言辞，产生于人心便会危害政治，体现于施政便会危害政事。如果再有圣人出现，一定会听从我的话！"

养气与知言是不可分割的修养功夫。孔子曾说："不知道天命，没办法成为君子；不知道礼，没办法立足于社会；不知道言辞，没办法了解别人。"[1]知言就是知人，养成了浩然之气，内心不再恐惧疑惑，从而对人性、对义理、对天道有了深刻的把握，才能具备衡量他人言辞与心志的尺度。

孟子养气的学说，超越了训练心性使之符合道德规范的层次，也超越了曾子道德自觉的层次，不是一般的君子之学，而是成圣之道或大人之学。冯友兰说："曾子由守义而得的大勇，虽大，而仍是关于人与人的关系者。孟子由集义而得的浩然之气，则是关系人与宇宙的关系者。""有浩然之气者，堂堂立于宇宙间，虽只是有限的七尺之躯，而在此境界中，已超过有限，而进于无限矣。"[2]所以，养浩然之气是人的精神通过对自性

---

[1] 《论语·尧曰第二十》3章。
[2] 冯友兰《孟子浩然之气章解》。

[1] *Analects*, "Yao Saying," 20.3.
[2] Feng Youlan, "Explanation of Mencius' chapter on Flood-like *Qi*."

one's own nature and moral cultivation.

What Mencius meant by flood-like *qi* is inseparable from his understanding of human nature. The source of this *qi* is in the human mind; after growing it nurtures the mind. The course of its growth is as natural as that of rice sprouts; but it requires the cultivation of both "wisdom" and "action" with not even a bit of external force. This type of thought has often been regarded as a mysterious spiritual experience by modern philosophers because within ancient Chinese thought *qi* is hard to pin down. It can be explained as man's blood and vapor, character, feelings, or life force; it can also be explained as the source, construction, and energy of the universe. But viewed from the angle of Mencius, flood-like *qi* is not a kind of private and personal experience, but is a kind of *qi* that is born in the mind, that collects goodness and stores up righteousness, and externally fills the universe. It can be manifested as a true moral and spiritual force. Mencius said: ❶

> "Wealth and honor cannot make me besotted or promiscuous; poverty or baseness cannot make me lose my integrity; power or military might cannot make me submit; this is called being a great man!"

Actually, as for those who nurture the flood-like *qi*, originally being able to become a great man meant reaching the highest realm. Zhu Xi once said that the flood-like *qi* "was like a Yangtze River and great stream, onrushing like a flood. Wealth and honor, poverty and baseness, power and military might and other unmovable things—these realms are too low, and cannot be compared with it." ❷ Therefore, flood-like *qi* is more so a power of beauty and a power of sacredness. Mencius said , ❸

> What makes men close to each other is "goodness," when goodness truly exists within the self it forms "faithfulness;" when it fills the body it forms "beauty;" it not only enriches but also emits splendor which forms "greatness;" when splendor shines universally, it transforms and adapts to form "sageliness;" the marvelous qualities of sagely virtue which cannot be totally comprehended is "sacredness."

的发挥和道德的修炼而参与宇宙运动的过程。

孟子所说的浩然之气是与他对人性的认识分不开的，这些气根源于人心，长成之后又养护着心，它们的生长过程也如禾苗一样自然而然，需要"知"与"行"两方面的培育却不得有半点外力的作用。这样的思想往往被现代哲学家们看成神秘的精神体验，因为，气在中国古代思想范畴中很难被清晰地界定，它可以被解释成人的血气、气质、情感、生命力，也可以被解释成宇宙的源泉、构成与能量。但从孟子的角度看来，浩然之气决非一种私密的经验，而是一种生于内心，积善聚义，外发充塞于宇宙的气。它可以表现为真实的道德力量和精神力量。孟子说[1]：

> 富贵不能让我淫乱，贫贱不能让我变节，威武不能让我屈服，这就叫做大丈夫！

其实，对于养成浩然之气的人来说，能做个大丈夫远未到达最高的境地。朱熹曾说浩然之气"如长江大河，浩浩而来也。富贵、贫贱、威武，不能移屈之类，境界都低，不能与它相提并论。"[2]所以，浩然之气更是一种美的力量和神圣的力量。孟子说[3]：

> 令人亲近就是"善"，善真实地存在于自我就是"信"，充满于身体就是"美"，不仅充实，而且绽放出光辉就是"大"，光辉普照，融化变通就是"圣"，圣德之妙不可尽知就是"神"。

---

[1]《孟子·滕文公下》2章。
[2]《朱子语类》卷五十二。
[3]《孟子·尽心上》4章。

---

[1] Mencius, " Duke Wen of Teng," Ⅱ 2.
[2] Zhu Xi, *Classified Sayings of Zhu Xi*, Vol. 52.
[3] Mencius, " Jinxin," Ⅰ 4.

孟庙牌坊
The memorial arch of Mencius' Temple

孟庙古碑：孟母断机处、孟母三迁处、子思作《中庸》处
The ancient tablets of Mencius' Temple: the place of Mencius' mother
breaking the strings of her loom, the place of Mencius' mother moving
three times, the place of Zisi creating *Zhongyong*

五 知人论世，以意逆志——文化传统的阐释

Chapter Ⅴ   Judging People and the Times, Letting the Mind
Meet Intent: Expounding the Cultural Tradition

Confucius founded the Confucian school, the first of the scholarly schools among many philosophical streams during the Spring and Autumn and Warring States Periods. This school followed the format of masters, students, and a school as opposed to the format followed by Mohists based on masters, students, and trade associations. It was also different from the Taoists who plowed the fields as peasants or who lived as hermits, and was even more different from bodies of religious monks and mendicants. Confucius was the first man to extend the education for aristocrats to the common man. The content of these educational forms may be divided into two parts, techniques of self-cultivation, and the transmission of literary documents. The techniques of self-cultivation are called the "Six Arts," that is, ritual ceremonies, music, archery, chariot driving, calligraphy, and mathematics. Literary documents that were chanted and studied were in the main the *Book of Poetry* and the *Book of History*. Confucius edited and revised the *Book of Poetry* and the *Book of History* as well as the rites and music; according to tradition, late in life he selected the *Spring and Autumn Annals* and the *Book of Changes* from among other documents in the possession of official historians and edited and annotated them. Afterwards, during the Warring States, Qin, and Han eras, Confucians composed more than ten types of *Commentaries* on the *Book of Changes*, all ascribed to the authorship of Confucius. They also composed three types of commentarial records on the *Spring and Autumn Annals*, the *Mr. Zuo*, *Gongyang*, and *Guliang* commentaries. They also organized the various rites into various ritual handbooks, such as one devoted to personal cultivation the *Rites of Comportment*, *the Rites of Zhou* which explain the ritual and musical systems, and the *Record of Rituals*, which contains as contents the rites and music, etc. By the Han Dynasty, the Confucian school already had in its possession the five canonical classics of the *Book of Poetry*, *Book of History*, *Record of Rituals*, *Book of Changes*, and the *Spring and Autumn Annals* (the *Book of Music* had long since become lost; only a "Record of Music" was included in the *Record of Rituals*.)

In the *Analects* we can see that, in addition to discussing such ancient literary documents as the *Book of Poetry* and the *Book of History*, he himself reverently participated in ritual ceremonies, edited music, and mastered archery and chariot driving; he therefore advocated to "Set the ambition on the Great Way, maintain moral conduct, rely on humaneness and righteousness, relax by wandering amid the Six Arts." ❶ This explains that in the time of Confucius, the cultural tradition inherited by the Confucian school still included the two parts of technique and literary documents. But from *Mencius*

孔子开创的儒家学派，是春秋、战国时代许多思想流派中的第一个学派。这个学派以师生和学校的方式组成，不同于以师徒和行帮方式组成的墨家，也不同于以自耕农或隐士自居的道家，更不是宗教僧侣团体。孔子是第一个将古代贵族教育带至民间的人，这些教育内容可以分为修养技艺和文献传承两部分，修养技艺称为"六艺"，即礼仪、音乐、射箭、御车、书法、数学；文献以诵习《诗》、《书》为主。孔子对《诗》、《书》和礼、乐都作过整理、修订，据说他晚年又从史官的文献中选择了《春秋》和《周易》加以编纂阐释。后来，战国秦汉之际的儒家为《易经》写了十多种《传》，都托之于孔子的名下；他们又为《春秋》写了《左氏》、《公羊》、《谷梁》三种传记；还将古代的礼整理为许多礼书，如讲个人修养的《仪礼》、讲国家制度的《周礼》和诠释礼乐制度、礼乐内涵的《礼记》等，到了汉代，儒家已经拥有《诗》、《书》、《礼》、《易》、《春秋》的五经体系（《乐经》亡失，仅有《乐记》存于《礼记》）。

我们可以从《论语》中看到，孔子除了谈论《诗》、《书》等古代文献之外，他自己恭行礼仪、整理音乐、并且擅长射箭、御车，所以他主张"立志于大道，据守于德行，依凭于仁义，游憩于六艺" ❶。这说明在孔子时代，儒学传承的文化传统尚且包括技艺与文献两部分。可是从《孟子》一书中就看不到孟

---

❶《论语·述而第七》6章："子曰：'志于道，据于德，依于仁，游于艺。'"

❶ *Analects*, " Shu'er," 7.6.

we cannot see any evidence of Mencius being well-versed in these techniques or having inherited the Six Arts. The techniques of archery and chariot driving are merely metaphors that appear in his discourses and debates. For example, those who practise humaneness are like men shooting arrows, they certainly need to first correct their postures and then shoot their arrows. If they missed the target, they would not complain about those who shot better than themselves, they merely examined their own selves." ❶ Therefore, Mencius lived in the age of the Warring States when the rites and music had thoroughly broken down, and the cultural tradition that he had inherited was mainly in the form of literary remains and legends and other such spiritual legacies from the distant past and was not in such physical things as implements or techniques. This tradition was more abstract, and the difficulty in explaining it was even greater. Of course, the space in which to create new interpretations was even greater.

The Mohist school which was formed after the Confucians also acclaimed the *Book of Poetry*, the *Book of History*, and venerated morality. But profit and gain was the basis of their moral system and rites and music; they did not pay any attention at all to the spiritual value of rites and music. The Taoists and Legalists were the critics and deniers of traditional culture. Only the Confucians expressed the greatest respect and love for the traditional rites, music, and literary remains handed down from the Zhou Dynasty; they also edited, expounded, and transmitted the ancient ritual and musical canons as the basis of their own careers. Confucius said, "I only expound and transmit the ancient rites and musical canons, but do not create or innovate; I am thus a 'transmitter but not an innovator,' because I 'believe in and am fond of the ancients.' " ❷ He also said, "*Poetry* inspires me, rituals establish me, music completes me." ❸ The entire process of a person being inspired by morality and thereupon establishes his own aspirations and accomplishes something is based on the utilization of the resources of traditional culture; culture thus causes one to become a true person.

But, if we understand Confucius' veneration for ancient culture as a conservative return to ancient ways, this would be a great mistake. Confucius said, "Through reviewing the old and gaining the new, one is able to become a teacher." ❹ Therefore, "reviewing the ancient and learning the new," as he literally put it, refers to the new experiences of humanity and the sources of wisdom possessed in the experiences and wisdom of men of the past. Cultural

子娴熟或传授六艺的场景。射、御之技仅仅是他谈辩时的譬喻。
比如他说："实践仁的人就好像射箭一样，一定要先端正自己
的身体再放箭。如果射不中，绝不会抱怨比自己射得好的人，
只会反躬自省。"❶因此，孟子处在一个礼乐彻底崩溃的战国
时代，他所传承的文化传统更多的是文献、传说等更为遥远的
精神遗产，而不是器物或技艺，这个传统更为抽象，解释的难
度更大，当然，创发新义的空间也越大。

继儒家之后形成的墨家也称道《诗》、《书》，推崇道德，
但他们以功利作为道德和礼乐的根据，并不顾及礼乐文化中的
精神价值；道家和法家则是传统文化的批判者和否定者。只有
儒家对西周以来的礼乐传统和古代文献表示出极大的尊重和热
爱，并以整理、阐释、传授古代的礼乐典章作为自己的事业。
孔子说："我只阐释、传授古代的礼乐典章，并不创始制作，
是个'述而不作'的人，因为我'信而好古'，相信并且热爱
古人。"❷他还说："《诗》感发了我，礼树立了我，乐成就了
我。"❸一个人从受到道德的感召、确立自我的人生理想进而
有所成就的整个过程都在享用着传统文化的资源，文化使人成
为真正的人。

但是如果将孔子对古代文化的推崇理解为复古守旧就大错
特错了，孔子说："通过温习旧的而获得新的，就能做别人的
老师了。"❹所以，"温故知新"指出了人类新的经验与智慧来
源于人类已经具备的经验与智慧，文化创新与文化传承在儒家

---

❶《孟子·滕文公下》1章。
❷《论语·述而第七》1章。
❸《论语·泰伯第八》8章。
❹《论语·为政第二》11章。

❶ *Mencius,* " Duke Wen of Teng," Ⅱ 1.
❷ *Analects,* " Shu'er," 7.1.
❸ *Analects,* " Taibo," 8.8.
❹ *Analects,* " On Administration," 2.11.

innovation and cultural tradition in Confucian theory are almost the same thing. Therefore, Confucius advocated, while studying ancient culture, being able to "Raise one side and get the other three sides in response," "Telling him how to go allows one to know how to come," ❶ and allows one to innovate. Another point is of great significance, that of Confucius' innovation of the Confucian study of ancient culture not being completely for the sake of gaining knowledge; it was rather to understand others and to learn how to be a better person. Study implied training in the rites, music, and moral practices. In the opening chapter of the *Analects* Confucius said, "Constantly practicing what one has learned, isn't this a joyful thing? Having a friend come from a distance, isn't this a happy thing? When others do not understand me I am not troubled, isn't this being a gentleman?" ❷ To Confucius, the processes of learning the ritual and musical canons and making intimate friends who are mutually compatible are intimately related. Perhaps one can say that seeking a bosom buddy and friends is the content of learning. Zengzi also said, "The gentleman uses studying the ritual and musical canons to meet with like-minded friends, and depends on friends for mutual aid and to implement the Way of Humaneness." ❸

Mencius developed Confucius' thought about knowing others by their words ❹. Mencius considered that studying ancient culture is an expansion on interacting with worthies, and is an enlargement of one's own moral realm. He proposed an interpretive method of "Judging Men and the Times" as follows ❺ :

A gentleman considered to be a man of goodness in a district will make friends with other gentlemen in the district. A gentleman considered to be a man of goodness in a state will make friends with other gentlemen in the state. A gentleman considered to be a man of goodness in the world will make friends with other gentlemen in the world. If making friends with the gentlemen of goodness in the world is

学说中几乎是一回事。所以，孔子主张在学习古代文化时能够
"举一反三"、"告诉他怎么去就知道怎么来"❶，能够有所创
发。还有一点非常重要，那就是孔子及其开创的儒家学习古代
文化的目标并不完全是为了获得知识，而是了解人、学习做人。
学习意味着礼乐训练与道德实践。在《论语》的开篇，孔子就
说："学了以后时时复习，不也很愉悦吗？有朋友从远方来，
不也很快乐吗？别人不了解我但我并不烦恼，这难道不是君子
吗？"❷在孔子看来，学习礼乐文章与知交朋友，相互理解的
过程紧密相关，或者说，寻求知音与朋友也是学习的内容。曾
子也说："君子用讲习礼乐文章来会集志同道合的朋友，依靠
朋友互相帮助，推行仁道。"❸

　　孟子发展了孔子知言而知人的思想❹。孟子认为，研习古
代的文化，是与贤人交往范围的扩大，是自我道德境界的扩充。
他提出了"知人论世"的阐释方法❺：

　　　　能算得上是一乡之中的善良君子会和那一乡的君子
　　　们交朋友，能算得上是一国之中的善良君子会和那一国
　　　的君子们交朋友，能算得上是天下的善良君子会和天下
　　　的君子们交朋友。如果结交天下的善良君子还不满足，

---

❶《论语·述而第七》8章、《学而第一》15章。
❷《论语·学而第一》1章。
❸《论语·颜渊第十二》24章。
❹ 陈昭瑛《孟子"知人论世"说与经典诠释问题》一文认为："从儒学史的角度来看，孟子
　'知人论世'说乃继承孔子有关'知言'、'知人'及论'文'与'友'之关系等言论。"见
　刘小枫、陈少明主编《经典与解释的张力》，上海三联书店，2003年，第321页。
❺《孟子·万章下》8章。

---

❶ *Analects*, "Shu'er," 7.8; "Xue'er," 1.15.
❷ *Analects*, "Xue'er," 1.1.
❸ *Analects*, "Yan Yuan," 12.24.
❹ In an article entitled "Mencius' theory on 'Judging People and the Times' and the Problem of
　Classical Hermeneutics," Chen Zhaoying felt, "Judging from the perspective of the history of
　Confucianism, Mencius' theory on 'Judging Men and the Times' succeeded Confucius'
　theories such as 'Knowing others by their Words,' 'Knowing Others,' as well as the relationship
　between 'literary studies' and 'friendship.'" See Liu Xiaofeng and Chen Shaoming, eds., *The
　Tension between Classic and Interpretation* (Shanghai : Sanlian Publishing House, 2003), p. 321.
❺ Mencius, "Wanzhang," Ⅱ 8.

not enough, then one can only seek out the worthy of ancient times, recite their *Poetry*, and read their *Histories*, but if one does not understand them as people, is this doable? This is to make friends with the ancients."

At this time, Mencius had already established an important tenet for the hermeneutics of ancient Chinese classics, that is, such texts as the *Poetry* and *Histories* of the ancients which are the products of the spirits and lives of the ancients. Yet in the course of interpreting texts, the method of the so-called "Judging People and the Times" is precisely using our own personal experiences to return to ancient times to enter into the spirits and times of the ancients and to experience what they went through, and to know them as men and to know their societies and times. From this, we can enrich our own insights and experiences, while at the same time through our own personal regeneration, extend the spirits and lives of the ancients. History exists in this type of interpretive process, and is transmitted amid the lives of people, thereby transcending institutions, implements, and even the written word, symbols and other material media. The reason that Mencius declared that every five hundred years a king will appear, and the reason that he selected a legitimate line of succession from Yao to Shun, Yu, Tang, Wen, Wu, the Duke of Zhou, and Confucius directly to himself, is precisely based on this type of interpretive theory.

Why are men able to experience the spirits and life experiences of other people through the written word and symbols? Mencius felt that all men shared the same sentiments; that is to say, a commonality and universality exist among men's spirits and lives; this is precisely our foundation for understanding and interpreting the ancients. Therefore, in Mencius' view, to be able to read and understand the ancient classics, ceremonies, institutions, written word and other types of symbols, even understanding their significance and thought, are not the endpoint of understanding. The only way to accomplish this would be to take an additional step in understanding the spiritual realm of the ancients, and to let our own spirits interact and fuse with the spirits of the ancients. In this way, the self and the ancients can understand one another, be sympathetic with each other, and form friendships.

We know that, regardless whether trying to understand our neighbors or the ancients, both attempts must go through the media of language, practice, the written word, or physical relics. Confucius advocated that, to understand individuals, one had to listen to their words and observe their actions. This is

只有再追溯古代的贤人。吟诵他们的《诗》，阅读他们的《书》，却不了解他的为人，可以吗？因此要探讨他所处的世道。这就是与古人交朋友。

此时，孟子已经确立了中国古典解释学的一条重要原理，即古人的《诗》、《书》等文本是古人精神和生命的产物。而我们阐释文本的过程，即所谓的"知人论世"的活动，正是我们通过自身的体验返回古代，进入到古人的精神和生命之中，体验他的经历，知其为人，知其社会与时代，从而丰富自我的体验与经历，同时也通过自我来复活、延展古人的精神和生命。历史就存在于这样的阐释过程，传递于人的生命之间，因而就超越了制度、器物甚至文字、符号等物质载体。孟子之所以声称五百年必有王者兴起，之所以拈出一个从尧、舜、禹、汤、文、武、周公、孔子直至他自己的道统，正是基于这样的阐释理论。

那么，人为什么能够通过文字和符号来体验别人的精神和生命经验呢？孟子认为人同此心，心同此理，也就是说，人的精神和生命之间存在着共同性与普遍性，这正是我们理解、阐释古人的基础。所以，在孟子看来，能够解读古代的经典、礼仪、制度、文字等符号，乃至于理解了其中的意义和思想，这并没有达到理解的终点。只有进一步理解了古人的心灵世界，并且让自我的心灵与古人的心灵产生交流与融合，自我与古人才能相知、同情，结为朋友。

我们知道，无论是了解身边的人，还是了解古人，都要通过语言、行为、文字或遗物等媒介。孔子主张，了解一个人，

because words and actions are both the external embodiment of the thoughts of the internal heart. However, Mencius had a more direct and sensitive method, that of observing the eyes of others. He said, "To observe a person, there is no better way than to observe his eyes, because the eyes cannot conceal his evil. When a man has an upright heart of goodness, his eyes are then bright; when a man has a heart that is dark and ignorant, his eyes are dim. When you hear somebody talking, pay attention and look at his eyes, for none of the good or evil thoughts of the inner heart can be concealed." ❶ The eyes are the window to the heart and spirit, therefore Mencius advocated the directive observation of the human heart. However, we cannot possibly observe the eyes of the ancients, therefore we must actively enlighten our own hearts to seek to understand the background motivations of the words and deeds of the ancients. Therefore, Mencius further proposed another important tenet for interpreting ancient Chinese classics, that of the explanatory technique of "Letting the Mind Meet Intent."

One day, the disciple Xianqiu Meng and Mencius were discussing some problems in ancient legends and literary documents; both concerned Shun and his father Gusou. Shun was the greatest filial son in ancient China, but he happened to have the world's worst father. Gusou was in league with his second wife as well as their young son and plotted all day how to kill Shun. Shun lost the ethical and emotional support of that come from reverencing his parents, at the very least he suffered bitterly. He went to the fields to cry and complain to Heaven. But he still worked tirelessly to take care of his parents. Afterwards, Shun was recommended to Heaven by Yao, to become the Son of Heaven. At this time, his parents became his subjects. So how should they treat each other? The *Mencius* records the following passage ❷:

> Xianqiu Meng asked, "A common saying has it that 'A ruler should not regard a gentleman of the loftiest morality as his subject, nor should a father regard him as a son.' I have heard that when Shun became the Son of Heaven, even Yao personally led the feudal lords to pay homage to him at court, so Gusou also should have paid homage to him. At this time, upon seeing Gusou, Shun's face revealed that he was ill at ease. Confucius commented on this matter, saying, "At this time and this moment, the empire was in danger!" Given the circumstances, did it really happen as this passage says?"

要听其言，观其行。因为言、行都是一个人内心思想的外在体现。可是孟子还有更为直截而敏锐的办法，那就是观察别人的眼睛。他说："观察一个人，没有比观察他的眼睛更好的方法了。因为眼睛没法掩饰他的邪恶。一个人良心端正，他的眼睛就明亮；一个人良心昧失，他的眼睛就浑浊。当你在听一个人说话时，注意看他的眼睛，他心中的善恶之念都无法隐匿。"❶眼睛是心灵的窗户，所以孟子主张直观人心。可是我们没有办法看到古人的眼睛，所以我们就要积极地启动自己的心去揣摩古人言行背后的用心。于是，孟子又提出了中国古典解释学的另一条重要原理，即"以意逆志"的阐释方法。

有一天，弟子咸丘蒙与孟子讨论了一些古代传说和文献中的问题，都是关于舜和他的父亲瞽瞍的。舜是古代最大的孝子，可他偏偏摊上了一个天下最坏的父亲。瞽瞍伙同后妻以及他们生的小儿子成天谋划如何杀死舜。舜失去了孝敬父母的伦理与情感寄托，尽管痛苦之极，到田里去向天哭诉，但他仍然不懈地眷恋着父母。后来，舜被尧推荐给上天，成为天子。此时，他的父亲成了他的臣民，他们之间应该如何面对呢？《孟子》中有这样一段记载❷：

> 咸丘蒙问道："俗语说：'道德极高的君子，君主不能视他为臣民，父亲不能视他为儿子。'我听说舜做了天子，连尧都亲率诸侯向他朝拜，瞽瞍也得向他朝拜。此时，舜见到瞽瞍，脸上露出不安的神色。孔子评论此事说：'此时此刻，天下岌岌可危啊！'当时的情形，真如这话所说的那样的吗？"

❶《孟子·离娄上》15章。
❷《孟子·万章上》4章。

❶ *Mencius*, "Lilou," I 15.
❷ *Mencius*, "Wanzhang." I 4.

Mencius answered him, saying, "Wrong, this description did not come from the mouth of a gentleman. It was circulated by those rustic men in the East of Qi, that is the country folk of the state of Qi. Because Yao was old at the time, he only yielded power to Shun to act as regent. He could not have possibly led the feudal lords to pay homage to Shun. The *Book of History*, 'Canon of Yao' chapter says, 'After Shun acted as regent for 28 years, Yao passed on. The common people mourned him as if he were their own father or mother. During three years, no music was performed or entertainment performed within the four seas.' Confucius once said, 'There are not two suns in the sky, nor do the people have two lords.' If things really happened as those people said, Shun was the Son of Heaven before Yao died, but he also personally led the feudal lords in the world to mourn Yao for three years; isn't this the case of having two Sons of Heaven?"

Xianqiu Meng said, "I understand the Yao did not serve as Shun's subject. Yet I have read in the *Book of Poetry*, a line in the poem 'Northern Mountain' that says, 'All over the world, not even a single piece of earth does not belong to the Son of Heaven; in the four quarters of the great world not even a single man is not the subject of the Son of Heaven.' Well, after Sun became the Son of Heaven, how can Gusou not be considered his subject.' May I inquire what is this doctrine?"

Mencius said, "The poem 'Northern Mountain' does not mean what you say it means. Its author sighed with emotion at the matter of his lost state, that he could not return home and care for his parents. His meaning is, 'These are all matters of the Son of Heaven, but why am I alone labored?' Therefore, those who explain this poem should not get bogged down in language and rhetoric and misinterpret what the author meant to say. One must be able to let the mind meet the intent of the poem before one can truly understand it. If one gets bogged down in the language and rhetoric , then, just as the poem 'Cloudy Han' in the *Book of Poetry* has it, 'Of the people of the Zhou Dynasty, not a single one will remain.' If you believe that this line is true, well then the Zhou Dynasty will truly lose every single living man. The highest degree of filial piety for those who are filial, is that extended towards one's parents. The highest degree of respect for those who are filial, is to use the world to nurture one's parents. The *Book of Poetry* poem called 'Later Succession' says 'Forever maintain a filial heart, then the Filial Way will become the law of the world.' This embodies this type of

孟子回答说："不对，这些话不是从君子口中说出来的，是那些齐东野人，也就是齐国的乡下人说的话。因为尧只是在年老之时，让舜代他摄政罢了，不可能率领诸侯向舜朝拜。《书》中的《尧典》说：'舜摄政二十八年后，尧驾崩。百姓们如丧考妣，三年之内，四海未曾奏乐欢娱。'孔子曾说：'天无二日，民无二主。'如果真如那些人所言，舜在尧死前就做了天子，而他又在尧死后亲率天下诸侯为尧服丧三年，这岂不是有两个天子了吗？"

咸丘蒙说："尧没有做过舜的臣子这件事，我算是明白了。不过我读过《诗》，其中的《北山》有这么一句，说：'普天之下，没有一块土地不属于天子；大地四方，没有一个人不是天子的臣民。'那么舜做了天子之后，瞽叟却不能算是他的臣民，请问这是什么道理呢？"

孟子说："《北山》这首诗，不是你说的那个意思！作者是感慨忙于国事，不能回家奉养双亲。他的意思是说：'这些都是天子的事，可为何都让我一个人操劳啊！'所以，解说诗的人，不要拘泥于文字修辞而误解作者要说的话，不要拘泥于作者说出来的话而误解作者的心志。要能够以意逆志，也就是用你自己的心意去推测作者的心志，才能获得真实的理解。如果拘泥于文字修辞的话，那么《诗》里的《云汉》说：'周朝的百姓，没有一个留存的。'如果你相信这话是真的，那么周朝就真的没有一个活人了。孝子们孝顺的极至，没有大过对父母的孝；孝子们尊敬的极至，没有超过用天下来奉养父母。瞽叟做了天子的父亲，尊贵到了极至；舜拿天下来孝养他，孝顺到了极至。《诗》里的《下武》说：'永远保持孝心，

doctrine. The *Book of History* says, 'Shun reverently and respectfully came to see Gusou, and was prudent and ill at ease. Gusou was moved, and became reasonable and sensible.' Isn't this the same as that common saying 'A father cannot regard him as a son' ?"

"Judging People and the Times," and "Letting the Mind Meet Intent" share the same process of interpretation but are different aspects of it. Modern scholar Wang Guowei regarded the former as the method of achieving the latter, which is to say that "Judging People and the Times" is the premise for allowing "Letting the Mind Meet Intent" become the correct manner of interpretation and not turn into conjecture and error. He felt that notwithstanding the truth of what Mencius said "Those who interpret poetry must be able to let the mind meet the intent of the poem," the intent is in the body; with intent in the body how can one avoid misinterpreting the intent of the ancients? This must depend on following the method of "Judging People and the Times," and through a profound understanding of the ways of the ancients in order to understand them as people; one can infer their intents through this understanding of them as people. If this is true, then there are very few ancient poems that cannot be understood. ❶

If no one possesses the ability to "Judge People and the Times," and cannot enter into the life experiences of the ancients, to experience their times and how they were as men, but distorts the poems since they merely base themselves on the words and are subject to misunderstanding or erroneous conjectures of the intent of the poets; to Mencius this results in laughable, dogmatic, and rigid interpretations. The discussion below concerning poetry demonstrates Mencius' criticism of just such types of interpretation as well as his profound yet refined observations concerning human nature.

One poem in the *Book of Poetry*, "Small Cap," according to tradition was composed by the last prince of the Western Zhou Dynasty Yi Jiu. His father King You had married a wicked woman called Bao Si and was beguiled by her. King You deposed his original queen, and drove off the prince. Thereupon in the poem we see birds and beasts leisurely soaring or gamboling around, and water plants growing closely together, and the people enjoying the pleasures of home life. Yet the poet took this as a springboard to contemplate his own tragic situation: because of the intervention of petty men he had to lose forever the trust of his father. The poet's sorrow, grief, and solitary hopelessness were uncontrollable, so he left with a cry. However, a scholar called Gaozi regarded this poem as having been composed by a petty person. Mencius' disciple Gongsun Chou conveyed Gaozi's opinion to Mencius. Mencius asked, "Why

孝道就成了天下的法则。'指的就是这样的道理。《书》里面也说:'舜恭恭敬敬地来见瞽叟,谨慎而不安。瞽叟也受到感动,变得通情达理。'这难道是俗语说的'父亲不能视他为儿子'吗?"

"知人论世"和"以意逆志"是同一个理解过程中的不同方面,近代学者王国维认为前者是实现后者的方法,也就是说"知人论世"是"以意逆志"能够成为正确阐释而不流为臆断与误读的前提。他认为尽管像孟子说的那样:"解说诗的人,要能够以意逆志",可是心意在我身上,心志在古人身上,怎样才能使得我的心意不误解古人的心志呢?这就要依循"知人论世"的方法,通过探讨古人所处的世道了解他的为人,通过了解他的为人推测他的心志。果真如此的话,古代的诗很少有不能理解的了。❶

如果没有"知人论世"的能力,没有进入古人的生命历程,去体验他的时代与为人的能力,仅仅根据文辞来曲解或臆断诗人的心志,在孟子看来,都是一些可笑的、教条的、死板的解释。下面一则有关诗的讨论,向我们展示了孟子对上述解释方法的批评以及孟子对人性深宏而细微的体察。

《诗》中有一首《小弁》,据说是西周最后一位太子宜臼写的。他的父亲周幽王娶了一位叫褒姒的坏女人,受她的迷惑,幽王废黜了王后,驱逐了太子。于是我们在诗中看见鸟兽悠闲地飞翔奔跑、水草茂密地生长,人民享受着家居的快乐,而诗人却由此想到自己的悲惨处境:因为小人的离间而永远失去了父亲的信任。诗人忧怨伤痛与孤苦绝望之情不能抑制,呼号而出。可是有一位被称为高子的学者,认为这首诗是小人写的。

---

❶ 见王国维《玉谿生诗年谱会笺序》。

❶ See Wang Guowei, "Collected Comments on the Chronological Poems of Yuxisheng, Preface."

did he say this?" Gongsun Chou said, "Gaozi said that his poem contains the sentiments of someone who has been wronged." Mencius said, "This old master Gaozi truly interprets the *Book of Poetry* too rigidly. Think about it, if someone had been shot at by an archer from the southern state of Yue he probably would talk about it later in a half-joking manner. The only reason would be that the man from Yue had only a distant relationship with him. But if his elder brother had been shot at with an arrow, he would certainly cry as he talked about it. And the only reason would be that the elder brother was his own relative. The reason that this poem "Small Cap" has the sentiment of resentment is due to the family feeling that exists between relatives. This type of family feeling is precisely humane love. This is too rigid! This is the interpretive approach to the *Book of Poetry* by this old fellow Gaozi!

At this time, Gongsun Chou who was able "raise one side and get the other three sides in response" thought of one poem "Victorious Wind" in the *Book of Poetry*. The poem mentioned a warm wind in the southern region that was wafting gently over some brambles bushes, resembling a benevolent mother diligently nurturing some good-for-nothing sons like us; a very deep cold spring is always able to water the earth, but we seven brothers are unable to serve our mother very well. An oriole on a tree is still able to warble its clear and mild song, making one relaxed and joyful. But we seven brothers are unable to console or cheer our mother. The ancients all knew the background to the composition of this poem. This was a widowed mother who had seven sons; she decided to remarry, and no longer live in chaste widowhood. At this point her sons were very hurt, but they did not complain about their mother, instead merely repeated their feelings of self-blame. Therefore, Gongsun Chou asked Mencius, "Why doesn't his poem 'Victorious Wind' contain sentiments of resentment?" Mencius said, "The faults of the mother in 'Victorious Wind' were minor individual matters; but the faults of the father in the 'Small Cap' were great ones. When a father or mother commits a great error but one does not complain, this distances one from his parents; when a father or mother commits some minor errors and one complains without end, this is too extreme. Creating distance from one's parents is to be unfilial; being too extreme is also unfilial. Therefore Confucius said, 'Shun truly was the ultimate in filial piety, he still loved and clinged to his parents at age 50.' " ❶

Well, how can one gain the ability to be like Mencius in "Judging People and the Times" and in "Letting the Mind Meet Intent?" We know that in

孟子的弟子公孙丑将高子的意见转告孟子。孟子问:"为什么这样说呢?"公孙丑说:"高子说这首诗中有怨恨之情。"孟子说:"这个高老先生解说《诗》,真是太死板了!你们试想啊,如果有个人曾经被南方的越国人开弓射击过,事后他可能有说有笑地谈论这件事。没有别的原因,越国人与他的关系很疏远。可如果这个人被他的哥哥开弓射击,那他一定会哭泣着诉说这件事。没有别的原因,哥哥是自己的亲人。《小弁》这首诗之所以有怨恨之情,是出于亲人之间的亲情,这种亲情正是仁爱。太死板了啊!这个高老头居然这样解说《诗》!"

这时,能够举一反三的公孙丑想起了《诗》中一首叫《凯风》的诗。诗中说南方的暖风吹拂着荆棘灌木,好像慈爱的母亲辛勤地养育我们这些不能成材的儿子;再深的寒泉都能滋润土地,我们兄弟七个却不能好好地侍奉母亲;树上的黄鸟,尚能唱出清和婉啭的歌声,让人心旷神怡,我们兄弟七个却不能让母亲感到安慰愉快。古人都知道这首诗的创作背景: 这是一位有七个儿子的寡母,她已决定改嫁他人,不再守节。此时做儿子的尽管非常难过,但他们并没有抱怨母亲,只是一再地表达自我责备的心情。于是公孙丑问孟子:"《凯风》这首诗里为什么没有怨恨之情呢?"孟子说:"《凯风》里的母亲,她的过失属于个人小节;而《小弁》里的父亲,他的过失就大了。父母有大的过失却不抱怨,这就与父母更加疏远了;父母有些小过失却抱怨不止,这就是过激的表现了。疏远父母是不孝,过激也是不孝。所以孔子说:'舜真是孝顺到极至了,到了五十岁还那么依恋父母。'"❶

那么,如何能够像孟子那样具备"知人论世"、"以意逆志"

---

❶《孟子·告子下》3章。

❶ Mencius, "Gaozi," II 3.

Western intellectual scholarship there is a rich tradition of hermeneutics. This tradition originated in the interpretation of the Bible, and its interpretive goal was to understand God and the truth through the text of the Bible. Hermeneutics considers that one can understand the meaning of the words of ancient texts merely through the knowledge of the commentator; but in order to gain a revelation from God or the truth, one needs faith as well as knowledge. Therefore, the activity of interpretation is not the normal understanding of a text, neither can interpretation stay at the technical level of linguistics, but must deeply enter into sacred faith, and implement actual religious and theoretical practice. Viewed from this angle, both Confucius and Mencius can be regarded as the founders of ancient Chinese hermeneutics. Confucius transmitted but did not innovate; during his life he edited the *Book of Poetry* and the *Book of History*, but he absolutely was no pedant, instead his creed was "believe in and be fond of antiquity." With regard to research into ancient culture, Confucius was not mired in objective reality and historical knowledge, but wanted to grasp and carry out the moral spirit of the ancients. He once said, "I can explain the rites of the Xia Dynasty, but the rites of the state of Qi which was founded by their descendants are lacking in sufficient evidence; I can also explain the rites of the Shang Dynasty, but the rites of the state of Song which was founded by their descendants are lacking sufficient evidence. This is because the records and worthies of the states of Qi and Song are all lacking; if enough of them were extant, then I would use them to verify the ritual systems of the Xia and the Shang." ❶

Mencius grounded himself on this type of creed, that is, what the classics reveal to us about the spirits and human goodness of the ancient sages and worthies. He himself also had the experience of "nurturing the *qi* and know the words," and deeply realized the need to train the self to cut through the power of understanding through words and language before being able to understand the ancients and recognize the Great Way. This ability is not the power to understand words and sentences but to enact humaneness and righteousness and perfect one's own moral force. Because in order to become friends with the ancient sages and worthies, one must become "a gentleman of goodness in the world," only then will one be able to understand their intentions. Otherwise, one will only be able to judge the feelings of the ancients with the mind of a petty man. Although Mencius was very familiar with the ancient literature, he maintained a high degree of distrust and skepticism toward words and language, even denying to a degree the classics. He said, "It would be better to not read the *Book of History* than to completely believe it; when I read

的能力呢？我们知道，西方古代学术也有深厚的阐释学传统，这个传统源自对《圣经》的解释，其解释的目的是通过《圣经》的文本，理解上帝和真理。阐释学认为，仅仅理解古代文献中的文字意义，解释者具备知识就可以了；而要获得上帝的启示或者真理，除了知识，还需要信仰。所以，阐释的行为就不是对文本的一般理解，阐释也不能停留在语文学的技术层次，而要深入到对神圣的皈依，落实到宗教与伦理的实践。如果从这个意义上看，孔子和孟子也可以称得上是中国古代阐释学的奠基者。孔子述而不作，一生删订《诗》、《书》，但他决非是一个学究，"信而好古"是他的信仰。孔子对古代文化的研究，决不停留在对客观事实与历史知识的研究之上，而是要把握和履践古人的道德精神。他曾说："我能够阐释夏代的礼，可是夏人后裔封国杞的礼不足为证；我也能阐释商代的礼，可是商人后裔封国宋的礼不足为证。这是因为杞国和宋国的典籍与贤人都很缺乏，如果很充足，我就将它们作为阐释夏、商礼制的证明了。" ❶

　　孟子也基于这样的信仰，即经典向我们昭示着古代圣贤的心灵和人类的善性。他自己也有"养气知言"的体验，深知必须锻炼自己穿越文字和语言的理解能力，才能理解古人，知晓大道。这个能力决非破解文字和语句的知识能力，而是履践仁义，完善自我的道德能力。因为与古人的圣贤为友，必须先成为"天下的善良君子"，才能体察他们的用心，不然的话就只能以小人之心度君子之腹了。尽管孟子非常娴熟古代的文献，但是对文字与语言保持着高度的警惕与反思，甚至有一些否定

❶《论语·八佾第三》9章。
❶ *Analects*, "Bayi," 3.9.

the *Book of History*, I feel that in the 'Chapter on Concluding the War' with its record of the conquest by King Wu of the Shang and its bloody battles, I only believe the words on two or three bamboo strips. Think about it, the humane man has no enemy in the world. When such a humane man as King Wu chastised such an inhumane man as King Zhou of Shang, the entire world followed his lead and he became invincible. So how could it have been as recorded in the 'Chapter on Concluding the War' with its killing until rivers of blood flowed until even heavy war clubs floated off ?" ❶

He wasn't even constricted by the superficial reading of either the words or deeds of Confucius. Confucius said of himself that he "transmitted but did not innovate;" but Mencius regarded Confucius the same as the Great Yu and the Duke of Zhou, who harbored the great aspirations of saving the age, of wishing to save the people from floods and fires, and of assisting the ways of the world that were in danger of disappearing; so he absolutely did make some innovations. Confucius' innovation was to compose the *Spring and Autumn Annals*. Mencius said, "Confucius composed the *Spring and Autumn Annals* to make rebellious ministers and disorderly sons fearful." ❷ We know that the *Spring and Autumn Annals* is a historical work that records the Spring and Autumn Period. During the age of Confucius, this period of time would have been equivalent to recent contemporary history for Confucius. According to the ancient ritual system, only the king of Zhou could establish an office of historian to record the Way of Heaven and human affairs, never mind someone with the status of a knight, not even the feudal lords had the authority to edit histories. The ancient office of historian was a hereditary post to manage cultural affairs, and existed right up to the destruction of the Western Zhou. When the king of Zhou re-founded the capital in the east, official historians scattered among the various feudal kingdoms; in this way some of these kingdoms gained historical materials such as records of historians. In the state of Lu in which Confucius resided, because it was set up by as a feudal kingdom by the Duke of Zhou, therefore ritually speaking it enjoyed a higher status than the other feudal states. Perhaps when it was established it also set up the office of historian. Because of this it possessed rather ample historical sources, and provided historical materials for Confucius to edit and finalize the *Spring and Autumn Annals* late in life. Mencius considered that composing the *Spring and Autumn Annals* embodied his fine and painstaking effort. He said, "Just when the customs were declining, evil heresies and violence were breaking out, ministers were murdering their lords, and sons were killing their fathers. Confucius became worried and fearful, and so composed the *Spring*

经典的色彩。他说："完全相信《书》，还不如不读《书》。我读《书》时，对其中记载周武王伐商、流血战斗的《武成篇》，只认可其中两、三根竹简上写的文字。试想，仁人是天下无敌的。周武王这样的仁人去讨伐商纣王这样不仁的人，天下风从，所向披靡，怎么会像《武成篇》中说的那样：杀得血流成河，连木槌这样重的兵器都漂了起来？" ❶

他甚至对孔子的言行都不拘泥于表层的阅读。孔子说自己"述而不作"，孟子却认为孔子与大禹、周公一样，怀有伟大的用世之心，想要拯民众于水火、扶世道于危亡，决不是一个无所创作的人。孔子的创作就是作《春秋》。他说："孔子作《春秋》，使得乱臣贼子们惧怕。" ❷我们知道，《春秋》是记载春秋时代的史书，在孔子时代，相当于近现代史。按照古代的礼制，只有周天子才可以设立史官记录天道与人事，不要说是一个士人，就是诸侯王也没有修史的资格。古代的史官是世袭的文化职掌，直到西周灭亡，周天子东迁，史官流散到诸侯国，一些诸侯国才有了史记类的文献。孔子所处的鲁国因为是周公的封国，所以在礼制上可能高于其他诸侯国，或许在分封时就设置了史官，因而拥有较为丰富的历史文献，为孔子晚年编订《春秋》提供了史料。孟子认为，作《春秋》这件事体现了孔子良苦的用心。他说："当世道衰微之际，邪恶的学说和暴力萌发，有臣下杀君主的事，有儿子杀父亲的事。孔子感到忧惧，写作了《春秋》。作《春秋》本是天子的职责，所以孔子说：

---

❶《孟子·尽心下》3章。
❷《孟子·滕文公下》9章。

❶ *Mencius*, "Jinxin," Ⅱ3.
❷ *Mencius*, "Duke Wen of Teng," Ⅱ9.

and Autumn Annals. Composing a *Spring and Autumn Annals* was originally the duty of the Son of Heaven, therefore Confucius said, 'I will probably be known by the *Spring and Autumn Annals*; I will probably also be blamed because of the *Spring and Autumn Annals.*' " ❶ Mencius also said ❷:

> When the reign of the kings died out, the age of the *Book of Poetry* perished. When the *Book of Poetry* perished, then the *Spring and Autumn Annals* was composed. The *Cheng* of the state of Jin, the *Taowu* of the state of Chu, and the *Spring* and *Autumn Annals* of the state of Lu are similar in being historical works recording the Spring and Autumn Period. The contents all concerned the events of the hegemons Duke Huan of Qi and Duke Wen of Jin, and the language recorded according to the format of the historian's office. Confucius said, "I only render its general meaning, and make use of it in my own way."

The rule of the Royal Way consisted of the enactment of humane government by King Wen, King Wu, and the Duke of Zhou. At that time, poets spontaneously composed poems to criticize or laud the government and social mores, and expressed the voices of their hearts. Yet after the king of Zhou moved the capital eastward, he was unable to marshal the feudal lords, the rites collapsed and music deteriorated; poets no longer composed poems. During this age of decay and chaos, Confucius composed another *Spring and Autumn Annals* based on the historical materials in the state of Lu. Even though he adopted the historical genre normal for the time, he emphasized more "deriving meaning" from historical records. The word "meaning" from the phrase "deriving meaning" means to praise the good and blame the bad, and was the judgmental power to affix rebellious ministers and disorderly sons to an historical pillar of shame. Therefore, Mencius even regarded Confucius as possessing the nature to become a Son of Heaven, it was just that no one recommended him. He said, "A commoner being able to become the Son of Heaven would certainly have the same moral conduct as Shun and Yu; however he would still need a Son of Heaven to recommend him. Therefore Confucius was unable to become one!" ❸ Although Mencius was not a disciple of Confucius, he was the first man able to understand Confucius' writings, and thereby invent the spiritual tradition of Confucius. He also self-consciously took up the burden of inheriting this tradition.

Learning and teaching combine in one person, just as Confucius claimed for himself, "I learn without tiring, and teach without wearying." ❹ The same as Confucius, Mencius not only was a man good at studying ancient culture, he

'知道我的，大概就是因为《春秋》了；怪罪我的，大概也是因为《春秋》了。'"❶孟子还说❷：

> 王者的政治熄灭，《诗》的时代便消亡了。《诗》消亡了，《春秋》便写了出来。晋国的《乘》，楚国的《梼杌》，鲁国的《春秋》，都是一样的记载春秋时代的史书：其中的内容都是关于齐桓公、晋文公这些霸主的事迹，其中的文字都是按照史官的体例记录。孔子说："不过其中的大义，我私下取用了。"

王者的政治是文王、武王、周公施行的仁政。在那个时代，诗人们自发地创作诗歌讽颂政治和社会风气，表达心声。而周天子东迁之后，不能号令诸侯，礼崩乐坏，诗人也就不再作诗。在此衰乱之世，孔子根据鲁国的史书重新写作了一部《春秋》，尽管在书写上采用了当时的史书体裁，但是孔子更注重从历史记录中"取义"。这个"义"就是褒善贬恶，就是将乱臣贼子们钉在历史耻辱柱上的审判力量。所以，孟子甚至认为孔子具备做天子的资质，只可惜没有人推荐，他说："一个平民而能够做天子，他的德行一定要和舜、禹一样，不过还得有天子来推荐他，所以孔子做不成天子啊！"❸孟子虽然不是孔子的弟子，但他是第一个能够读懂孔子的人，从而发明了孔子的精神传统，并自觉地担当起这个传统的继承者。

学和教是集于一身的，正如孔子自称的那样："学而不厌，诲人不倦。"❹和孔子一样，孟子不仅是一个善于学习古代文

❶《孟子·滕文公下》9章。
❷《孟子·离娄下》21章。
❸《孟子·万章上》6章。
❹《论语·述而第七》2章。

❶ Mencius, "Duke Wen of Teng," Ⅱ 9.
❷ Mencius, "Lilou," Ⅱ 21.
❸ Mencius, "Wanzhang," Ⅰ 6.
❹ Analects, "Shu'er," 7.2.

was also a man who was able to transmit ancient culture. Therefore he considered that gaining brilliant talent from all over the world and teaching them is one of the three great sources of joy for a gentleman. He also said, "The gentleman uses five methods to teach others: transform others just like a timely fall of rain that nurtures the trees and grasses; complete the moral virtues of others; nurture the talent of others; resolve others' doubts, and let the residual effects of his own virtue transform the men of later ages." ❶ Although both the teaching and learning of Confucians included the transmission and study of knowledge, what was more important was moral enlightenment and training, because the purpose of teaching was to nurture sages, worthies, and gentlemen, and not merely nurture men of knowledge and skills. Mencius especially stressed the moral conduct of teachers, because the premise for teaching others was after becoming enlightened oneself, to enlighten others, and after establishing oneself, to establish others. If one always aims to teach others, this demonstrates that he has not yet become self-aware. Later on he will consider himself to be infallible, and forever forfeit any growth. Therefore he said in a satirical manner, "One defect of man is his delight in being somebody else's teacher!" ❷

Mencius' educational thought also expressed a striking difference in style from that of Confucius. Confucius was a tireless teacher of others, but Mencius was different; not everyone could become his student. He regarded that "There are many methods of educating others, and I am not willing to teach everyone, this in itself is a sort of teaching." ❸

A man called Cao Jiao visited the state of Zou to seek instruction from Mencius, "Everyone is able to become a Yao or a Shun; is this a true saying?" Mencius said, "Of course." But I, Cao Jiao, I have heard that King Wen of Zhou was ten Chinese feet tall, Tang of Shang was nine feet. And I for some strange reason have grown nine feet four inches. All I can do is sit around and eat, so how am I able to become a Yao or a Shun?" Mencius said, "Why are you worried about this? All you have to do is strive to achieve it then you can. If a man cannot even lift up a small bird, he would be considered to lack strength. If a man were able to lift up something that weighed three thousand catties, then he would be considered to be a strong man. If one were able to lift up the same great weight which that Hercules Wu Huo was able to lift up, then one would be a Wu Huo. How can one worry that he will not live up to his capacity? It is only that one will not go and do it. To walk slowly behind an

化的人，还是一个能够传授古代文化的人，所以他认为得天下英才而教育他们是君子的三大快乐之一。他又说："君子教育人的方式有五种：像及时雨滋润草木那样感化别人；成就别人的道德；培养别人的才干；解答别人的疑惑；让自己的美德余韵泽被后世之人。"❶儒家的教与学尽管包括知识的传授与学习，但更重要的是道德的启发与训练，因为教学的目标是培养圣贤君子而不仅仅是培养具有知识和技能的人。孟子特别强调教师的德行，因为教育别人的前提是自觉然后再去觉悟他人，自己有所建树然后再去树立别人，如果一个人总是以教诲别人为目的，就说明他自己尚未自觉，以后也会自以为是，永远不会有所长进。所以孟子讥讽道："人的毛病就在于喜欢做别人的老师！"❷

　　孟子的教育思想也表现出一些与孔子迥然不同的风格。孔子是一个诲人不倦的老师，可孟子就不一样了，不是什么人都可以得到他的教诲的。他认为："教育人的方法很多，我不屑去教诲一个人，这也是一种教诲。"❸

　　一个叫曹交的人到邹国来请教孟子："人人都能成为尧舜，有这话吗？"孟子说："当然！""可我曹交听说周文王身高十尺，商汤身高九尺。而我枉长了九尺四寸之高，只会吃饭，怎样才能成为尧舜啊？"孟子说："这有什么可担心的？只要努力去做就是了。如果有个人，连只小鸡都提不起来，那真是个没有力气的人；如果能举起三千斤的东西，就是个有力气的人了；如果能举起大力士乌获能举起的重量，那他就是乌获了。

❶《孟子·尽心上》40章。
❷《孟子·离娄上》23章。
❸《孟子·告子下》12章。

❶ *Mencius*, "Jinxin," Ⅰ 40.
❷ *Mencius*, "Lilou" Ⅰ 23.
❸ *Mencius*, "Gaozi," Ⅱ 12.

elder is to be called fraternal; to rush on ahead of an elder is called not fraternal. How could it be impossible to walk a little slower? It is only that one does not want to do it. To enact the Way of Yao or Shun is nothing more than enacting filial piety and fraternity. If you were to put on Yao's clothing, and speak his words, do his deeds, you then would be a Yao. If you were to put on the clothing of Jie, speak his words, and do his deeds, you then would be a Jie." Mencius clearly told Cao Jiao that moral accomplishments lay in the self-conscious effort to put them into practice. However, Cao Jiao still could not understand, but said, "I plan to go have an audience with the ruler of Zou, and request a place to live to stay around to listen to your teachings." Mencius refused, saying, "The Way of Yao and Shun is like a large highway, how could it be that you still do not understand? One defect of men is the lack of willingness to go out and search on one's own! It is best that you return home and make a good search on your own, some there are teachers!" ❶

Mencius also developed the theory of the so-called "Five Un-Teachables." His disciple Gongduzi asked him, "Although Teng Geng is the younger brother of the ruler of the state of Teng, while you were residing in the state as a retainer, you should have treated each other with ritual courtesy. But you did not respond to him this way, why was this?" Mencius answered, "To depend on one's own authority and position to ask about this and ask about that, to suppose that one has the ability to ask this and ask that, to presume on age or seniority to ask this and that, to depend on merit and honor to ask this and that, borrowing the friendship of friends to ask this or that—I answer none of them. But Teng Geng presumed on two out of these five types of conditions." ❷

Actually, one additional condition should be that of a father not teaching his son. Disciple Gongsun Chou asked him, "What does it mean when a gentleman does not act as his son's teacher?" Mencius said, "This is an awkward case. Teaching other people must be done according to the proper way; if one day it is no longer effective, then one will get angry. If one gets angry, then it will cause hurt feelings. Then the son will say, 'You are using great principles to teach me, but what you do and how you act do not conform very well with these principles.' This would hurt the feelings that should exist between father and son, the worst thing that could happen. So the ancients educated each other's sons, so father and son would not demand perfection of each other. If fathers and sons demanded perfection of each other, then

一个人怎么能担心自己不胜任呢？只是因为不去做罢了。在长者后面慢慢走，这就叫悌；抢在长者前面走，就叫不悌。走慢一点难道不能吗？只是不肯做罢了。尧舜之道做起来不过是孝、悌而已。您穿上尧的衣服，说着尧话，做着尧的事，您就是尧了。您穿着桀的衣服，说着桀的话，做着桀的事，您就是桀了。"孟子明明白白告诉曹交，道德的成就在于自觉地去履践。可是曹交还是不能了悟，说："我打算面见邹君，借个住的地方，留下来聆听您的教诲。"孟子拒绝道："尧舜之道就像大路一样，难道您还不明白吗？人的毛病就在于不愿意去寻求啊！您还是回家好好寻求吧！有的是老师！"❶

孟子还有所谓"五不教"之说。弟子公都子问他："滕更虽是滕国国君的弟弟，在您门下的时候，似乎应该以礼相待，可您并不搭理他，这是干吗呢？"孟子答道："凭借自己的权势和地位来问这问那，自以为有本事来问这问那，倚老卖老地来问这问那，仗着有功劳来问这问那，借着朋友的交情来问这问那，我都不会回答他们，而滕更在这五条里占了两条。"❷

其实还应该加上一条，即父不教子。弟子公孙丑问他："君子不做儿子的老师，这是何道理？"孟子说："这是因为情理上有些别扭。教育别人一定要用正道，一旦不奏效，就要发怒。一旦发怒，就伤了感情。做儿子的会说：'您拿大道理来教训我，可您的所作所为也不见得合乎道理。'这样父子之间就伤了感情，这是最不好的事情。所以古人互相交换儿子来教

❶《孟子·告子下》2章。
❷《孟子·尽心上》43章。

❶ *Mencius*, "Gaozi," Ⅱ2.
❷ *Mencius*, "Jinxin," Ⅰ43.

closeness would no longer exist; the lack of closeness between fathers and sons is the most inauspicious thing in the world!" ❶

Mencius refusing to teach some was due to their prejudices or stubbornness, making it impossible for their minds to be sincere and respectful. Regardless of whether intimate feelings, friendship, or imposing position are the specific factor involved, all of these would prohibit the establishment of a relationship between teacher and student that allowed for the transmission of a teaching or passing on of information. To be true and sincere is not only a psychological preparation for being taught, it is also the beginning of learning to conduct oneself properly. This type of correct and enlightened heart is the precursor, and single-minded devotion is the key educational ideal, and is a great source of enrichment to the Confucian educational theory created by Confucius. It is just like what *Doctrine of the Mean* says, "The gentleman reverently and respectfully maintains his own moral nature, and then through learning understands the Great Way."

育，父子之间不求全责备。父子之间如果求全责备，父子之间就不再亲密，父子不亲是天底下最不吉祥的事情！"❶

　　孟子这些不教，是因为人们有所挟持或执着，使得受教之心不诚不敬，无论是亲情、交情还是显赫的地位，都会妨碍传道授业这一师生关系的确立。正心诚意，既是受教前的心理准备，也是学习做人的开始。这种以端正和启发人心为先导，以专心致志为关键的教育理念，是孟子对孔子开创的儒家教育学说的极大丰富，正如《中庸》里所说的那样："君子恭恭敬敬地奉持着自己的德性，再通过问学知晓大道。"

❶《孟子·离娄上》18章。

❶ *Mencius*, "Lilou," Ⅰ18.

北京故宫　二千年来，孔子、孟子学说占据中国官方意识形态的主流
Forbidden City, Beijing
Since two thousand years the thought of Confucius and Mencius
taking the mainstream of Chinese official ideology

六　仁政——政治理想与社会批判

Chapter VI　Humane Government: Government Ideals and Social Criticism

Confucian political theory developed out of the teachings on the feudal rites and music of the Western Zhou Dynasty. The target of the performance of these rites and music was the aristocracy, which was a synthesis of kinship ties and traditional culture, and who enjoyed the privilege of education. The relationship they shared with one another was that of father and son, and also that of lord and subject; from the lowest to the highest there were the five ranks of the knights, the grandees, the high ministers, the feudal lords, and the Son of Heaven; they may be all called "Gentlemen." But the common people and slaves were the targets of the performance of legal punishment, and were called anciently the "commoners," "common people," "the people," or just the "petty men." Because the ancient feudal society was a class society, government by rites and music was the rule of virtue, not the rule of law.

Different than many of the aristocracy, Confucius did advocate the rule of gentlemen over petty men, but he steadfastly believed that the reason a gentleman was able to govern petty men was because the gentleman was educated, and possessed morality. The responsibility of a gentleman was to guide petty men towards goodness, causing them to become gentlemen and not to punish them. He said that the moral nature of a gentleman was like wind, the moral nature of a petty man was like grass; grass will always sway before the wind. When rulers pursue goodness, the mass of the people will certainly seek goodness. Ruling the mass of the people does not depend on murdering methods to root out evil men, but depends on placing upright men among the mass of the non-upright men, and from this cause the non-upright to change to be upright men❶.Therefore, for Confucius, the content of a gentleman even more pointed towards moral conduct instead of social classes. Mencius also felt that as long as one was a humane man he possessed the qualifications to be a ruler. If an inhumane man occupied a lofty position, that simply would spread evil around among the people. When a ruler is immoral and violent, the mass of the people have no legal recourse. When the government does not adhere to morality, then workers and carpenters will not adhere to their compasses or squares. When a gentleman violates the rites and righteousness, petty men will violate the penal code. A country such as this would find it extremely difficult to survive in the world ❷.

Confucius was born into the knightly class, which was a low level aristocrat. But he lived in an age when the rites had collapsed and music had decayed, the state government where he resided had been continuously controlled by the three great families of the Ji's, Meng's, and Shu's. Confucius constantly criticized their despotic dominance, excessive extortion, and their

儒家的政治学说是从西周封建礼乐教化中发展出来的。礼乐施及的对象是由血缘宗法文化结合起来的、享有受教育权利的贵族们。他们之间的关系既是父子，又是君臣，从低到高分为士、大夫、公卿、诸侯、天子五个等级，可以统称为"君子"；而庶民与奴隶则是刑罚施及的对象，古代称为"庶人"、"庶民"、"民"或"小人"。由于封建社会是一个阶级社会，所以礼乐政治是德治而不是法治。

与很多旧贵族不同的是，孔子虽然主张君子统治小人，但他坚信君子之所以能够统治小人，是因为君子受过教化，具备道德。君子的责任就是引导小人向善，使之成为君子，而不是对小人施加刑罚。他说君子的德性就像风，小人的德性就像草，草总是随风倒。统治者追求善，民众一定会追求善。治理民众不是用杀戮的方法铲除恶人，而是将正直的人放在不正直的人群之中，从而使不正直的人变得正直❶。所以在孔子这里，君子的内涵更多地指向了道德品行而不是社会等级。孟子也认为，只有仁人才有资格成为统治者。如果一个不仁的人身居高位，那简直是将罪恶流播于民众。统治者无道残暴，民众就无法可依。政府不遵守道义，工匠就不遵守规矩。君子违反礼义，小人就触犯刑律，这样的国家能在世上存在就算万幸了❷。

孔子出身于士的阶层，是低级的贵族，可是他生活在一个礼崩乐坏的时代，他所在的鲁国一直是大贵族季氏、孟氏、叔氏三家把持国政。孔子经常批评他们专横跋扈、横征暴敛和僭越礼制的行为，他说："天下有道，大夫不会专政；天下有道，

---

❶《论语·颜渊第十二》19章、22章。
❷《孟子·离娄上》1章。

❶ *Analects*, "Yan Yuan," 12.19, 22.
❷ *Mencius*, "Lilou," Ⅰ 1.

actions in overstepping the bounds of the ritual system. He said, "When the Way operates in the world, grandees will not become dictators; when the Way operates in the world, petty men will not discuss political affairs." ❶ His student Ran Qiu was the household steward of the Ji clan, and helped them to amass wealth. Confucius unexpectedly cried out to his disciples, "My children, knock on drums and attack him with sound!" ❷ But when the head of the Ji clan was enjoying a performance of military music at home that was resereved for the Son of Heaven, Confucius said with a sigh, "This type of thing, if they have the heart to do it, what won't they dare to do!" ❸ He observed that gentlemen were surprisingly the first to destroy the rites and music, especially those dukes, ministers, and grandees with high positions of authority who had given up moral and cultural cultivation. They indulged their own desires, destroyed the order of the rites, and were unable to act as examples for the mass of the people, even going so far as to plot against and murder their own fathers and brothers and lords and rulers. Therefore they had lost all qualifications to be rulers, and the petty men would act the same in encroaching against their betters and acting rebellious. When Confucius visited Qi, Duke Jing of Qi inquired of him concerning governance; Confucius answered with eight words, "Lord, lord; minister, minister; father, father; son, son." This meant that "A lord had to be a good lord, a minister had to be a good minister, a father had to be a good father, and a son had to be a good son." ❹ Late in Confucius' life, the head of the Ji clan frequently inquired of him concerning governance. Confucius told him, "The main root in the term 'governance,' is the same 'correct' as in 'correct conduct.' If you are yourself correct, then who would dare not to be correct?" ❺ The head of the Ji clan further asked, "Nowadays, with robbers and thieves multiplying, what would you do about it?" Confucius satirized him, "All you have to do is to rid yourself of greed, then even if you offered a reward to the people to go out and steal, they would not do so." ❻ Therefore, strive to advocate governing the state based on the rites, and maintain political and cultural order.

His disciple Zilu asked him, if you are asked to govern a state, what would you do first? Confucius asked, "Rectify names." Jilu said, "Master, you are really pedantic! What is there about names that are worth rectifying?" Confucius' countenance turned stern, and he said, "How could you be so

庶人们不会议论政治。"❶他的学生冉求做季氏的家臣，帮助季氏聚敛财富，孔子竟对弟子喊道："小子们，敲着鼓去声讨他！"❷而当季氏在家里欣赏周天子的舞乐时，孔子叹道："这样的事情，他们都忍心做得出来，还有什么事做不出来呢？"❸他看到君子们竟然是首先破坏礼乐的人，特别是公卿大夫这些权重位高的君子们失去了道德与文化修养，放纵自己的欲望，破坏礼的秩序，不能为民众树立榜样，甚至谋杀自己的父兄与君主，所以他们失去了统治者的资格，小人们也会按照他的样子犯上作乱。孔子到齐国时，齐景公向他询问政治，孔子回答了八个字："君君、臣臣、父父、子子"。也就是说，"君主要做好君主，臣子要做好臣子，父亲要做好父亲，儿子要做好儿子。"❹孔子晚年，季氏经常向他咨询政治。孔子告诉他："所谓'政治'的'政'，就是'端正'的'正'。你自己端正，谁还敢不端正？"❺季氏又问："现在盗贼如此之多，您看有何办法？"孔子讥讽他说："只要您没有贪欲，就是悬赏庶民们去盗窃，他们也不会干的！"❻所以，孔子竭力主张以礼治国，维持政治与文化秩序。弟子子路问他，如果让您来治理一个国家，您第一件事做什么？孔子说："端正名分。"子路说："夫子真是迂腐！名分有什么值得端正的呢？"孔子正

---

❶《论语·季氏第十六》2章。
❷《论语·先进第十一》16章。
❸《论语·八佾第三》1章。
❹《论语·颜渊第十二》11章。
❺《论语·颜渊第十二》17章。
❻《论语·颜渊第十二》18章。

❶ *Analects*, "Ji Clan," 16.2.
❷ *Analects*, "Xianjin," 11.16.
❸ *Analects*, "Bayi," 3.1.
❹ *Analects*, "Yan Yuan," 12.11.
❺ *Analects*, "Yan Yuan," 12.17.
❻ *Analects*, "Yan Yuan," 12.18.

uncouth? A gentleman does not talk nonsense about things he does not understand. If names are not rectified, then language cannot be used smoothly; if language is not used smoothly, then things cannot be managed well; if things are not managed well, then neither rites nor music will flourish; if the rites and music cannot flourish, then punishments will not be proper; if punishments are not proper, then the commoners will not know how to act." ❶

Mencius also felt that the basis of governance was in each individual's moral cultivation. He said that the basis of the world lies in the state, the basis of the state lies in the family, and the basis of the family lies in the individual ❷. However, the age of Mencius was greatly different from the age of Confucius; education in the rites and music had already collapsed and had almost disappeared, the feudal lords swallowing up each other with violence, warfare was continuous, the people fled homeless, the government lost its moral ideals, and became entirely the tool of achieving private gain and enacting coercive authority. Therefore, Mencius no longer deliberately imposed an external order on the rites and music; instead he emphasized the internal content of rites and music, and called for the enactment of humane government and advocated righteousness and opposed private gain, advocated protecting the people and opposed coercive authority. He regarded the reason that the three dynasties of the Xia, Shang, and Zhou being able to rule the world was due to humaneness; the reason that they lost the world as due to lack of humaneness. The rise and fall of states was all due to humaneness and the lack of it. If the Son of Heaven was not humane, then he would be unable to govern the four seas; if the feudal lords were not humane, then they would not be able to govern their states; if the great ministers were not humane, then they would not be able to protect their own ancestral temples; if the knights and common people were not able to be humane, then they would not be able to preserve their own lives. People nowadays are all afraid of death yet they act without humaneness or righteousness; this is just as preposterous as fearing to be drunk yet insisting on drinking wine ❸.

The ideal of administering a humane government for the people was first proposed by Confucius. He said, "If a king were to rise up, it would take thirty years before he would be able to enact humanity and morality in the world ❹." "If a good man were allowed to govern a state, it would take one hundred years before he could eliminate violence and warfare ❺." However, the two words "humane government" were first voiced by Mencius as he expounded and enriched the content of humane government.

色道："你怎么如此粗野？君子对于不明白的东西决不妄说。名分不端正，话就没法说得顺；话说不顺，事就办不好；事办不好，礼乐就不兴起；礼乐不能兴起，刑罚就不会适当；刑罚不适当，百姓就会手足无措。" ❶

　　孟子也认为政治的根本在于每个人的道德修养。他说天下的根本在于国，国的根本在于家，家的根本在于身 ❷。但是孟子的时代与孔子的时代大不相同了，礼乐教化已经被摧毁殆尽，诸侯兼并剧烈，战乱不休，民众流离失所，政治失去了道德理想，完全成为实现私利和强权的工具。所以，孟子不再刻意地强调礼乐的外在秩序，而是强调礼乐的内涵，呼吁行仁政；主张道义，反对私利；主张保民，反对强权。他认为夏、商、周三代能够得天下是因为仁，失天下是因为不仁。国家兴废存亡都是因为仁与不仁。天子不仁，不能统治四海；诸侯不仁，不能统治国家；卿大夫不仁，不能保有自家的宗庙；士与庶民不仁，不能保全性命。现在人的都害怕死亡却乐于做不仁不义的事，这和害怕醉酒又非要喝酒一样荒唐 ❸。

　　对民众施行仁政的理想首先是由孔子提出的，他说："如果有王者兴起，一定要经过三十年才能让仁道施行于天下 ❹。""如果让一位善人来治一个邦国，要经过一百年才能消除残暴和杀伐 ❺。"不过，"仁政"二字最早由孟子喊了出来，他阐发和丰富了仁政的内涵。

---

❶《论语·子路第十三》3章。
❷《孟子·离娄上》5章。
❸《孟子·离娄上》3章。
❹《论语·子路第十三》11章。
❺《论语·子路第十三》12章。

❶ *Analects*, "Zilu," 13.3.
❷ *Mencius*, "Lilou," Ⅰ5.
❸ *Mencius*, "Lilou," Ⅰ3.
❹ *Analects*, "Zilu," 13.11.
❺ *Analects*, "Zilu," 13.12.

Mencius said, "Everyone possesses the feelings of pity for others. Because the ancient sage kings possessed this kind of heart, they were able to enact a humane government that took pity on the people." ❶ The basis of humane government is universal humane nature; this is an important point of departure for Mencius' political theory. Humane government derives completely from setting good human nature in motion and moral motivations. Humaneness is the goal of government, but cannot in any shape or form become a political tool. Mencius said, "Yao and Shun enacted humaneness and righteousness; this comes completely from their original natures; Shang, Tang and the Duke of Zhou all depended on personally putting into practice humaneness and righteousness. Yet the five hegemons of the Spring and Autumn Period borrowed as pretext humaneness and righteousness to seek for personal gain. Since they were borrowed over a long period without being returned, none of them realized that these things were not originally their own." ❷However, according to Mencius' logic, even a violent, greedy, brazen and shameless lord possessed the Heavenly-endowed nature to implement a humane government. It is just that this nature is concealed by greed and profit, and the fact that he has lost his innate moral sense. King Xuan of Qi was this type of ruler.

One time King Xuan of Qi invited Mencius to lecture on the historical events associated with the Spring and Autumn Period Dukes Huan of Qi and Wen of Jin and their hegemony of the world. Mencius assertively rejected them, saying, "Confucius and his disciples never mentioned these events; as a student who came along much later, I was also unable to hear of the matter of these hegemons. If you, great king, want me to discuss the matter of conquering the world, then we should talk about the use of government by the Royal Way to unite the world."

King Xuan of Qi answered vaguely, "What type of virtue is necessary to unite the world using the Royal Way?"

Mencius said, "Comfort and protect the people and you will be able to unite the world, and you will have no enemies in the world!"

King Xuan of Qi was a man of self-knowledge, who answered, "Is a man such as I able to comfort the people?"

Mencius said, "Of course you will be able to do so!"

"How do you know this?" Mencius said, "Your retainer Hu He told me that one day you great king were sitting in your hall, and saw an official leading an ox cross below the hall. You great king asked, 'Where are you

孟子说："人人都有怜悯别人的心情。古代的圣王因为有这样的心，才推行怜悯人民的仁政。"❶普遍的人性是人类政治的根据，这是孟子政治学说的重要出发点。仁政完全出于善性的发动，完全出于道德动机；仁是政治的目的，丝毫不能成为政治的工具。孟子说"尧舜推行仁义，完全出于本性；商汤和周武王靠的是亲自履践仁义；而春秋时代的五位霸主只是假借仁义来谋求私利。长期借着不还，都不知道这东西原来不是自己的了。"❷不过按照孟子的逻辑，即便是残暴贪戾、厚颜无耻的君主，也具备推行仁政的天性，只是他们为贪欲和利益所蔽，丧失了天良。齐宣王就是这样的一位君主。

一次齐宣王请孟子讲讲春秋时代齐桓公、晋文公称霸天下的事迹。孟子断然拒绝道："孔子和他的学生们从没谈过这些事，作为后学者，我也不可能听过这些霸主们的事。大王如果要我谈论征服天下的事，那就与您谈谈以道德统一天下的王道政治吧！"

齐宣王渺茫地问道："那要具备什么样的道德才能够以王道统一天下啊？"

孟子说："安抚、保护人民就能统一天下，无敌于天下！"

齐宣王也是有自知之明的人，回答说："像我这样的人，还能够安抚人民吗？"

孟子说："当然可以！"

"您凭什么知道我可以呢？"

孟子说："您的侍从胡龁告诉我，有一天大王坐在朝堂上，见臣子牵牛从堂下经过。大王您问道：'牵牛上哪儿？'臣子

---

❶《孟子·尽心上》21章。
❷《孟子·尽心上》30章。

❶ *Mencius*, "Jinxin," Ⅰ 21.
❷ *Mencius*, "Jinxin," Ⅰ 30.

leading this ox?' The official answered, 'To be sacrificed to the spirits.' You said, 'Let it go, I cannot stand to look at its pitiable, innocent appearance.' The official said, 'Well then should we sacrifice?' You then said, 'Change it for a sheep!' Did this really happen?"

"It really happened."

Mencius said, "With such an intention, great king, it is sufficient to unite the world! The people all think that you substituting a sheep for the ox meant that you were cheap and stingy. But I early on realized that your motivation derived from not being able to bear it."

King Xuan said, "Right. Some people really said that about me. Although the state of Qi is not large, can't it stand the loss of an ox? It is just that I could not stand to see its trembling and innocent appearance, so I had somebody substitute a sheep."

Mencius said, "Yet you great king still need to understand why the people are talking about you in this way. Substituting a small sheep for a large ox, how can the people understand the thoughts of your heart? They felt that if your motivation was pity, what difference would there be between killing an ox and killing a sheep?"

After hearing this, King Xuan of Qi couldn't help but laugh, saying, "This time, even I cannot make sense out of this. I certainly did not substitute a sheep for the ox because I was stingy. Since the people are so ignorant about this, all I can do is to let them talk like this!"

Mencius said, "It does not matter whether the people talk like this. Your heart of mercy, great king, is precisely the way of humane love! It is because you saw the ox but did not see the sheep. When a gentleman sees flying fowl and running beasts, viewing their living appearances means he cannot stand to see them die; when he hears their cries, he cannot stand to eat their flesh. Therefore, the gentleman stays away from the slaughterhouse and the kitchen."

King Xuan of Qi quickly brightened up, saying, "You truly appear like it is chanted in the *Book of Poetry*, 'The intentions of others, I can conjecture.' I just act in a spontaneous manner, and if I engage in self-examination, I still do not know why it is like this. Your kind words entered into my heart. However, you mention that the heart of mercy is commensurate with government by the Royal Way, just what does this mean?"

Mencius said, "If someone declared that he was able to lift up something that weighed three thousand catties, yet was actually unable to lift a single feather, or that he was able to discern the fine downy autumn feathers on a bird yet could not make out a cartload of firewood in front of his eyes, can you

回道：'宰了祭钟。'您说：'放了它吧，我实在不忍心看它无辜可怜的样子。'臣子说：'那么就不祭钟了？'您说：'怎么可以呢？换只羊吧！'确有此事吗？"

"确有此事。"

孟子说："大王有这样的用心，就足以统一天下了！老百姓们都认为您用羊换牛是小气吝啬，我早就知道你是出于不忍。"

齐宣王说："是啊！确实有人这样议论我。齐国虽然不大，但不至于舍不得一头牛吧？我就是不忍心看它颤抖无辜的样子，这才让人用羊代替。"

孟子说："不过大王也要理解为什么百姓们这样说您。用小的羊来代替大的牛，老百姓哪能理解大王的深意。他们认为，如果大王是出于怜悯的话，那么杀羊与杀牛又有什么不同呢？"

齐宣王听了，无可奈何地笑道："这下连我自己都搞不清楚了。我的确不是因为吝啬才用羊代替牛的。老百姓如此不理解，只得让他们去说了！"

孟子说："百姓这样说您没有关系。大王您的这种不忍之心正是仁爱之道啊！因为您见到了这头牛而没有见到那只羊。君子对于飞禽走兽，看到它活着的样子，就不忍心看到它死；听到它的哀叫，就不忍心吃它的肉。所以君子远离屠宰场和厨房。"

齐宣王高兴了起来，说："您真是像《诗》里唱的那样：'别人有心，我能揣测。'我只是自然而然地做了，反躬自问，却不知道为何如此。夫子您这样一说，说到我的心里去了。不过，您说我这种不忍之心合乎王道政治，这又是为什么呢？"

孟子说："如果有人向您声称能举起三千斤重的东西却拿不动一根羽毛；能辨察秋天鸟儿身上长出的细绒毛却看不见眼

believe what he says?"

"Of course not."

Mencius analyzed it further, "Now your humane love, great king, is able to be extended to birds and beasts, yet is unable to extend to commoners. What is this all about? Therefore, being unable to move a feather is not a matter of being unable to, rather a matter of not being willing to expend the energy; not seeing a cartload of firewood, is not a matter of being blind in the eyes, rather a matter of not being willing to use the eyes. Commoners not being comforted, and their lives not being stabilized, is not the case of you great king not being able to protect them, rather it is a case of not extending grace and dispensing humaneness. Therefore, you great king not being able to use the royal way to unite the world is a matter of you not being willing to do it, not because you cannot do it!"

"What is the difference between not being able to do something and not being willing to do something?"

Mencius said, "If you say you want to clasp Mt. Tai and cross over the Northern Sea, and then conclude 'This is impossible,' it would truly be impossible. If you want to snip off a tree branch to give to an elder, but then say, 'This is impossible,' it would be a matter of not being willing to do it rather than not being able to do it. Therefore, if you, great king, do not implement a humane government, it is not a matter of clasping Mt. Tai under your arm and crossing the Northern Sea, but rather a matter of snipping off a tree branch for an elder." ❶

During the Warring States Period, because of the expanding scale of warfare between states, each seeking to be the leading hegemonic state, they each encouraged agriculture, and vied to attract the masses of the people. But the goal of these measures was for the sake of guaranteeing tax levies and the conscription of troops within the states; advocating enriching the state and strengthening the army only meant regarding the people as tools, and increasing the exploitation and oppression of the people. Mencius deeply sensed the change in the times, and the crisis of survival facing the people. He warned these lords of states, "The feudal lords possess three types of treasures: the land, the people, and politics. Yet precious jewels and fine jade all are disasters that threaten lives." ❷ Among these three precious things of course what must be lent special emphasis are the people and the people's hearts. He said, "The people are the most precious, next are the spirits at the altars of soil and grain, and the position of the lord of state is the least important. He who is able to gain the support of the people can become the Son of Heaven; he who

前的一车木柴，您能相信他的话吗？”

"当然不信！"

孟子分析道："如今大王的仁爱能够施及到禽兽，却不能推及到百姓。这到底是为什么呢？所以，拿不动一根羽毛，不是没力气，而是因为不肯用力气；看不见一车木柴，不是眼瞎了，而是不肯看一眼；老百姓得不到安抚，生活不能安定，不是大王不能保护，而是不愿意推恩施仁。所以，大王不能以王道统一天下，是您不愿意去做，而不是您不能做！"

"不愿意做和不能做有什么区别呢？"

孟子说："挟持泰山超越北海，说：'这可做不到。'是真的不能做。给长者折个树枝，却说：'这可做不到。'就是不愿意做而不是不能做。所以大王您不推行王道，不属于挟持泰山超越北海之类的事情，而是属于给长者折个树枝之类的事情。"❶

战国时代，由于各国的争霸战争规模扩大，纷纷奖励农耕，争夺民众。但这样做的目的是为了保证国内的赋税与兵役的征用，富国强兵的主张只是将人民当作工具，不断地加重对他们的盘剥与压榨。孟子深感时代的变迁和百姓的生存危机，他警告这些国君："诸侯有三宝：土地、人民、政事。而那些珠宝美玉，都是危害性命的祸殃。"❷三宝之中当然应该特别重视人民和民心。他说："人民最为贵重，社稷神灵为次，而君主

---

❶《孟子·梁惠王上》7章。
❷《孟子·尽心下》28章。

❶ *Mencius*, "King Hui of Liang," Ⅰ7.
❷ *Mencius*, "Jinxin," Ⅱ28.

is appreciated by the Son of Heaven can become a feudal lord; he who is appreciated by the feudal lords can become a grandee. A feudal lord who threatens the state altars of soil and grain must be removed and replaced. A spirit who receives fat and pure sacrificial offerings in a timely manner yet is unable to preserve the people in avoiding floods and droughts, would have his sacrifices removed and offered to another spirit." ❶

The only way to obtain the support of the people is to enact a humane government. He said, "The reason the two violent rulers of Jie of Xia and King Zhou of Shang lost the world was due to losing the people; the reason they lost the people was due to losing the hearts of the people. Having a workable method that can be implemented in the world and gaining the people will gain the world; gaining the people is also a workable method, and gaining the hearts of the people will gain the world; gaining the hearts of the people is also a workable method for increasing the things which they hope for and reducing despicable and evil things. When the people submit to humane government, it is like water flowing toward a lower place, and beasts racing towards the wilderness. Therefore, otters drive schools of fish onward in deep pools, sparrow hawks drive flocks of birds onward in deep forests, and those who drove the people onward towards Tang of Shang and King Wu of Zhou were Jie and Zhou. Now all that is needed is for one feudal lord to enact humane government and all of the feudal princes in the world would drive the people to him. Even if he did not desire to unite the world it would happen anyway. However, those feudal lords who want to unify the world at the present time are like those men who have been sick for seven years and want to use old mugwort that is three years out of date to be healed; this is the saying that goes 'One with a seven-year sickness seeks for three-year mugwort.' If one does not usually store mugwort, then it will be hard to find one's whole life. If one does not desire to enact humane government, worry and shame will follow one for one's entire life, even up until death." ❷

He had a profound view of the great power of humane government and the heart of the people. He said, "The timeliness of seasons is not as important as the benefits of the earth; the benefits of the earth are not as important as the harmony of the people. Each border town has only a small moat of three *li*. Its outer walls are only seven *li* long on each side, but those who lay siege to capture it are not successful. Think for a moment, those who lay siege to it have certainly been conferred by Heaven with a golden moment for fighting,

的地位最轻。能得到民众拥戴的人便可以做天子，得到天子赏识的人便可以做诸侯，得到诸侯赏识的人便可以做大夫。诸侯危害社稷国家就撤换他。用肥美干净的祭品按时供奉神灵，可是这个神灵仍不能保佑人民免遭水旱灾害，那就改祭其他的神灵。"❶

要拥有民心，只有施行仁政。他说："夏桀和商纣王这两个暴君之所以丧失天下，是因为丧失了人民；之所以丧失了人民，是因为丧失了民心。获得天下有可行的方法，拥有人民就拥有了天下；拥有人民也有可行的方法，拥有民心就拥有了天下；拥有民心也有可行的方法，增加他们所希望的东西，去除他们厌恶的东西。人民归附仁政，就像水流向低处，兽奔向旷野。所以，为深池驱赶来鱼群的是水獭，为森林驱赶来鸟群的是鹞鹰，为商汤和周武王驱赶来人民的是桀、纣。现在只要有一个诸侯施行仁政，天下的诸侯就都为他驱赶人民来了。他就是不想统一天下，也做不到了。可现在这些想要统一天下的诸侯们，好像是那些害了七年病的人，要用放了三年的陈旧艾草来医治一样，所谓'七年之病求三年之艾'，平时不贮存艾草，那么终身都得不到。如果不想推行仁政，终身都伴随着忧患与耻辱，甚至死亡。"❷

他深刻地看到了仁政和民心的伟大力量。他说："天时不如地利，地利不如人和。每边城墙只有三里长的小城池，它的外廓每边仅长七里，围着它攻打却不能取胜。试想能围着它攻打，一定得到了上天赐予的战机；可是却不能攻占，这说明上天的时机不如地理的便利。如果城墙不是不高，护城河不是不

---

❶《孟子·尽心下》14章。
❷《孟子·离娄上》9章。

❶ *Mencius*, "Jinxin," Ⅱ 14.
❷ *Mencius*, "Lilou," Ⅰ 9.

yet are unable to take the town. This verifies that timely seasons given by Heaven are not as important as the earthly advantages given by geography. If the walls are high, the moat deep, the weapons and armor particularly durable or sharp, and the stored provisions very plentiful, yet the enemy abandons the siege and flees, this would verify that the geographical advantages are not good as the harmony in the human heart. Therefore I feel that restraining the people does not depend on boundaries and borders; guarding the state does not depend on relying on the dangers and defiles of mountains and rivers; overawing the world does not depend on weapons or armor. A just cause enjoys abundant support, while an unjust cause gets little support. This means that if one is based on the Way and righteousness and enacts humane government, then those who are willing to help him will be abundant; if one does not enact humane government and loses the Way and righteousness, then those who are willing to help will be few. When helpers reach the absolute minimum, then even one's relatives will turn on him. But when those who help reach the absolute maximum, all men in the world will follow him. If all the world follows him and he attacks the one whose relatives have turned away, then although the humane and righteous man may not necessarily initiate warfare, when he does he will certainly prevail, do not doubt it!" ❶

Mencius even warned the rulers of states, saying that the survival of the people inherently depends on the rulers' hearts of humaneness and righteousness. However, the safety or peril of the lords of state and the altars of soil and grain must depend even more on the hearts of humaneness and righteousness of the subjects and people. When Mencius visited King Hui of Liang, the king said, "Old master, you have not considered a thousand miles too far to come to our state of Wei, you certainly have some beneficial and profitable teachings for me, right?" Mencius resolutely refuted him, saying, "Great king! Why should the first words out of your mouth be about benefit and profit? It is enough to talk about humaneness and righteousness. If the ruler of a state all day long seeks how to benefit his state, and the grandees all day long seek how to benefit their own holdings, and the knights and the people all day seek how to benefit themselves, then all, above and below, will only contend among themselves for benefit; this state would be on the verge of a disaster within a day. In a great state armed with ten thousand chariots of war, the one who attempts to assassinate the lord is certain to be a grandee with a thousand chariots. In a small state with a thousand chariots, the one who attempts to assassinate the lord is certain to be a grandee with a hundred chariots. States that possess ten thousand or a thousand chariots, compared to

深，兵器和盔甲不是不坚利，贮存的粮食不是不充足，但大敌当前便弃城而走，这说明地理的便利又不如人心的和合。所以我认为：制约人民并不依靠国家疆界，守卫国家并不依靠山川险阻，威服天下并不依靠兵器甲胄。得道多助，失道寡助，也就是说，根据道义，施行仁政，帮助他的人就多；不行仁政，丧失道义，帮助他的人就少。帮助的人少到极至，连亲戚都背叛他；帮助的人多到极至，天下所有的人都顺从他。如果天下都顺从的人去攻打亲戚都背叛的人，尽管仁义之人不用发动战争，如果发动了战争，必胜无疑！" [1]

孟子还警告国君们：人民的生存固然要靠你们的仁心与仁政，可是，国君和社稷的安危更要依靠臣民们的仁义之心。孟子见到梁惠王时，梁惠王问道："老先生，您不远千里来到我们魏国，一定有给我带来利益的教诲吧？"孟子断然拒绝道："大王！你何必开口就谈利益？只要讲仁义就行了。如果做国君的人成天追问如何对我的国家有利；做大夫的成天追问如何对我的封邑有利；士与百姓也会成天追问如何对我个人有利。上上下下都在相互追逐利益，这个国家就危在旦夕了。装备了一万辆战车的大国，谋杀国君的一定是装备了一千辆战车的大夫。装备了一千辆战车的小国，谋杀国君的一定是装备了一百辆战车的大夫。在这些万辆、千辆战车的国家里，大夫们拥有

---

[1]《孟子·公孙丑上》1章。

[1] *Mencius*, "Gongsun Chou," I 1.

grandees with a thousand or one hundred chariots, have to be described as great. Yet if their rulers only know how to plot for private gain and do not recognize humaneness and righteousness, then the others will not stop until they have seized the wealth and property of those lords. Nevertheless, there has never been a man of humane love who would abandon his own parents, and there has never been a man of the Way and righteousness who would insult his own lord. Great king, all you have to do is mention humaneness and righteousness and that is enough, why must you mention benefit and profit?" ❶

Nevertheless, Mencius was not naive. He realized in a profound manner that some rulers are infatuated with becoming the hegemon of the world, with ordering around the people, and engaging in endless warfare. Therefore, in addition to having to speak out in exhortation, he criticized and attacked sternly and mercilessly. He berated King Hui of Liang, saying, "Your pigs and dogs eat human food, yet you know nothing about self-introspection and restraint. With corpses on the road that died from starvation you still do not open up your storehouses to distribute grain and relieve the poor in their calamities. When your subjects die of starvation, you say instead, 'It is no crime of mine; it is due to the poor harvest.' It is the same as using a knife to kill someone then saying, 'I did not kill him, it was the knife;' how is this any different? As long as you do not shift the blame to the weather or the harvest, then all the common people in the world will come in haste to live under your rule!" ❷

There is nothing worse in violating a humane government than to extort and levy exorbitant taxes and initiate warfare. Mencius said, "There are three types of levies on the people: fabrics and silk, foodstuffs, and corvee labor. When a gentleman levies a tax of one kind, he should not levy taxes on the other two kinds. If he levies two kinds at the same time, then some among the commoners will starve to death. If he levies all three at once, then fathers will not be able to take care of their sons, nor will sons be able to nurture their fathers with filial piety." ❸ He said to his students, "A minister like Ran Qiu, who served his ruler in extorting exorbitant taxies, would always be held in contempt by Confucius, how much more so in the case of those who initiated warfare on behalf of their rulers? To fight for territory, slaughtered men would fill the fields; to fight for cities, slaughtered men would fill the cities. This is to use the earth to eat men; the greatness of their crimes is worse than death. Therefore those who are good at manipulating campaigning should be assigned the ultimate punishment; those who are good at foreign diplomacy should be assigned a severe punishment. Those who urge the people to open up new

千辆、百辆战车，这不能不说是家大业大了。可是如果他们只知道谋求私利而不知仁义，那么这些人不将国君的财产侵占就不会罢休。然而，从来没有仁爱的人会抛弃自己的父母，也从来没有道义的人会轻慢自己的君主。大王您只要讲仁义就行了，何必要讲什么利益呢？" ❶

不过孟子并不天真，他深知这些统治者迷恋于称霸天下，驱使民众，无休无止地征战。所以，他除了无可奈何地劝说，就是严厉无情地批判与抨击。他指责梁惠王："您的猪狗吃着人吃的食物，却不知道检点制约；路上有人饿死却不知道开仓放粮，赈灾济民。老百姓饿死了，您却说：'不是我的罪过，是今年的收成不好。'这与拿刀杀了人，却说'不是我杀的，是刀杀的'有什么不同？您只要不委过归罪于年景和收成，这样，天下的百姓就会来投奔您了！" ❷

最违背仁政的事莫过于横征暴敛和发动战争。孟子说："对百姓征收的东西有三种：布帛、粮食和劳役。君子征收其中的一种，就不应该征收另外两种。如果同时征收两种，老百姓就会有人饿死。如果同时征收三种，那么父亲便照顾不了儿子，儿子也不能孝养父亲了。" ❸他对学生说："像冉求那样为统治者横征暴敛的臣子，都遭到孔子的唾弃，更何况那些为君主发动战争的人？为争夺土地而战，杀人遍野；为争夺城池而战，杀人满城，这就是用土地来吃人，其罪恶之大，死有余辜。所以善于征战的人应该处以极刑；善于操纵外交的人应该处以

❶《孟子·梁惠王上》1章。
❷《孟子·梁惠王上》3章。
❸《孟子·尽心下》27章。

❶ *Mencius*, "King Hui of Liang," Ⅰ1.
❷ *Mencius*, "King Hui of Liang," Ⅰ3.
❸ *Mencius*, "Jinxin," Ⅱ27.

territory, to develop new fields should be subject to punishment." ❶ Compared to ministers, the crimes of tyrannical lords are even greater. King Xuan of Qi asked him, "Tang of Shang once sent Jie of Xia on exile, and King Wu of Zhou invaded King Jie of Shang; did these things really happen?" Mencius replied, "They are recorded in the historical records." The king asked further, "Isn't this the case of a minister murdering his lord ruler?" How can this be tolerated?" Mencius answered, saying, "He who destroys humaneness is called a thief, he who destroys righteousness is called a savage. Men who are savage or thieves are also termed 'autocrats.' I have only heard that King Wu of Zhou executed the 'autocrat' King Jie; I never heard of him killing his lord ruler!" ❷

Mencius frequently posed some questions for rulers of states to answer, forcing them into embarrassing circumstances. He asked King Hui of Liang, "What is the difference in killing someone with a wooden club and killing someone with a knife?" King Hui of Liang answered, saying, "There is no difference." Mencius inquired further, "Well is there a difference in using a knife to kill someone and using the government to kill someone?" King Hui of Liang answered, "There is still no difference." Thereupon Mencius pointed out with severity, "Your kitchen is filled with fat meat hung on racks; your stables are filled with fat horses, but your people are pale-faced and emaciated, and the starving drop dead in the suburbs. In this case you are leading wild beasts to swallow up and eat your own people! They feel disgusted when they see wild animals eating each other. The lord ruler of the common people and senior officials are the parents of the people, but when government policies are enacted it is as if they were leading wild beasts to devour men; how are such men worthy of being the parents of the people? Confucius said, 'The first one to have devised earthen figurines and wooden figures to serve as grave goods should die without posterity, right?' This is because earthen figurines and wooden figures are similar to the forms of men. Such immoral behavior, as setting a bad example, should be censured; well then what should happen to those who permit the people to starve to death?" ❸ He asked King Xuan of Qi, "Supposing you, great king, had a minister who went to Chu to look around. He left his wife and children in the care of a friend. When he returned to Qi, he saw that his wife and children were suffering from cold and hunger; how should he treat this friend?" King Xuan of Qi replied angrily, "Cut off contact

重刑；督促百姓开垦荒芜，拓耕田地的人也该处以刑罚。" ❶
与臣子相比，暴君的罪恶更大。齐宣王问他："商汤曾经流放
了夏桀，周武王讨伐过商纣王，有这些事吗？"孟子说："史
传上记载过。"齐宣王又问："这不是臣子杀害君主吗？这难道
是可以的吗？"孟子答道："败坏仁的人叫做贼。败坏义的人
叫做残。残、贼这样的人又称为'独夫'，我只听说周武王诛
杀了'独夫'纣王，从未听说他杀害君主！" ❶

　　孟子经常设计一些问题让国君们回答，将他们逼到尴尬的
境地。他问梁惠王："用木棒打死一个人和用刀杀死一个人有
什么不同吗？"梁惠王答道："没什么不同啊？"孟子又问：
"那么，用刀杀人和用政治杀人有什么不同？"梁惠王答道：
"也没什么不同！"于是孟子严正地指出："你的厨房里挂满了
肥肉，马厩里站满了肥马，可您的人民面黄肌瘦，饥饿者倒毙
于郊外，您这是率领野兽来吞食您的人民啊！人们见到野兽自
相残食都觉得恶心；老百姓的君主和长官们，是百姓的父母，
可是施行起政治来却好像率领野兽来吃人，这样的人怎能配得
上做人民的父母？孔子说：'最早制作土俑木偶来作殉葬品的
人都应该断子绝孙吧？'因为土俑木偶很像人的形状。像这样
不人道的行为都应该受到谴责，那么让人民饥饿至死又应该如
何呢？" ❸他问齐宣王："大王您有个臣子去楚国游历，将妻
子儿女托付给他的朋友。等他回到齐国，见到妻子儿女饥寒交
迫，他应该如何对待这个朋友呢？"齐宣王愤然地说："和他

❶《孟子·离娄上》14章。
❷《孟子·梁惠王下》8章。
❸《孟子·梁惠王上》4章。

❶ *Mencius*, "Lilou," Ⅰ 14.
❷ *Mencius*, "King Hui of Liang," Ⅱ 8.
❸ *Mencius*, "King Hui of Liang," Ⅰ 4.

with him!" Mencius said further, "If a judge were unable to manage his underlings, how should you treat him?" "Remove him from office!" Mencius then asked again, "If a state is managed poorly, what should be done?" King Xuan could only turn his head with a look of distress, and gaze out to the left and right mumbling something about another matter. [1]

Even more valuable is that Mencius not only criticized and attacked the violent regimes of the feudal lords, he also devised a meticulous plan and description of humane government.

The humane government advocated by Confucians was quite simple, and very much in conformity with modern political ideals: to first enrich the people then to teach them. The former is the foundation, and the later is the goal. Once when Confucius travelled to the state of Wey, he offered praise, stating, "It is so densely populated!" Ran Qiu who was driving said, "Such a large population, how would you govern them?" Confucius said, "Enrich them!" Ran Qiu further inquired, "And after they get wealthy?" "Educate them!" [2] However, other thinkers during the Warring States Period did not necessarily endorse this position of the Confucians. For example, the Taoist Laozi advocated letting the people be well fed, live comfortable lives, and be strong and healthy, but not be educated, or let them gain knowledge or bravery. When the people are kept ignorant and lack aspirations, then those with knowledge will not dare to act; this would result in peace in the world [3]. Then there were the Legalists who also advocated encouraging agriculture and warfare, enriching the state and strengthening the army; they also opposed educating the people. They even regarded the *Book of Poetry*, the *Book of History*, rites, music, filial piety and fraternity, humaneness and righteousness, sincerity, etc. as sources of disaster for states [4]. Confucians regarded the people as the chief

绝交！"孟子又问："如果一个法官不能管理好他的下级，应该如何对待他呢？""将他撤职！"孟子再问："如果一个国家治理得不好，那又该怎么办呢？"齐宣王只得窘迫地回过头去，左右张望，胡乱扯些别的事了。❶

更为可贵的是，孟子不仅仅批判和抨击诸侯们的暴政，而且对仁政有着精致的设计和描绘。

儒家主张的仁政非常简单，也非常符合现代政治的理念，那就是先富民，后教民。前者是基础，后者是目的。有一次孔子到卫国去，称赞道："人口多稠密啊！"给他驾车的冉求说："有这么多的人，如何治理他们呢？"孔子说："让他们富起来！"冉求又问："富起来以后呢？"孔子说："让他们受教育！"❷不过，战国时代的其他思想家并不见得赞同儒家的主张。比如道家的老子就主张让老百姓吃得饱，过得安逸，身体强壮，但不要让他们受教育，有智慧，有胆识。老百姓没有知识，没有欲望，那些有知识的人也不敢有所作为，这样天下就太平了❸。还有主张奖励耕战、富国强兵的法家，也反对教育民众，甚至将《诗》、《书》、礼、乐、孝悌、仁义、诚信等当作国家的祸害❹。儒家以人民作为国家的主体，而道家和法家

---

❶《孟子·梁惠王下》6章。

❷《论语·子路第十三》9章。

❸《老子》第三章："圣人治：虚其心，实其腹，弱其志，强其骨。常使民无知无欲，使知者不敢为，则无不治。"

❹《商君书·靳令》："六虱：曰礼乐，曰《诗》《书》，曰修善，曰孝弟，曰诚信，曰贞廉，曰仁义，曰非兵，曰羞战。国有十二者，上无使农战，必贫至削。"

❶ *Mencius*, "King Hui of Liang," Ⅱ 6.

❷ *Analects*, "Zilu," 13.9.

❸ *Laozi*, 3. Or, as it is literally put: "In the rule of a sage, empty their minds, fill their bellies, weaken their resolves, and strengthen their bones. Constantly keep the people from knowledge and desires, this would cause those with knowledge to not dare to act, if so then all would be governed."

❹ The *Book of the Lord Shang*, "Harnesses and Orders" says, "The Six Vermin categories are known as rites and music, the *Book of Poetry* and the *Book of History*, self-cultivation and goodness, filial piety and fraternity, sincerity, frugality, humaneness and righteousness, the negation of arms, and shame towards warfare. If a state has all twelve of these, the lord wouldn't have people farm and fight, and the state would be impoverished to the point of being carved up."

element of the state, but Taoists and Legalists took the ruling lord as the chief element.

When Mencius discussed with King Hui of Liang and King Xuan of Qi the role of ruling lords of great states, he described just what an acceptable life for the people was❶:

> If you do not recruit corvee laborers or draft soldiers during the busy season when peasants are planting their fields, then grain would be too much to eat; if you do not use finely woven nets in small ponds to catch all the fish in them, then the fish and turtles would be too many to eat. If you fell trees in the forest at the appointed seasons, then wood would be so much that it could not be used up. When foodstuff and products from the rivers are too many to consume and when timber cannot be used up, the people would be able to support their wife and children, bury their parents, and have no regrets. When the people have no regrets, this is the starting point of the Royal Way.
>
> When households of five *mu*❷ of land plant mulberry trees, fifty year-old peasants can wear coats with silk wadding. When chickens, dogs, pigs, and such domestic animals are able to be grown into large flocks, seventy-year-old men are able to eat meat. When each home is able to have a hundred *mu* of land, and there is no hindrance making it productive, several households will no longer fear starving to death. Afterwards, operate some schools in a fine manner, educate the populace concerning being filial and respectful to parents, to venerate older brothers and elders, and when one's hair turns white, you and other oldsters will not have to shoulder heavy burdens and rush about on the roads. Seventy-year-olds will be able to wear silk and eat meat, and the people will not suffer either cold or hunger. If at this point one is not able to gain the support of the people of the world, then no one has ever done so!

He systematically expounded the content of humane government to the insignificant ruling lord of a petty state, Duke Wen of Teng, saying that, ❸

> Concerning matters of the people, one cannot lose a single minute. Doesn't it state in the *Book of Poetry*: "Cut grass in the day, at night weave ropes. Rush to raise a dwelling, plant the five grains in season." The doctrine of the common people is, to have a stable livelihood is to have a stable heart; without a stable heart, then they would act in defiance of the law. Yet waiting until they committed a crime to punish

则以君主作为国家的主体。

孟子对梁惠王和齐宣王这样的大国君主描绘过什么是像样的人民生活❶：

> 不在农民忙于种田的时候征派劳役兵役，谷物就多得吃不完。不用细密的网到小池沼里一网打尽，鱼鳖也多得吃不完。在规定的季节里砍伐林木，木材也多得用不完。粮食和水产吃不完，木材用不尽，如此，老百姓就能养活家小，安葬父母，没有什么遗憾。老百姓没有什么遗憾，就是王道的起点。
>
> 五亩❷大的家园，种上桑树，农夫到了五十岁就能穿上丝绵袍袄。鸡、狗、猪等家禽家畜都能够喂养繁殖，七十岁的人都能吃上了肉。每家能有一百亩土地，不要妨碍他们的生产，几口之家就不再饿肚子。然后再好好地办些学校，教育百姓孝敬父母，尊重兄长的道理，头发斑白，上了年纪的人就不用头顶背负着重物，奔波于道路之上。七十岁的人能穿上丝绵吃上肉，老百姓不受饥寒，这样还不能受到天下人的拥戴，从来就没有过啊！

他也对一个微不足道的小国君主滕文公系统地阐述过仁政的内容❸：

> 老百姓的事情，一刻都不能迟缓。《诗》里面不是说吗："白天割茅草，晚上搓成索。赶紧修房屋，按时播五谷。"老百姓的道理是，有稳定的产业就有安定的心，没有稳定的产业就没有安定的心。如果没有安定的心，就

---

❶《孟子·梁惠王上》2章、7章。
❷ 亩，地积单位，合1/15公顷。
❸《孟子·滕文公上》3章。

❶ *Mencius*, "King Hui of Liang," I 2, 7.
❷ *Mu*, a unit of area (=1/15 hectares).
❸ *Mencius*, "Duke Wen of Teng," I 3.

them was the same as setting them up. How could a man of humane love govern his people in this way? Therefore a worthy and capable lord of state was certain to be respectful and frugal, treat his underlings with ritual courtesy, and levy taxes on the people according to a set system. Once the family steward of the Ji clan Yang Hu said, "To become wealthy one cannot have humane love, to have humane love one cannot become wealthy."

The Xia Dynasty implemented the one in fifty *mu* "tribute" system; the Shang Dynasty implemented the one in seventy *mu* "aid" system; the Zhou Dynasty implemented the one in one hundred *mu* "pervasive" system. These three systems had different names, but were all based on the tax rate of ten percent. The so-called term "pervasive" means "universal," verifying that this type was the common system of taxation. The so-called term "aid" , means "to support," verifying that it was designed to assist the labor of the people in working the public section of the field. Anciently a worthy named Longzi once said, "As for the taxes on the fields, there was none better than the 'aid' system; and there was nothing worse than the 'tribute' system." This was because the "tribute" system was similar to a system based on a percentage of the annual harvest. During good years, grain and rice were everywhere, so taking in more as taxes was not considered harsh; yet following the "tribute" system of taxation did not allow for collecting more taxes. In bad years, the crop of grain was insufficient to leave some for fertilizing the next year's crop; yet following the "tribute" system did not allow for collecting less taxes. All claim that the lord of the state is the parent of the people, but he makes the people labor the entire year, busy with no rest, and cannot provide for their own parents, let alone have to borrow to pay their taxes. This makes the elderly and young drop into ditches from cold and hunger. How can such a one claim to be the parent of the people? Gentlemen and the aristocracy both receive income from inherited land taxes; this practice dates from early on in your state of Teng. But just as the *Book of Poetry* has it, "The rain falls on the public fields, and also falls on our private fields." This verifies that the common people during the Zhou Dynasty had income from their private fields, and only the "aid" system had so-called "public fields" . From this we can tell that the Zhou Dynasty also implemented the "aid" system.

After gaining an income, the people need to establish such schools as the *xiang, xu, xue,* and *xiao* to provide for their education. The

要胡作非为。而等到他们犯了罪再加以处罚，这等于是陷害他们。哪有仁爱的人会如此治理他的人民的呢？所以贤能的国君一定恭敬节俭，礼待臣下，按照一定的制度征收人民的赋税。从前鲁国季氏的家臣阳虎曾经说过："想要致富就不能仁爱，想要仁爱便不能致富。"

夏代实行五十亩一"贡"的制度，商代实行七十亩一"助"的制度，周代实行一百亩一"彻"的制度。这三种制度名目不同，但都是十分抽一的税率。所谓"彻"，就是"通彻"的意思，说明这是一种通行的征收赋税的制度；所谓"助"，就是"借助"的意思，也就是说要借助人民的劳力耕种公共的土地。古代有位叫龙子的贤人曾经说过："就田赋来说，最好的莫过于'助'的制度，最不好的莫过于'贡'的制度。"因为"贡"的制度是比较若干年的收成定出来的征收成数。丰年时谷米到处都是，多征一些算不上苛刻，而遵守"贡"的制度就不能多收；灾年收获的粮食还不够来年施肥的费用，而遵守"贡"的制度就不能少收。都说国君是人民的父母，却让人民终年劳作，忙碌不休，不能好好地赡养自己的父母，还要借贷举债来交纳赋税，使老人、儿童饥寒倒毙于沟壑之中，这怎能称得上是人民的父母呢？贵族君子们都有世袭的田赋俸禄，这在你们滕国早就实行了。可是正如《诗》里所说的那样："雨下到了公田里，再落到我的私田里"。这说明周代的老百姓也有自己的私田收入，只有"助"的制度才有所谓的公田，由此可见周代也是施行"助"的制度的。

人民有了收入，就要设立庠、序、学、校来教育他们。庠，就是养老的意思；校，就是教育的意思；序，

meaning of *xiang* is to nurture the old; the meaning of *xiao* is to educate; the meaning of *xu* is to study the art of archery. These three were all primary level schools, and the Xia Dynasty called it primary level school a *xiao*; the Shang Dynasty called its school a *xu*; the Zhou Dynasty called its school a *xiang*; but a *xue* was the name of the government school set up in all three dynasties. All of these schools were set up to expound ethical morality. When upper strata gentlemen adhere to ethical morality in a self-aware manner, the commoners will love each other. All you have to do is act in this way, and in the future if a king were to arise, he would certainly imitate your state of Teng and hence you would become the teacher of the king.

In the *Book of Poetry* it says, "Although our state of Zhou is ancient, the destiny of the state is newly arisen." What is being praised is the rise of King Wen of Zhou; continue to work hard to implement it! Let your state of Teng thrive and flourish!

Therefore, the essence of humane government is the goal of an economic system that insures the people's livelihood; the goal of the educational system is ethical morality. What is worth noting is that Mencius especially praised the "aid" system. In *Mencius*, this type of plowing and lifestyle were described as the "Well Field" or "Well Land." One time Duke Wen of Teng sent his great minister Bi Zhan to inquire of Mencius just what the well field was. Mencius said that humane government starts from dividing up the field. If it is divided inaccurately, then the well field will be unequal, and the income derived from it for aristocrats will be unfairly received. All tyrannical lords and corrupt officials will divide the fields erroneously in order to exploit the people. As long as the well field is divided accurately, such matters as how to apportion fields to the people or how to determine the income that goes to the aristocracy, etc., can be decided easily as sitting down.

The land of your state of Teng is narrow, yet it has gentlemen and farmers. Without gentlemen it would be impossible to rule the people, but without farmers it would be impossible to support the gentlemen. I advise you all to enact the "aid" system for the farmers, with one part in nine; for the craftsmen and merchants of the towns you should enact the "tribute" system of one part in ten. All knights below the rank of great ministers should have ownership of the labor on fifty *mu* of tillage for use in sacrifices. If other households have excess labor, each one should have twenty-five more *mu*. These farmers, whether when settling down

就是学习射术的意思。这三者都是基层的学校，夏代称为校，商代称为序，周代称为庠，而学则是夏商周三代都设置的国立学校，这些学校都是为了阐明伦理道德。上层的君子们自觉遵守伦理道德，下层的百姓就会相互亲爱。您只要这样去做，将来如果有王者兴起，一定会来效法你们滕国的，这样您就成为王者的老师了。

《诗》里说："我周邦虽古，但国运新兴。"歌颂的是周文王的兴起。您努力地实践吧！让您的滕国欣欣向荣！

所以，仁政的精髓，就是经济制度以为民置产为目标，教育制度以伦理道德为目标。值得注意的是，孟子对"助"的制度特别赞赏，在孟子那里，这种耕作与生活方式被描绘成"井田"或"井地"。一次滕文公让大臣毕战来向孟子请教何为井田。孟子说：

仁政一定从划分田界开始。田界划分得不标准，井田就不均匀，作为贵族俸禄的田赋就会收得不公平。凡是暴君和贪官们都会乱划田界以剥削百姓。只要田界划得正确，如何分给百姓田地，如何制定贵族的俸禄等事情，容易得坐下来就可以决定。

你们滕国土地狭小，可也有君子，有农夫。没有君子无法治民，没有农夫无法养活君子。我建议你们对农夫实行"助"的制度，九分抽一；对城市的工商业者实行"贡"的制度，十分抽一。公卿以下的士应该拥有耕种五十亩供祭祀的土地的劳力，如果他家还有多余的劳力，可以每人再配给二十五亩。这些农夫们无论居住或死葬，都不出乡里。同乡同井，在平常的生活中相互友

or being buried, should not leave their native places. Fellow countrymen and neighbors normally should be friendly with each other, care for each other, help each other in their daily lives, and should nurse each other in case of illness; only this way will the people be even more close and harmonious. One square *li* is one well; each well has nine hundred *mu* of well fields. One hundred of these *mu* are open to common use, and are called public fields. The other eight hundred *mu* are distributed to eight families as private fields, one hundred per family. These eight families collectively work the general use fields; after finishing work on these public fields, then they work their own private fields. The harvest from these public fields provides the salaries for the aristocrats and officials; the harvest from the private fields constitutes the wealth of the farmers. This is how noble and commoner, honorable and humble, are distinguished.

Of course, the well field system that Mencius spoke of was an ancient system of village communes under the rule of feudal lords. In these ancient communes, the harvest of public fields was used to support public expenditures. Later on, society progressed to become a feudal state; after the land in a village commune and the people associated with it were assigned to a particular nobility, the income from the public fields became the salary of the nobility. Of course, the ideal nobility should use the income from the public fields for public works or to aid the poor in distress or disaster. However, as early as the later part of the Western Zhou, the people were no longer willing to till the fields of feudal lords for no compensation. By the Spring and Autumn Period, public fields even more so became vacant and overgrown, and many farmers left their home villages and opened up private fields. In the year 645 B.C., the state of Jin issued two regulations; the first recognized that newly opened up private fields were legal private property; the second levied taxes on these fields to support military expenses. In this way, the farmers in village communes who were collectively plowing became various households of land-owning peasants. Whichever state implements this type of system is the state whose ruler can levy more taxes and become more powerful. As early as before the birth of Confucius, in 594 B.C., his native place of Lu had implemented a system of taxation based on fields, acknowledging the legality of private fields. During the Warring States Period, the well field system went from bad to worse. Probably right around the birth of Mencius, Shang Yang enacted legal reform in the state of Qin. He encouraged opening up new land for tillage, abolished the well field system, acknowledged the private

爱、关照、帮助，有了病相互帮扶看护，这样百姓们便亲爱和睦。方圆一里为一井，每井有井田九百亩，当中一百亩作为公共的田地，叫公田，其他八百亩分给八家作为私有的田产，每家一百亩私田。这八家共同耕种公共田地，公共田地里的事干完了再来料理自家的私田。公共田地里的收获是供养贵族官吏们的俸禄，私田里的收获是农夫们的财富，以此区别贵贱尊卑。

当然，孟子说的井田制是封建领主统治下的古代农村公社土地制度。在古代的公社中，公田里的收获是用作公共开支的。后来，社会进入了封建制国家，当一个农村公社中的土地和人民都分封给某个贵族之后，公田里的收入就成了贵族的俸禄。当然，理想的贵族也应该用公田里的收获进行公共建设或赈济贫困灾荒。不过，早在西周后期，人民便不愿意白白地耕种领主的公田了。到了春秋时代，公田更是大量荒芜，很多农夫离开乡井村社开垦私田。公元前645年，晋国就曾颁布了两道法令，一是承认平民们新开垦的土地是他们的合法财产，二是征收他们的田赋用作军费。这样，农村公社中集体耕作的农夫们纷纷变成了一家一户的自耕农。哪个国家施行这样的制度，哪个国家的国君便能征到更多的税，变得强大起来。早在孔子诞生之前，他的家乡鲁国于公元前594年就实行了按田亩征税的制度，承认私田的合法性。战国时，井田制度更是江河日下。

ownership of land, and allowed the public sale of land. Farmers with no fields to plow were given one hundred *mu* of land by the government and households were registered. Taxes were levied according to individuals, laying the foundation for the land system of a united empire in the future. Moreover, government officials were no longer assigned land but were issued grain by the state as their salaries. A system of officialdom based on the centralization of authority replaced the system of assigning land to the aristocracy. Mencius advocated the well field system, which has been derided by many historians. Why would Mencius like this old obsolete land system?

Actually, what Mencius liked was not the productive capabilities of the well field system, but the cultural tradition of the village commune included in the system; he liked its moral force and human sentiments. The well field system merely borrowed the strength of the people and did not levy taxes; in this way the masses could be organized and within them the spirit of public sacrifice and sense of one large family could be nurtured, and cultivation and a lifestyle based on the cohesiveness of ethical morality could be utilized. Yet at the time when the land-holding peasants during the Warring States Period were being tempted by the benefits of the new land system, they were deeply affected by the callous exploitation of this new type of system. This was because both the state and landlords controlled the land-holding peasants more directly through political and economic means, and extorted excessive taxes. Small fragile families often could not resist these new disasters, and given the fact that they could find no help, could only sell off or abandon their own land, becoming hired help or refugees. The well field system could guarantee the income of the hundred *mu* of private fields, letting farmers lead a life that could support a small family and bury their parents with no regrets. But the new land system not only made farmers lose their lands, it also made them lose their close and harmonious lifestyles and their homes based on traditional culture. In addition to this, Mencius saw that Teng was a state with small territory, and had no uncultivated land to make into new fields to increase state income. He wanted to use the well field system to erect a moral order to implement humane government, and to unite what was most valuable in the state, the hearts of the people. Mencius said, "Depending on military might, and borrowing humaneness and righteousness to conquer the people of the world, one would be able to proclaim himself a hegemon. But the one who claims to be the hegemon must have a strong and powerful state. But when a man who is based on morality implements humaneness and righteousness and is able to proclaim himself king, all the people in the world would submit their hearts to him, therefore there would be no need to depend on the power of a large state. Tang of Shang based himself on a

大概在孟子出生的年代前后，商鞅在秦国变法，奖励垦荒，废除井田，承认土地私有，允许土地公开买卖，无田耕种的农夫，由政府授田一百亩，并统计户口，按人征赋，奠定了此后统一帝国的土地制度。并且，官吏们不再受封土地，而是由国家发给粮食作为俸禄，中央集权的官僚制度代替了贵族封爵领地的制度。孟子主张井田制，遭到了许多历史学家的讥笑。那么，为什么孟子如此喜欢这套老掉牙的土地制度呢？

其实孟子看重的并不是井田制的生产能力，而是看重井田制中包含的农村公社的文化传统，看重其中的道德力量和人类温情。井田制只借助民力，不征收租税，这样便可以组织民众，培养民众为公奉献的精神和大家庭式的亲情，是用伦理道德凝聚起来的耕作与生活方式。而战国的自耕农在受到新土地制度利益诱惑的同时也深受这种制度的冷酷盘剥，因为国家和地主更加直接地通过政治和经济手段控制自耕农，横征暴敛。单薄贫弱的小家庭往往抵抗不了天灾人祸，在无助的情况下只有出卖或放弃自己的土地，成为雇佣或流民。井田制可以保有农夫一百亩私田的收入，过上能够养活家小，安葬父母，没有什么遗憾的生活。而新的土地制度不仅能让农夫丧失土地，而且丧失亲爱和睦的风俗生活与传统文化的家园。此外，孟子看到滕国是一个土地狭小的国家，也没有荒地可供开垦以增加国家的收入，他想让一个小国借此建立道德秩序，推行仁政，凝聚一个国家最为宝贵的民心。孟子说："凭着武力，假借仁义来征服天下的人能够称霸，可是称霸的人一定要有一个强大的国家。而以道德推行仁义的人能够称王，天下人都打内心归服他，所

small frontier state of seventy *li* to proclaim himself king; King Wen of Zhou based himself on a small frontier state of one hundred *li*." ❶

Although Mencius did not discuss matters concerned with seeking profit, he did have some independent views on trade. The state of Qi was on the seashore and the fishing and salt industries were flourishing. During the Spring and Autumn Period, Guanzi aided Duke Huan of Qi to proclaim himself hegemon through such economic means as expanding trade and regulating the prices of commodities and goods. Linzi, the capital of Qi, was replete in households of commoners and was luxurious and flourishing. It was an international, commercial metropolis. Flourishing trade brought to a state ample taxes from commerce. At that time, there were three types of taxes on commerce and industry in the states of feudal lords: first was the "lot" tax, that is, the tax on building sites; second was the "market" tax, that is, a tax on business; third was the "customs" tax, that is, the tariff on international trade between states. Mencius advocated that states which implement humaneness and righteousness should implement a zero tax system. Merchants operate their businesses in the markets, the government provides sites to store goods and does not levy building site taxes; for goods not sold, the government can purchase them according to the law, and not let goods pile up for too long. In this way, all merchants in the world are willing to store their goods in the markets of this state. At border checkpoints just inspect goods but do not levy taxes on them; in this way, travelling merchants of the world will all be willing to pass through this state. All the people of the world will all be willing to move to this state to settle down; the people of neighboring states would support the lord of this state just like their own parents. If the lord of a neighboring state were to drive the masses of his people to attack a state, it would be just like driving children to attack their own parents; ever since humanity has existed this type of thing has never existed. It is only this way that the phrase no enemy under heaven makes sense; it would be strange indeed if one could not unite the world in this way! ❷

What is even more interesting is that in modern Chinese, the rather high-frequency economic technical term of "monopoly" derives from Mencius' explanation; possibly he was the first man in history to advocate opposing monopolies. One time, while discussing the case of a nobleman giving offices to his own sons and nephews, Mencius said, "This should be called a 'monopoly.' Ancient country fair trade was for the sake of trading one's own property for something in shortage; it was a matter concerned with the mechanism of market management. But this despicable fellow insisted on

以不必依靠强大的国家。商汤凭借七十里的小邦国便称了王，周文王凭借上百里的小邦国也称了王。"❶

孟子虽然不谈论谋求利益的事情，但对于贸易也有独到的见解。齐国是海滨国家，渔业和盐业非常发达。春秋时代，管子通过发展贸易，调整物价货币等经济手段辅佐齐桓公称霸。齐国的首都临淄家给户足，奢侈繁华，是个国际化的商业都市。贸易的繁荣给国家带来了充足的商业税收。当时诸侯国的工商业税收有三种，一是"廛"，即屋基税；一是"市"，即营业税；三是"关"，即国际间的关税。孟子主张行仁政的国家应该实行零税收制度。商人在市场上营业，政府提供场地储存货物而不征收屋基税；货卖不出去，政府依法收购，不让货物积压太久。这样，天下的商贾都乐意把自己的货物存放在这个国家的市场上。关卡之上只对货物进行稽查而不征收关税，这样，天下的商旅都乐意打这个国家经过。天下的人民都乐意到这个国家居住，邻近国家的人民也会像对待父母一样爱戴这个国君。如果邻国的君主要驱使民众攻打这个国家，就如同率领他的子女来打他们的父母，自打有人类以来，还没有过这样的事。这样才叫无敌于天下，要不能统一天下才怪呢！❷

更有趣的是，现代汉语中使用频率相当高的经济学术语"垄断"恰恰出自孟子的解释，或许他也是人类历史上第一个主张反垄断的人。一次，他在谈论某个贵族把官职都分给自己的子侄们，孟子说："这应该叫做'垄断'。古代的集市贸易，是为了拿自己拥有的东西换取自己短缺的东西，由市场的机构管理相关的事务。可是就有那么一个卑鄙的家伙，非要登上一个

---

❶《孟子·公孙丑上》3章。
❷《孟子·公孙丑上》5章。

❶ *Mencius*, "Gongsun Chou," Ⅰ 3.
❷ *Mencius*, "Gongshun Chou," Ⅰ 5.

climbing up an isolated ridge, gazing out left and right, and controlling the market to gather all its advantages within his own net. Everybody feels that he was hateful, and so took steps to tax him. This resulted in the system of levying taxes on merchants." ❶ We absolutely cannot regard Mencius' advocacy of zero taxes and opposition to monopolies as something similar to the modern economic advocacy of free markets. He was only criticizing from a moral point of view politics oriented towards making a profit; still we cannot help be surprised at his wisdom.

Similar to Confucius, Mencius was a man who was anxious to serve the state. However, during the Warring States Period, the relationship between lord and minister changed. Because of the continuous decline of the great aristocracy, more and more common people were being educated; commoners and knights became more and more active on the political and diplomatic stages. In order to enrich the state and strengthen the army, and to gain hegemony over the world, rulers of each state supported the knights and vied to recruit talent. The relationship between officials who had been born commoners and ministers from foreign states with the lords of state was not one of kinship ties; therefore the relationship between lords and ministers no longer resembled that which existed during the Spring and Autumn Period when it had been an extension of the father-son relationship. Legalist Han Feizi considered that the relationship between lord and minister actually was one of the exchange of benefits. The ruler used the two methods of rewards and punishments to control the great ministers; in order to gain benefits, great ministers feared the lord. But the way the Confucians managed the lord-minister relationship was much more complicated.

Mencius advocated that between ruler and ministers the Way and righteousness should be united in one. This is to say that lords and ministers must share the same political ideals and moral realm; it is a composite of morality and culture, not a composite of benefits. The significance of this means rulers and ministers are equal, and both roles need to be played by sages or gentlemen. He said, "The square and the compass are the standards for circumference; the sage is the standard for being human. If one is a ruler, then he has to fulfill the way of a ruler; if one is a minister, then he needs to fulfill the way of a minister. These two ways merely imitate Yao and Shun. If one does not adopt the methods of Yao and Shun to serve one's lord, then this would be disrespectful to one's lord. If a lord does not adopt the methods of Yao and Shun to govern the state, then this would wreak havoc among the people." ❷ It is precisely because of this that Mencius, though admittedly

断耸的垄冈之上，左右张望，操纵行市，想把好处一网打尽。大家都觉得他可恨，便发动起来抽他的税。因此就有了向商人征收税的制度。"❶我们千万不要以为孟子的零关税和反垄断的主张与当今自由贸易的经济主张不谋而合，他只是从道德的角度批评以谋利为目标的政治而已，但我们不得不为他的睿智感到惊讶。

和孔子一样，孟子也是一个汲汲于用世的人。不过，战国时期，君臣关系发生了变化。由于大贵族不断衰落，越来越多的平民受过教育，平民士人在政治和外交舞台上愈加活跃。各国统治者为了富国强兵，争霸天下，纷纷养士、争夺人才。出身平民的官僚和来自其他国家的客卿与国君之间没有宗法血缘关系，因此君臣关系不再像春秋时代那样仅仅是父子关系的延伸。法家韩非子认为君臣之间其实是利益交换的关系。君主用赏罚两种手段驾御大臣，大臣由于要获得利益，所以畏惧君主。而儒家处理君臣关系的原则就复杂得多。

孟子主张君臣之间凭借道义结合在一起，也就是说，君与臣必须具有共同的政治理想与道德境界，是一个道德与文化的共同体，而不是一个利益共同体。在这个意义上，君臣是平等的，都需要由圣人或君子来担任。他说："规矩是方圆的标准，圣人是做人的标准。如果做君主，就要尽君主之道；如果做臣子，就要尽臣子之道。两种道都不过是效法尧舜罢了。不以尧舜的方法事奉君主，就是对君主不敬；不以尧舜的方法治理国家，就是残害人民。"❷正因为如此，孟子固然主张臣下敬重

---

❶《孟子·公孙丑下》10章。
❷《孟子·离娄上》2章。

❶ *Mencius*, "Gongsun Chou," Ⅱ 10.
❷ *Mencius*, "Lilou," Ⅰ 2.

advocating ministers reverencing their lords, also stressed even more that lords must respect worthies and gentlemen. This type of respect was not in the form in conferring wealth but in being able to allow them to achieve their individual missions. Mencius said, "Back then Duke Mu of Lu constantly asked after Zisi, sending meat to him. Zisi was very unhappy, and finally drove those who came to present gifts out of the front gate. After performing ritual greetings towards the direction of the court, he severely rejected it, saying, 'Today I finally realize that the lord of the state merely regards me as a dog or horse to be raised.' Probably afterwards Duke Mu no longer dared to present gifts to Zisi. He liked worthy men, but was unable to respect them, and was not able to support them in accordance with ritual courtesy and righteousness; is one able to call this behavior liking the worthies?" ❶ Someone called Chenzi asked Mencius, "What was the principle anciently for gentlemen emerging to take office?" Mencius responded, "There was the so-called theory of 'three taking office and three leaving office.' If a lord is not only ritually courteous but also receptive of his suggestions, then he will emerge and assume office; if the ritual courtesy is not reverential enough, and his suggestions are not accepted, then he will leave office and depart. Next, although his suggestions are not accepted, still he is treated with great ritual courtesy, then he will emerge and assume office. The worst kind is when in the morning there is nothing to eat, and there is nothing to eat in the evening, he is too hungry to leave his dwelling. At this time the lord of the state realizes what is happening, and says, 'I am unable to implement his ideals, and also am unable to accept his suggestions. But letting him starve to death in my state is intolerable, this is my shame!' Thereupon he sends relief to him. In this case it can be accepted only to preserve life and limb." ❷

The greatest responsibility of an upright great minister is to correct the lord in a moral sense. He said, "Petty men who abuse power in office are not even worth censuring; the government that they administrate is itself not worthy of discussion. Only great upright men and gentlemen are able to correct the improper intentions of a lord. If a lord emphasized humaneness, then everybody would be humane; if the lord emphasizes righteousness, then everyone would be righteous; if the lord emphasizes correctness, then all would be correct. If one day one can cause the lord to emphasize correctness, then the nation and great households would be secured." ❸ In the eyes of Mencius there were three kinds of great ministers. One is the kind that serves the ruler; all that is necessary is to please the ruler and to make him happy, and that is good enough. One kind is the minister who stabilizes the state and great

君主，但更强调君主对贤人君子的尊重，这种尊重不是赏赐财富而是能让他实现自己的抱负。孟子说："当年鲁缪公经常问候子思，送肉食给子思。子思非常不高兴，终于将送东西的人赶出大门。他向朝廷的方向行礼后严正地拒绝说：'我今天才知道，国君只不过将我当作犬马一样来豢养！'大概从此鲁缪公不敢再给子思送礼了。他喜欢贤人，却不能重用，还不能合乎礼义地供养他们，这能称得上是喜欢贤人吗？"❶有个叫陈子的人问孟子："古代君子出来做官的原则是什么？"孟子说："有所谓的'三就三去'之说。君主对他既有礼貌又听从他的建议，便出仕就职；礼貌不够恭敬，又不听从建议，便离他而去。其次呢，虽不听从建议，但非常有礼貌，便出仕就职；礼貌不够恭敬，便离他而去。最差的一种呢，早上没有吃的，晚上也没有吃的，饿得连门都出不了。这时国君知道了，说：'我不能推行他的理想，又不能接受他的建议，让他在我的国家饥饿不堪，这是我的耻辱！'于是周济他。这也可以接受，只是保全性命罢了。"❷

一个真正的大臣，他最重要的责任就是在道德上匡正君主。他说："那些弄权执政的小人们是不值得谴责的，他们搞的政治也不值得去议论。只有正直的大人君子才能校正君主不正当的用心。君主仁，就没有人不仁；君主义，就没有人不义；君主正，就没有人不正。一旦使得君主端正了，国家也就安定了。"❸在孟子眼里，大臣有三种，一是专门侍奉君主的，那

❶《孟子·万章下》6章。
❷《孟子·告子下》14章。
❸《孟子·离娄上》20章。

❶ *Mencius*, "Wanzhang," Ⅱ 6.
❷ *Mencius*, "Gaozi," Ⅱ 14.
❸ *Mencius*, "Lilou," Ⅰ 20.

households; as long as they are stabilized, then he will be happy. There is also the kind of man who may be called the "Man of Heaven." He takes serving the whole world as his responsibility; when the Way and righteousness are able to circulate throughout the world, he will go implement them. And reaching the highest realm is the so-called "Great Man;" as long as he corrects himself, all things in the world will follow him in becoming correct. ❶

Mencius himself acted in this manner. One time he prepared to see the King of Qi; at this time it so happened that the king sent somebody to say to Mencius, "I originally wanted to come visit you, but I have caught a chill, and cannot afford to be out in the wind. Are you able to come to see me instead?" Mencius knew that this was merely an excuse for the king to not come and see him, so he answered, "I am sorry, I am myself ill, and cannot attend court." The next day, Mencius had to go out to mourn at a funeral. His disciple Gongsun Chou said, "Yesterday you pled illness for not going to the court, but today you go out to mourn at a funeral, this is probably not appropriate, right?" Mencius replied, "Yesterday I was sick, today I am fine, what is wrong with that?" Right at this moment the king sent someone to bring a doctor to see how Mencius' illness was doing. His disciple Meng Zhongzi handled the messenger by stating that Mencius' illness was somewhat better and was already on his way to court, and at the same time sent someone to notify Mencius to go to court. Mencius had no other choice and could only take refuge in the home of Jing Chou to stay out of sight for a while.

Jing Chou asked Mencius, "The relationship in a home between father and son and the relationship between a lord and minister are the two most important human relations. Between father and son there needs to be familial love; between lord and son there needs to be reverence and respect. I perceive that the King of Qi is treating you with great respect, but you do not pay the king much reverence!"

Mencius replied calmly, saying, "Oh, what are you saying? There is none in the state of Qi who is willing to discuss humaneness and righteousness with the great king, can it be that they regard humaneness and righteousness as bad things? It is just that they think in their hearts, 'How is it worthwhile to discuss humaneness and righteousness with this person, the great king?' This is the greatest form of disrespect to him! But I never dare to discuss anything with the king if it does not pertain to the Way of Yao and Shun; therefore out of all the men in Qi I am the most respectful of the great king!"

Jingzi said, "You, sir, err in your words! According to ritual courtesy and

只需讨好君主，让他高兴就行。一是安定国家的社稷之臣，只有社稷安定了他才会高兴。还有一种人可以称之为"天民"，他以天下为己任，只有道义能通行于天下时，他才去推行。而达到最高境界的是所谓的"大人"，他只要将自己端正了，天下万物都随之而端正。❶

孟子自己就是这样做的。一次他准备去见齐王，这时恰巧齐王派人来说："我本来想来看看您，但是我受了风寒，不能吹风。不知您是否能来见我？"孟子知道这是齐王不愿来见他的借口，便回道："对不起，我也有病，不能上朝了。"第二天，孟子要外出吊丧。弟子公孙丑说："您昨天刚托病不上朝，今天却出去吊丧，这不太合适吧？"孟子说："昨天我生病，今天好了，有何不可？"就在这时，齐王让人带了医生来探问孟子的病情。弟子孟仲子一边应付来人说先生病好了一点，已经上朝去了；一边让人赶紧通知孟子上朝。孟子无可奈何，只得到景丑家里避一避。

景丑问孟子："家里的父子关系，国中的君臣关系，是两种最重要的人伦。父子之间要恩爱，君臣之间要恭敬。我看齐王对您很敬重，您却不太敬重齐王啊！"

孟子回敬道："唉，您这说的是什么话！齐国没有一个人愿意与大王谈论仁义，他们难道认为仁义是不好的东西吗？只不过他们心里想：'大王这个人，哪里值得与他谈论仁义！'这才是对齐王最大的不敬！而我，只要不是尧舜之道，从不敢对大王谈论，所以整个齐国都没有人比我更敬重大王！"

---

❶《孟子·尽心上》19章。

❶ *Mencius*, "Jinxin," Ⅰ 19.

righteousness, when a father calls to his son, the son merely utters one sound, 'hmm' and rushes off to him without even saying 'yes.' When a lord calls to his minister, the minister does not wait for a horse and carriage to be prepared, but sets off first. You originally were going to the court to see the great king, but as soon as you saw that the king had sent someone to summon you, you left instead; it seems that this is not too reasonable!"

Mencius said, "Is it really this way? Zengzi once said, 'The lords of the states of Jin and Chu can be called wealthy beyond compare. While they have wealth, I have humaneness; while they have power, I have righteousness. Do I then not have something comparable to them?' Zengzi would not say something unreasonable! There are three things in the world that by common consensus are honored and valued: one is rank, one is age, and one is morality. At court, rank is honored, in the countryside age is honored, in the aspect of assisting the lord in governing the people, morality is honored. How can the King of Qi use his rank to slight my age and morality? All lords of states who accomplished great things definitely had the experience of summoning ministers who would not come. If they wanted to discuss matters, they had to go visit the minister. If a lord of state does not honor morality and delight in humaneness and righteousness, then it isn't worthwhile to work with him. Therefore, Tang of Shang learned from Yi Yin before making him his minister, and with no effort at all unified the world. Duke Huan of Qi first learned from Guan Zhong before making him his minister, and with no effort at all established a hegemony of the world. Nowadays, the size of the territory and political power of each state in the world is roughly equal. Despite being evenly matched, some are unable to defeat other nations. There is no other reason for this than liking to have as ministers those obey them, and disliking to have as ministers those who are able to teach one's own people. If Tang had not dared to summon Yi Yin, or Duke Huan had not dared to summon Guan Zhong, or if Guan Zhong, the only one who was able to implement a hegemonic government, hadn't come immediately when summoned, what about others who could not stand Guan Zhong?" ❶

One who could not stand Guan Zhong was Mencius. His disciple Gongsun Chou was from the state of Qi. One time he asked Mencius, "Master, if you became a minister in power in Qi, would you be able to reduplicate the glorious achievements of Guan Zhong and Yanzi?" Mencius answered, saying, "You really are a man of Qi, only acquainted with Guan Zhong and Yanzi. Previously someone asked Zeng Xi, the son of Zengzi, 'How do you compare with Zilu?' Zeng Xi said, 'Zi Lu was a person respected by my father; how can

景子说："先生此言差矣！按照礼义，父亲召唤儿子，儿子只说一声'唯'，连'诺'都不说就赶紧去了。君主召唤臣子，臣子不等马车准备好就先走了。您本来是要去朝见大王的，可一见大王召您反而不去了，似乎不太合乎情理吧！"

孟子说："难道是这样吗？曾子说过：'晋国、楚国的国君可谓富不可及。可他们有财富，我有仁；他们有权势，我有义。我有什么比不上他们的呢？'曾子不会说没有道理的话！天下公认的尊贵的东西有三个，一是爵位，一是年龄，一是道德。在朝廷上以爵位为尊，在乡里以年龄为尊，在辅助君主治理人民方面以道德为尊。齐王怎能凭藉他的爵位来轻慢我的年龄和道德呢？凡是大有作为的君主一定有召唤不动的臣子，如要商量事情，他必须到臣子那里去。国君如果做不到尊重道德，喜爱仁义，就不值得与他共事。因此商汤先向伊尹学习再让他成为臣子，不费劲就统一天下。齐桓公先向管仲学习再让他成为臣子，不费劲就称霸天下。如今天下各国，土地大小和政治能力都差不多，可是旗鼓相当，不能有胜出的国家，没别的原因，喜欢让听话的人做臣子，不喜欢让能够教诲自己的人做臣子。汤不敢召伊尹，桓公不敢召管仲，管仲这种只能施行霸政的臣子尚且不能召之即来，何况那些看不起管仲的人呢？"❶

看不起管仲的人正是孟子。弟子中的公孙丑是齐国人，一次问孟子："老师如果在齐国做了当权的大臣，您能复兴管仲、晏子的功业吗？"孟子答道："你可真是个齐国人，只知道有管仲、晏子罢了。以前有人问曾子的儿子曾西：'你与子路比

❶《孟子·公孙丑下》1章。

❶ *Mencius*, "Gongsun Chou," Ⅱ1.

I compare with him?' He asked further, 'What about Guan Zhong?' Zeng Xi responded quite upset, saying, 'Why would you compare me with Guan Zhong? This guy was greatly trusted by his lord and his administration was so long, yet his accomplishments were so light as to be not worth mentioning. What the heck are you comparing me to him for?' Not even Zeng Xi was willing to be compared to Guan Zhong, can it be that you think I would be willing to imitate him?" ❶

On another occasion King Xuan of Qi inquired of Mencius about the duties of a high-ranking court official. Mencius asked which type of court official was in question. The King of Qi said, "Are there differences in high-ranking court officials?" Mencius said, "Of course there are differences. Some are royal relatives, and some are royal in-laws or otherwise have different surnames." The King of Qi said, "What about high-ranking ministers who are royal relatives?" Mencius said, "When a lord of state commits a grave error, then he must admonish him. If the king does not listen after repeated admonitions, then he should depose the lord of the state." The king flushed and changed color when he heard this. Mencius stated further, "Great king, do not be alarmed; you inquired of your minister, so I do not dare not to tell you the unvarnished truth." The king composed himself, then continued by asking about high-ranking court officials with different surnames. Mencius said, "If the lord of state commits an error, then he should admonish him, if after repeated admonitions he still does not listen, then he should leave his service." ❷

If the lord is too brutal, and has lost the Way and righteousness, those who act as his minister not only may leave him, they can even regard him as the common enemy of mankind. Mencius said, "Grandees can leave a lord who kills knights and the people even though they are not accused of a crime; knights can leave a lord who kills the common people even though they are not accused of a crime." ❸ He admonished King Xuan of Qi, saying, "When a lord ruler considers his ministers as his own brothers, his ministers will regard their lord as their own hearts and souls. But when the lord ruler regards his ministers as his dogs or horses, his ministers will regard their lord as an unrecognizable stranger on the road. When a lord ruler regards his minister as dirt or grass, his minister will regard him as an enemy." ❹ After 1,700 years or more, when the founder of the Ming Dynasty Zhu Yuanzhang read the above cited passage, he became furious. He was a tyrant with great ambitions for his state, yet he ordered the entire country to cease sacrifices to Mencius. But the thought of Mencius had already deeply influenced Chinese officialdom. The Minister of the Bureau of Punishments Qian Tang strode forward to protest

怎么样？'曾西说：'子路是我父亲敬畏的人，我怎能与他相比？'又问：'与管仲比呢？'曾西非常不悦地说：'你为什么拿我与管仲比呢？管仲这个人，国君对他如此信任，执政时间如此长久，可功业却如此微不足道。干嘛拿我和他相比？'连曾西都不愿意与管仲相比，难道你认为我愿意学他吗？" ❶

还有一次齐宣王向孟子询问公卿的责职。孟子问他询问哪一类公卿。齐王说："公卿还有不同的类别吗？"孟子说："当然不一样啦。有的是大王的贵戚公卿，有的是异姓公卿。"齐王问："请问贵戚公卿。"孟子说："国君有大的过失便要进谏，反复劝谏还是不听，就将国君废除。"齐王听了勃然变色。孟子又说："大王不要诧异。您咨询臣下，我不敢不说实话。"齐王定了定神，接着问异姓公卿。孟子说："国君有过失便要进谏，反复劝谏还是不听，便离他而去。" ❷

如果君主过于残暴，丧失了道义，做臣下的不仅可以离开他，甚至可以将他视为人类的公敌。孟子说："没有罪名而杀戮士人，大夫们可以离开这个君主。没有罪名而杀戮百姓，士人也可以离开这个君主。" ❸他告诫齐宣王说："君主将臣下看成自己的手足，臣下就会将君主看成自己的心腹。君主将臣下看成犬马，臣下就会将君主看成不认识的路人。君主将臣下看成泥土草芥，臣下就会将君主看成仇敌。" ❹一千七百多年以后，明朝的开国君主朱元璋读到上述文字，大为震怒。他是个有抱负的暴君，居然下令全国停止祭祀孟子。可是孟子的思想

❶《孟子·公孙丑下》2章。
❷《孟子·万章下》9章。
❸《孟子·离娄下》4章。
❹《孟子·离娄下》3章。

❶ *Mencius*, "Gongsun Chou," Ⅱ2.
❷ *Mencius*, "Wanzhang," Ⅱ9.
❸ *Mencius*, "Lilou," Ⅱ4.
❹ *Mencius*, "Lilou," Ⅱ3.

against the emperor, saying, "Your servant is willing to die for Mencius, it would be an honor!" The emperor's bluff was called; he had no other choice than to rescind his order❶. This spirit of protecting the Way and righteousness and fearlessness in the face of death are what Mencius meant by the "Flood-like *qi*" ; in ancient China it was also called integrity. It was precisely this kind of integrity that caused officials and ministers who were educated in the thought of Confucius and Mencius to forever maintain a strained relationship with expansionist tyrants and treacherous officials.

已深深影响了中国的士大夫们。刑部尚书钱唐站出来抗议皇帝说："臣愿为孟子而死，死了也光荣！"皇帝被迫无奈，只得收回成命❶。这种维护道义而不怕死的精神，就是孟子说的"浩然之气"，在中国古代又叫做气节。正是这种气节，使得受孔子和孟子思想教育的官僚士大夫们与私欲膨胀的暴君和奸臣们之间永远存在着紧张关系。

---

❶《明史》卷五十《礼志四》，中华书局，1974，第1296页。

❶ *History of the Ming*, Vol. 50, "Monograph on Rites," 4 (Beijing: Zhonghua Book Company, 1974), p. 1296.

砖画中反映的论辩场景

Discussing Scene from a brick painting

砖画中反映的百姓生活场面

Populace' living Scene from a brick painting

七　予岂好辩哉——雄辩的思想和语言

Chapter VII　How Can It Be Said that I Am Fond of Debate?
The Thought and Language of a Powerful Debater

None of the sages or worthies in highest antiquity composed personal works, but they highly emphasized passing along some aphorisms to others which they had crystallized, based on their moral cultivation and life experiences. Many of these sayings were very philosophical and were transmitted to later generations. This type of practice was called to "establish words," and was viewed as important as life itself. One aristocrat from the state of Lu named Mu Shu visited the state of Jin; an aristocrat from Jin named Fan Xuanzi asked him, "I have heard of the following maxim from the ancients, called 'Dead but Immortal.' My family has been distinguished for generations; can this be considered as being immortal?" Mu Shu ridiculed him, saying, "We have a story in Lu, 'Although a gentleman called Zang Wenzhong had died, the words that he had spoken were passed down.' This most likely is what is meant as 'Dead but Immortal,' right? I have also heard that the highest type of speech establishes morality; the next type establishes meritorious deeds; the next type accurately establishes discourse. All of these can be called immortal. You have been distinguished for generations, but this only means that for generations you have had enough food to eat, this cannot be considered to be immortal." ❶   Confucius offered a meticulous analysis of language. He said, "Those who are moral certainly have their own maxims, but those who spout maxims are not necessarily moral. Those who are humane are certainly brave, but those who are brave are not necessarily humane." ❷ Confucius detested most of all those who were fake and yet very glib. He said, "Those who can speak in flattering terms seldom possess the fine virtue of humane love!" ❸ Confucius taught his disciples, saying, "When a gentleman speaks he must be prudent and straight-forward, in action he must be diligent and quick." ❹ But Confucius also opposed a gentleman who was too plain and lacked refinement; he demanded a gentleman be refined and courteous, and emphasized his ability in language, and such cultural accomplishments as performing rites and ceremonies. This type of cultivation does not seek for external trappings, but seeks a better way to express inward virtue. During the Spring and Autumn Period a gentleman called Jie Zitui said, "Language is the decoration of the body." This means that language is the cultural pattern of the body. Cultural patterns are the natural manifestation of one's basic essence, and is completely different from the decorative patterns that adorn the outside. All in all, Confucius even more so advocated truth in language; this type of language derives from sincere sentiments and profound cultivation; it comes from moral practice in daily life.

　　上古时代的圣贤们都不撰写个人的著作，但很注重从自己的修养与经历中总结出一些格言赠给别人，很多话非常有哲理，于是流传后世。他们将这样的事称作"立言"，看得和生命一样重要。鲁国有个叫穆叔的贵族访问晋国，晋国的贵族范宣子问他："我听说古人有这样的格言，叫做'死而不朽'。我的家族世代显赫，可以算得上不朽了吧？"穆叔讥讽他说："我们鲁国人说：'有个叫臧文仲的君子，人虽死了，可他说的话流传了下来。'这大概才算得上'死而不朽'吧？我还听说，最上等的是树立道德，其次是建立功勋，再次是确立言论。这些都可以称得上是不朽。您世代显赫，只能算得上世世代代有饭吃，不能算作不朽！"❶孔子对语言有精到的判断，他说："有道德的人一定有格言，而能说出格言的人不一定有道德。仁爱的人一定有勇气，而有勇气的人不一定有仁爱。"❷孔子最痛恨虚伪而又能说会道的人，他说："那些花言巧语的人很少有仁爱的美德！"❸孔子教导弟子说："君子说话要谨慎木讷，做事要勤奋敏捷。"❹但孔子又反对君子质木无文，要求君子文质彬彬，注重语言、礼仪等文化修养。这种修养决不是寻求一种外在的修饰，而是如何更好地将内在的美德表现出来。春秋时期有个叫介子推的君子说："言者，身之文也。"意思是：语言是一个人自身的文理。文理是内在本质的自然表现，完全不同于外在装饰的花纹。总之，孔子更多地主张语言的真实，这样的语言来自真诚的性情和深厚的修养，来自于人生的道德

❶《左传》襄公二十四年。
❸《论语·宪问第十四》4章。
❸《论语·学而第一》3章。
❹《论语·里仁第四》24章。

❶ *The Commentary of Mr. Zuo*, Duke Xiang, 24th year.
❷ *Analects*, "Xianwen," 14.4.
❸ *Analects*, "Xue'er," 1.3.
❹ *Analects*, "Inward Virtue," 4.24.

Confucius' words and discourses recorded in the *Analects* are precisely wise maxims of eternal validity.

However, Mencius had not developed this type of restraint but was rather a forceful and powerful debater. Many thinkers appeared in the Warring States Period; similar to Confucius and Mencius, they were respectfully called by their own disciples as "Master;" later on, these thinkers were collectively called the "Various Philosophers and Hundred Specialists." The various philosophers opened schools and accepted followers, travelled around lecturing to the feudal lords, composed works and established theories, and debated among each other as each of them was great masters of language. Therefore, oral discourse even more so became the tool of thought and debate, no longer merely an accomplishment of life. Mencius wanted to promote the scholastic theories of the Confucians, so could only regard oral discourse as a weapon. One time his disciple Gongduzi asked him, "Outsiders all say that you, master, love to debate others. May I inquire why this is?" Mencius said, ❶

Can it be true that I love debate? I am forced into it!

Now sages such as Yao or Shun do not appear anymore and the feudal lords are self-indulgent and lack scruples. The knights and people also spout off their theories, the theories of Yang Zhu and Mo Di especially flood the world. Discourse in the world is either that of Yang Zhu or Mo Di. The theories of Yang Zhu advocate 'egoism;' they place the individual on top, and do not acknowledge any responsibility to the state, and recognize no lord. The theories of Mo Di advocate 'all-embracing Love;' they love all based on no principles, do not acknowledge being utterly filial toward parents, and recognize no parents. To lack regard for parents or lord, loyalty and filial piety in human relations, and not to do all to mourn parents, is to be a bird or beast. Zengzi's disciple Gongming Yi said, 'Having fat meat hanging from racks filling the kitchen and fat horses filling the stables, yet letting the common people become emaciated and starved, this is to lead wild animals to eat people!' If the theories of Yang Zhu and Mo Di are not eliminated, the theories of Confucius will not be able to be promoted. They are heterodoxies and heresies which deceive the people and block the pathway of humaneness and righteousness. When the pathway of humaneness and righteousness is blocked, then this is to lead wild beasts to eat people, and so people will swallow up each other. Because of this, I am deeply fearful; I have to guard the scholastic theories of the sages, oppose the theories of Yang Zhu and Mo Di, expel

实践,《论语》里记录的孔子的言论,正是一条条隽永而智慧的格言。

可是孟子就没有这样含蓄的修养了,他是个滔滔不绝的雄辩家。战国时代出现了许多思想家,他们和孔子、孟子一样被自己的弟子尊称为"子",后人统称他们为"诸子百家"。诸子们开坛授徒,游说诸侯,著书立说,相互辩难,他们个个都是语言大师。所以,言论已经更多地成为思想和辩论的工具而不仅仅是人生的修养。孟子要发扬儒家的学说,也只得将言论当作武器。一次弟子公都子问他:"外人都说老师您喜欢与人辩论,请问为什么?"孟子说: ❶

我难道喜欢辩论吗?我是迫不得已呀!

现在,尧舜这样的圣王不再出现,诸侯们肆无忌惮,民间的士人也乱发议论,特别是杨朱和墨翟的学说充斥天下。天下的言论不属于杨朱,便归于墨翟。杨朱的学说主张"为我",这是个人至上,不知道对国家负责,目无君主。墨翟的学说主张"兼爱",这是没有原则的泛爱,不知道对父母尽孝,目无父母。无视父母君主,忠孝人伦尽丧,便是禽兽。曾子的弟子公明仪说过:"厨房里挂满了肥肉,马厩里站满了肥马,可是老百姓面黄肌瘦,饥饿者倒毙于郊外,这是率领野兽来吃人!"杨朱、墨翟的学说不消灭,孔子的学说就不能发扬,这就是异端邪说欺骗人民,阻塞仁义之路啊!仁义之路被阻塞,就是率领野兽来吃人,人与人也将互相残噬。我因此深感忧惧,我要捍卫圣人的学说,抵制杨朱、墨翟的学说,

---

❶《孟子·滕文公下》9章。

❶ Mencius, "Duke Wen of Teng," Ⅱ 9.

absurd thinking, and let those who will oppose these heresies rise up! These heresies are produced in the heart and then harm human affairs; if they harm human affairs, then they will harm the government. If a sage were to appear again, he would approve of my words!

In the past the Great Yu controlled the flood waters, ensuring peace in the world. The Duke of Zhou assimilated the Yi and Di barbarians, drove out fierce beasts, ensuing tranquility for the people. Confucius composed the *Spring and Autumn Annals*, ensuing rebellious ministers and fractious sons turned fearful. I also need to correct the human heart, extinguish heretical thought, oppose extremism, refute the absurd, and inherit the great endeavors of these three sages!

Can it be true that I am fond of debate? I am forced to do so! To be able to use words to oppose the theories of Yang Zhu and Mo Di, is to be a disciple of the sages!

This passage from Mencius reveals that the strongest debate opponents he faced were Yang Zhu and Mo Di. Confucius founded the Confucian school, and also inaugurated the ages of the various philosophers. After the Confucian school, the power of the Mohist school was greatest. The status of the founder of this school Mo Di was not too clear. Some said that he was a grandee of the state of Song, some said he was a scholar from Lu; someone also claimed that "Mo" referred to a form of ancient punishment, and that Mozi was a convicted criminal who had done hard labor. But from the thought of his collected works, the *Mozi*, he and his followers were all skilled artisans who were masters of manufacturing appliances. His organization was extremely close-knit, had its own rules and regulations, with the head of each unit called "Great Master," and disciples who were willing to do anything for him. They were extreme pacifists, venerated Great Yu, championed the weak and administered righteousness to save the common people. They were expert at the crafts and arts, and went around helping defend their towns with moats and prevent warfare. They changed the Confucian concepts of humaneness and righteousness based on the closeness or distance in kinship ties to an all-embracing love between equals which made no such distinctions; they venerated the search for benefit in order to plan for the happiness of humanity, not like the Confucians who would only lecture on righteousness but not mention benefit. Additionally, they advocated frugality, inexpensive funerals, and opposed enjoyment; nor did they believe in destiny while still deeply believing in ghosts and spirits, and had a strong patriarchal spirit. These actions and motivations all represented the ideals of the common folk or the

驱逐荒谬的思想，让那些制造邪说的人兴不起来！这些邪说从内心产生，便会危害人事；危害人事，就危害了政治。如果再有圣人出现，也会赞同我的话！

过去大禹治理洪水使得天下太平，周公兼并夷狄，驱赶猛兽使得百姓安宁，孔子作《春秋》使得乱臣贼子们惧怕。我也要正人心，灭邪说，反对极端，驳斥荒谬，继承这三位圣人的事业！

我难道喜欢辩论吗？我是迫不得已啊！能够用言论来抵制杨朱、墨翟学说的人，就是圣人的门徒！

孟子的这段表白说明了他面对的最强大的论敌是杨朱和墨翟。孔子开创了儒家学派，也开创了诸子的时代。儒家学派之后，墨家学派势力最大。这个学派创始人墨子的身份也不太清楚，有人说他是宋国的大夫，有人说他是鲁国的学者，也有人说“墨”是一种古代刑法，墨子是刑徒劳役之人。不过从他的思想集成《墨子》看来，他和他的弟子们都是些杰出的工匠，擅长制作器械。他的组织极为严密，有自己的法律，团体的头目称作“巨子”，弟子可以为他赴汤蹈火。他们是极端的和平主义者，推崇大禹，行侠仗义，拯救人民。他们精于工兵技术，到处帮人守御城池，制止战争。他们将儒家有血缘亲疏等差的仁爱改变为平等无差的兼爱，推崇功利以谋求人类的福祉，不像儒家那样只讲义不讲利。此外，他们主张节俭、薄葬，反对享受，不信命运但笃信鬼神，有着强烈的宗教精神。这些举动

professional craftsmen. Their organization was in the form of trade unions instead of religious lineages or clan lineages. It may be said that Mohism was the most influential intellectual school of the common folk.

The intellectual school of Yang Zhu was the school of hermits. In the *Analects* and the *Historian's Records*, we can see many hermits ridiculing Confucius for his anxiety to serve the state and running into a wall wherever he went among the various states, like a "dog that has lost its home." It seemed that they lived as dirt farmers, so they ridiculed Confucius who neither toiled with his four limbs nor told the five cereals apart. They were all cool, pure philosophers, and possibly derived from the ranks of out-of-work palace historians, doctors, and chefs. Therefore, they saw right through human life, greed, social disturbance, and the collapse of culture; they felt pessimistically that this was an inevitable rule, therefore they advocated a return to eternal nature and opposed the search for knowledge, morality, skills, wealth, position and other social values, because these were all vain and the sources of contention. Yang Zhu regarded the ego as especially important, and advocated preserving one's body and life endowed by nature and not let them be destroyed be external things, especially by things such as fame and profit. If everyone was able to accomplish this, then why couldn't the world become peaceful?

As for the human world, the Mohists were too fanatic and Yang Zhu was too detached, but Mencius never adopt the mild position of neutrality to mediate between the two schools, but based himself on the Confucian stance to oppose them both. He said, "Yang Zhu advocates 'egoism,' and wouldn't even pluck out a single hair if it would benefit the world. Mozi advocates 'all-embracing love,' as long as something would benefit the world he would not fear the difficulty but would work hard enough to wear off the hair on his head and would injure his feet and do it willingly. A worthy man from Lu named Zimo adopted a middle of the road attitude. Although middle of the road is preferable, being middle of the road loses some adaptability and lacks flexibility, and actually is a little too rigid. Why do I detest rigidity? Because it harms the pathway of humaneness and righteousness; to grasp one end is to lose the rest!" ❶

Mencius' defect was his vigorous attacks against other schools even to the point of berating others, but even it was a lovable aspect. However, he was no

和主张都代表着平民或手工业者的理想，他们的组织也是行帮式的而不是宗法和家族式的，可以说，墨家是最有影响力的平民学派。

杨朱学派是隐士们的学派，也被后人看作早期的道家学派。在《论语》和《史记》中，我们可以见到许多隐士讥笑孔子汲汲于用世，周游列国却四处碰壁，如同"丧家狗"一样；他们似乎过着自耕农式的生活，所以还讥笑孔子"四体不勤，五谷不分"。他们都是一些冷静、纯粹的哲学家，可能来自于失业的史官、宫廷医生和厨师，因而对人类的生理、贪欲、社会的衰乱与文化的崩溃看得非常透彻，悲观地认为这是不可避免的规律，所以主张回归永恒的自然，反对追求知识、道德、技巧、财富、地位等社会价值，因为这些都是虚伪和争夺的原因。杨朱将自我看得特别重要，主张保全自然赋予自己的身体和性命，不能被外物，特别是名利这一类的东西破坏。如果每个人都能做到这样，天下岂不太平了吗？

对于我们的人世间，墨家过于狂热而杨朱过于冷酷，但孟子决不采取温和的中间立场去调和两家的学说，而是本着儒家的立场均予以反对。他说："杨子主张'为我'，拔一根汗毛就能有利于天下的事他都不会做。墨子主张'兼爱'，只要有利于天下，哪怕辛苦得头顶磨秃，脚踵走破都心甘情愿。鲁国的贤人子莫采取执中的态度。执中固然比较好，但是执中就失去了权变，没有了灵活性，其实是执著于一点。我为什么讨厌执著于一点呢？因为这样损害仁义之道，抓住一点不及其余！" ❶

孟子如此激烈地抨击别的学派，甚至会辱骂别人——这是

❶《孟子·尽心上》26章。

❶ *Mencius*, "Jinxin," Ⅰ 26.

autocrat or dictator, and would not force others to render allegiance to Confucianism. This was because he had sufficient faith in Confucianism and knew that recognizing the truth was the self-perception of the individual; one could not force awareness onto others given that they had not yet perceived it themselves. Others said that when Mencius was teaching, "he would not pursue past matters, and would not reject knowledge of the new." All that was necessary was for others to harbor an attitude of learning, and that was good enough.❶ Mencius once said, "Those who flee Mozi's teachings are sure to rush over to Yang Zhu. Those who flee Yang Zhu are certain to return to Confucianism. Since they return to the orthodox way, one should accept them. Do not be picky over anything! But now there are some who argue with Yangists and Mohists; it is like chasing after little pigs; you not only will need to catch them and bring them back to the pen, you but also will have to tie up their feet lest they run off again." ❷

The "all-embracing Love" of Mohist directly conflicted with Mencius' moral system centered on humaneness and righteousness. In Mencius' view, not only did the love taught by Mohist lack principles, it also lacked a foundation. It was on these grounds that Mencius started their argument.

While in the state of Teng, the Mohist scholar Yi Zhi charged Mencius' disciple Xu Bi with seeking an audience for him with Mencius. Mencius courteously refused, saying, "I am very willing to meet with him, but today I am ill; wait until I feel better then I will go pay my respects to him, there is no need for him to come!" After some time, Yi Zhi once again asked Xu Bi to go see him on his behalf. Mencius received him with sincerity, and said, "I can see him now. However, if I do not speak plainly, then I would not be able to express the truth; for now let me speak plainly. I have heard that Yi Zhi is a Mohist scholar. Those Mohist advocate shabby burials and frugal expenditures. Since Yi Zhi would promote this kind of thought, he naturally would preach shabby burials. However, when he buried his parents he actually was quite lavish; this means he treated his own parents in a way that he opposed."

Xu Bi conveyed Mencius' words to Yi Zhi, and Yi Zhi said, "Confucians think that the ancients loved the people just as they did their own children. Please may I enquire what does this mean? I think that it is the same as we Mohists teach: the love between people is not differentiated between closeness or distance of relationship or position; it is just that I started first with my own

他的缺点，也是他的可爱之处。不过他并不专制独裁，也不强求别人归顺儒家。因为他对儒家学说有足够的信心：对真理的认识是人的自我觉悟，不能在别人没有觉悟的情况下强加灌输。别人说孟子开课讲学的时候，"往者不追，来者不拒。"只要别人怀着学习的态度来就行❶。孟子曾说："离开墨家的人一定会跑到杨朱那里。离开杨朱的人一定回归到儒家。既然回归正道，接纳他就是了，不要再计较什么！可是现在有些与杨、墨两家辩论的人，就像追小猪一样，不仅要把小猪捉回猪圈里，还要拿绳子把小猪的脚拴住，生怕小猪跑了。"❷

墨家的"兼爱"与孟子道德体系中的核心范畴"仁爱"发生了直接的冲突。在孟子看来，墨家的爱不仅没有原则，而且缺乏根据，为此他与墨家展开了辩论。

在滕国的时候，墨家学者夷之委托孟子的弟子徐辟求见孟子。孟子客气地推托说："我很愿意见他，但今天我有病，等病好了我去拜望他，他不必来了！"过了些时候，夷之又委托徐辟求见。孟子见他有诚意，便对徐辟说："现在可以与他见面了。不过，不直截了当地说话，就不能表达真理，我姑且说些开门见山的话吧。我听说夷子是个墨家学者，他们墨家主张薄葬节俭，夷子向天下人推行这样的思想，自然也是主张薄葬的了。可是他办理自己父母的丧事却很丰厚，这就是拿自己反对的东西来对待自己的父母了。"

徐辟便将孟子的话转告给夷之。夷之说："儒家认为，古代的圣人爱护百姓，就像爱护自己的婴儿一样。请问这是什么意思呢？我以为这正如我们墨家所说的那样：人与人的爱是没

❶《孟子·尽心下》30章。
❷《孟子·尽心下》26章。

❶ Mencius, "Jinxin," Ⅱ 30.
❷ Mencius, "Jinxin," Ⅱ 26.

parents; therefore, I buried my parents lavishly in accordance with the Mohist principle of all-embracing love."

Xu Bi relayed these words to Mencius. Mencius said, "Does Yi Zhi really think that the love one has for the child of his brother is the same as the love for the child of a neighbor? He only knows one aspect of a thing. If a baby were to crawl over to a well, it would not be the fault of the baby. All who saw him would open up the heart of compassion and rush to the rescue, but instead Yi Zhi regarded this phenomenon as proof of undifferentiated love. How much more so when everyone only has one father and mother, this is a natural law. Love can only be produced towards one's parents for whom one feels a natural attachment and then be extended to others; there are natural gradations. But according to Yi Zhi's logic, the production of love has two roots, and there is no difference between one's parents and other persons; it is only a matter of the order in which love is implemented; tentatively he started out with his own parents. Probably in ancient times there was one who did not bury his parents, and so cast them into a ditch after they died. After a few days he came by and saw that his parents had been eaten by foxes and bitten by mosquitos and flies. That person could not help breaking out in sweat and could not raise his head out of shame. His sweat broke out because of the regret felt in his heart, not to show others, and naturally appeared on his face. He would certainly rush back home and get a hoe and scoop and go bury their corpses. This is correct. From this we can see that a humane man and filial son burying his parents is certainly according to principle."

Xu Bi once again conveyed the words of Mencius to Yi Zhi, who looked lost in thought for a moment then said, "I finally have been taught!" ❶

Mencius and the very influential Taoist scholar from Jixia Academy Song Xing once crossed swords. Song Xing thought profoundly about the original nature of man and nature and the spiritual activities of man, even influencing Mencius' views on the mind and nature. He advocated that one must control one's own original nature and spirit, not be dominated by external things, and not be influenced by right or wrong, glory or shame, or seek for profit or avoid failure but preserve the self. What was different from Yang Zhu's egoism was that Song Xing was similar to Mozi in actively trying to save the world. Zhuangzi said that Song felt that being taken advantage of was no insult; he only worried about resolving interpersonal conflict. He tried to stop military attacks wherever he found them, and to eliminate conflicts; he only worried about resolving intra-state warfare. He travelled around the world, admonishing the feudal lords above, and teaching the common people below.

有亲疏等差的，我只是先从对待自己的父母做起罢了，因此我厚葬父母符合墨家兼爱的原则。"

徐辟将这些话转告给孟子。孟子说："夷子真的认为人们爱自己兄弟的儿子会和爱邻居家的儿子是一回事吗？他只知其一不知其二。婴儿快爬到井里了，这不是婴儿的错，每个人看见了都会发动恻隐之心上去营救，夷子竟然把这个现象当成爱无等差的证明了。何况每个人只有一个父母，这是自然规律，爱只能产生于对自己父母的依恋，推及到他人，自然有等差。可是按照夷子的逻辑，爱的发生就有两个根源，自己的父母与其他人没有差别，只不过按照实行爱心的次序，姑且从自己的父母开始罢了。大概上古的时候曾经有过不埋葬父母的人，父母死了便抛入沟壑之中。过了几日经过那里，看到父母的尸体被狐狸吃着，被蚊蝇叮咬。那人禁不住汗流满面，见人抬不起头来。他的汗不是流给别看的，而是出于内心的悔恨，自然显露于颜面。他一定会赶紧回家拿了锄头畚箕来将尸体安葬了。这就正确了。由此可见仁人孝子安葬他的父母，一定是有道理的。"

徐辟又将孟子的话转告夷之。夷之怅然若失地想了一会儿，说："我终于受到教诲了！" ❶

孟子和稷下学宫中很有影响的道家学者宋钘也有过交锋。宋钘对人和自然本性和人的精神活动有深刻的思考，甚至对孟子的心性观念也有影响。他主张人要把握自己的本性和心灵，不受外在事物的左右，不受是非荣辱的影响，趋利避害，保全自身。与"为我"的杨朱不同的是，宋钘反而像墨子一样积极地救世。庄子说他受到欺侮也不以为耻辱，只管解救人民之间

---

❶ 《孟子·滕文公上》5章。

❶ *Mencius*, "Duke Wen of Teng," I 5.

Although no one accepted his teachings, he was still peaceful in visage as he pressed on in his teaching activities❶. Song Xing said, "Everyone feels that being taken advantage of is an insult, therefore they contend without end. If they understood that being taken advantage of was no insult, then they would stop contending." ❷ One time the states of Qi and Chu exchanged arms; he went to have an audience with the Chu king; on a stone hillock he ran into Mencius. Mencius asked him how he would persuade the two states to cease fighting. He said, "I would tell them that warfare is not advantageous to a state." Mencius said, "Your aspiration, sir, is good, but your doctrine is not too correct. You use 'benefit' to encourage Qin and Chu to stop fighting; it is because the lords of these two states have benefits to pursue that they are happy to cease fighting; the troops are happy to cease fighting because they have benefits to pursue. With things as they are, ministers serve their lords with the purpose of seeking benefits, sons serve their fathers for the purpose of seeking benefits, younger brothers serve their elder brothers for the purpose of seeking benefits; the relationships between lord and minister, father and son, brother and brother are based on seeking benefits; there is a complete lack of humaneness and righteousness. If this were to continue, it would be strange if the state did not fall. If you sir used humaneness and righteousness to persuade Qin and Chu, the lords of these two states would, because of humaneness and righteousness, be happy to cease fighting, and the troops would, because of humaneness and righteousness, be happy to cease fighting. If this were the case, ministers would embrace humaneness and righteousness to serve their lords, sons would embrace humaneness and righteousness to serve their fathers, younger brothers would embrace humaneness and righteousness to serve their elder brothers, and the relationships between lord and minister, father and son, and between brothers would abandon the goal of benefit and treat each other with humaneness and righteousness; if this were the case, it would be strange if a state did not unify the world. So why should you discuss 'benefit' ? " ❸

A small state such as Teng became a place which scholars of the school of agriculturalist of the time admired. A scholar of this school named Xu Xing came to Teng from Chu, and said to Duke Wen of Teng, "We who have come from a distance have heard that you implement a humane government; we are willing to come here and become your subjects." Duke Wen then assigned him a dwelling place. Xu Xing and his ten-plus disciples each day dressed in coarse

的争斗；到处阻止攻伐，平息干戈，只管解救国家之间的战争。他周行天下，上劝诸侯，下教百姓，尽管大家都不接受，还是恬着脸上前说教❶。宋钘说："人人都认为被欺侮是耻辱，所以他们争斗不休。如果明白被欺侮并不是耻辱，就不再争斗了。"❷一次秦楚两国交兵，他先去谒见楚王，走到石丘这个地方遇见了孟子。孟子问他将如何劝说两国休战。他说："我要告诉他们，打仗是不利于国家的事。"孟子说："先生您的愿望是很好的，但您的道理却不太对。您用'利'来劝说秦楚两国休战，秦楚两国的国君因为有利可图而乐于罢兵，军队也因为有利可图而乐于罢兵。如此一来，做臣子的怀着谋利的目的来事奉君主，做儿子的怀着谋利的目的来事奉父亲，做弟弟的怀着谋利的目的来事奉兄长，君臣、父子、兄弟之间相互谋利，完全没有仁义，这样下去，国家不亡才怪呢。如果先生用仁义去劝说秦楚两国，秦楚两国的国君因为仁义而乐于罢兵，军队也因为仁义乐于罢兵。如此一来，做臣子的怀着仁义来事奉君主，做儿子的怀着仁义来事奉父亲，做弟弟的怀着仁义来事奉兄长，君臣、父子、兄弟之间抛弃谋利的目的，相互以仁义对待，这样的国家不统一天下才怪呢。您又何必要谈论'利'呢？"❸

滕国这样的小国，当时还成了一些农家学派的人向往的地方。有个叫许行的农家学者从楚国来到滕国，对滕文公说："我们这些远方来的人听说您行仁政，愿意来您这里做个老百姓"。滕文公便给他安排了住处。许行和他的十来个弟子每天

---

❶《庄子·天下》。
❷《荀子·正论》。
❸《孟子·告子下》4章。

❶ *Zhuangzi*, "In the world."
❷ *Xunzi*, "Correcting Discourse."
❸ *Mencius*, "Gaozi," Ⅱ 4.

clothing, wove straw sandals and mats to earn a living[1]. The reason they acted in this fashion was because the agriculturalists worshiped the god of agriculture Shennong, advocated the just distribution of land by society, and opposed luxuriousness and waste; they lived simply without ostentation, and took as their ideal a small state with a few subjects living peacefully and happily. They also yearned for the equal gentile community life of agricultural society of high antiquity, in which one ate what one harvested; it was fundamentally different from the well field system as advocated by Mencius.

At this time, the disciple of the Confucian scholar from Chu called Chen Liang, Chen Xiang and his younger brother Chen Xin, also brought their farming implements to move from Song to Teng, and said to Duke Wen of Teng, "I have heard that you implement the government of a sage, and are therefore a sage yourself. We are willing to become the subjects of a sage." When Chen Xiang left, he encountered Xu Xing, and greatly admired Xu's theories; he therefore completely abandoned Confucian theory. Not only this, but Chen Xiang also attempted to influence Mencius. He went to visit Mencius and conveyed to him the words of Xu Xing: "Granted that the lord of Teng is a worthy and enlightened ruler; notwithstanding this, he still does not understand the truth. Worthies need to plow fields with their subjects, cook for themselves all while ruling the state. Now the state of Teng has grain and a national army; this actually is a case of exploiting the common people to support himself; how can he be considered to be worthy and good?"

Mencius answered, saying, "Are you certain that Xuzi has to eat grain that he has planted himself?"

Chen Xiang answered, "Yes."

Mencius asked, "Are you certain that Xuzi has to wear clothes of material that he wove himself?"

The response was, "No. Xuzi only wears clothes of coarse burlap."

Mencius then asked, "Does Xuzi wear a cap?"

The answer was, "He wears a cap."

Mencius asked, "What type of cap?"

The answer was, "A cap made of white silk."

Mencius asked, "Is it silk fabric that he personally wove?"

The answer was, "No, he traded grain that he had personally planted for it."

Mencius asked, "Why didn't Xuzi personally weave it?"

The answer was, "It would have hindered his planting."

穿着粗布衣裳，编织草鞋和席子为生❶。他们之所以这样做，是因为农家崇拜农业始祖神农，主张社会分配公正平均，反对奢侈消费，以俭朴无华、和平安乐的小国寡民生活作为理想。他们也向往上古时期平等的氏族公社式的农耕社会，但是要求君臣平等，自耕自食，与孟子主张的井田制有着根本的差别。

这时，楚国儒家学者陈良的门徒陈相和弟弟陈辛也带着农具从宋国来到滕国，对文公说："听说您推行圣人的政治，也就是圣人了，我们愿意做圣人的老百姓。"陈相住下后遇到了许行，对他的学说心悦诚服，而将儒家的学说全部抛弃。不仅如此，陈相还企图影响孟子，他来拜见孟子，向孟子转述许行的话："滕国的国君固然是贤明的君王，尽管如此，他还是不明真理。贤人要和人民一道耕作，自己做饭吃，同时治理国家。现在滕国有粮仓和国库，这其实是剥削百姓来供养自己，这怎么算得上贤良呢？"

孟子问道："许子一定要吃亲自种出来的粮食吗？"

陈相答道："是的。"

孟子问道："许子一定要穿亲自纺织的布做的衣服吗？"

答道："不。许子只穿粗麻布做的衣裳。"

孟子问道："许子戴帽子吗？"

答道："戴帽子。"

孟子问道："戴什么帽子呢？"

答道："戴白丝绸做的帽子。"

孟子问道："是他亲自织的丝绸吗？"

答道："不，拿他种的粮食换的。"

孟子问道："许子为什么不亲自纺织呢？"

---

❶ 《孟子·滕文公上》4章。

❶ *Mencius*, "Duke Wen of Teng," I 4.

Mencius asked, "Does Xuzi use a pot and steamer to cook, and use iron tools to plow and sow?"

The answer was, "Yes."

Mencius asked, "Did he personally manufacture the implements he uses to cook and to plow?"

The answer was, "No, he uses the grain that he planted to trade for them."

Mencius said, "According to the doctrine of Xuzi, trading grain to trade for clay implements to cook and for iron implements does not hinder potters or blacksmiths; then can it be true that potters and blacksmiths trading clay and iron implements for grain hinders farmers? Why doesn't Xuzi personally manufacture pots and smelt iron, and make everything that he uses in his own home?" Why should he want to continuously trade with various types of craftsmen? Why doesn't he fear all this trouble?"

Chen Xiang said, "These types of jobs cannot be done part-time while still plowing and planting!"

Thereupon, Mencius began to teach him without ceasing, asking that can it be true that only governing the world can be done while plowing part-time? There is work done by great men and gentlemen; there is work done by petty men and commoners, let alone having each person needing to manufacture all the tools he would need that are usually made by craftsmen and smiths. This would be the same as leading all the men in the world to be worn out in busy work. Therefore I say, some men labor with their spirits, some men labor with their strength. Those who labor with their minds govern others; those who labor with their strength are governed by others. Those who are governed support others, those who govern are supported; this is a common doctrine in the world.

During the age of Yao, the world was not very peaceful, floods flowed continuously, spreading unchecked everywhere; vegetation flourished, animals propagated, and the five grains did not mature. Birds and beasts attacked the human race and left their traces all over the great land of China. Yao alone was worried over this, and raised up Shun to command the affairs of governing the state. Shun sent Yi to manage the making of fire; but Yi ignited the forests and wetlands, burned up the grass and trees, making the birds and beast flee and hide. The Great Yu dredged the nine rivers, and channeled the Ji and Ta Rivers, directing them to flow into the great ocean. He dug out the Ru and Han Rivers, dredged the Huai and Si Rivers, directing them to flow into the Yangtze River. Afterwards, the land of China was finally able to be plowed and planted with crops. At this time, Yu travelled around for eight years, and passed by his own

答道："这样妨碍他耕种。"

孟子问道："许子用锅、甑做饭，用铁器耕种吗？"

答道："是的。"

孟子问道："这些做饭和耕田的工具都是他亲自制造的吗？"

答道："不，用他种的粮食换的。"

孟子说："按照许子的道理，拿粮食交换做饭的陶器和耕田的铁器，算不上妨碍陶工和铁匠；那陶工和铁匠拿陶器和铁器来交换粮食，难道损害了农夫了吗？许子为什么不亲自制陶冶铁呢，样样东西都从自己家里取用呢？干嘛要不停地与各种工匠们交易呢？许子为何这样不怕麻烦？"

陈相说："这些工匠们的工作本来就不可能一边耕种一边去做啊！"

于是孟子滔滔不绝地教训起来了："难道唯独治理天下这件事可以一边耕种一边做吗？有大人君子们做的事，有小人平民们做的事。何况每个人，都需要各种工匠制造的器物，如果一定要自己制作的才能使用，这等于率领天下人疲于奔命。所以说，有的人劳动心灵，有的人劳动体力；劳心的人统治别人，劳力的被别人统治；被统治的人供养别人，统治人的人被别人供养，这是天下通行的道理。

在尧的时代，天下还不太平，洪水横流，到处泛滥，草木茂盛，禽兽繁殖，五谷不熟。禽兽攻击人类，它们的足迹交织于中国大地。尧独自忧患，举拔舜统领治国之事。舜让益掌管火种，益点燃了山林沼泽焚烧草木，使禽兽逃跑躲避。大禹疏通九河，治理济水、漯水使它们注入大海，开挖汝水、汉水，疏浚淮水、泗水，使它们注入长江，此后中国的土地上才能耕

home three times without entering; even if he wanted to plow his own field, would it have been possible?

An ancestor of the Zhou people Houji taught the people how to plant crops, and to cultivate the five grains. After the five grains matured, the people would be able to sustain themselves. But if after eating their fill, dressing warmly, and settling down they were not educated, what difference was there from the birds and beasts? The sage Shun alleviated this by appointing Qi to the office of minister of personnel to exclusively manage civil administration and to teach the people about ethics and morality; this taught them about the love that should prevail between father and son, the Way and righteousness that should prevail between lord and minister, the distinction that should prevail between husband and wife, the order that should prevail between old and young, and the sincerity that should prevail between friends. Yao once said, "Encourage them, correct them, aid them, thus causing them to have a safe haven for living, and then take an additional step to rouse their characters and to nourish their virtue." A sage worrying to such an extent about the people, how could he have time to plow and sow?

Yao was concerned about not being able to gain such a man as Shun, Shun was worried about not being able to gain such men as the Great Yu and Gaoyao; those who worry about a poor harvest from a hundred *mu* or so of fields are precisely farmers. Sharing property with others is called being kind; teaching others the doctrine of being good is called being loyal; finding outstanding talent for the people in the world is called being humane. Therefore, yielding the world to another is easy, but it is hard to find a sage for the people of the world. Confucius said, 'It was actually very great of Yao to be the ruler of the world! Only Heaven above is greater, and only Yao could imitate Heaven above, so vast and limitless as to be indescribable! Shun was also an outstanding ruler! He loftily and greatly ruled the world but did not claim possession of it.' Can it be true that in governing the world, neither Yao nor Shun was attentive to it? It was only that they did not waste their thoughts on plowing and sowing!

I have only heard of using the Chinese to change the barbarians, but have never heard of doctrine being changed by barbarians. Your teacher Chen Liang is a southerner from Chu, but he yearned after the Duke of Zhou and the theories of Confucius, and came north to study with Chinese scholars. But northern scholars are not necessarily able to surpass him; he is what is known as a bold and daring knight! You two brothers have followed him for several decades; after your teacher died, you surprisingly turned against him. When

种庄稼。在这个时候，禹在外奔走了八年，三次经过自己的家门都没有进去，即使他想耕田，还可能吗？

周人的祖先后稷教导人民种庄稼，培植五谷。五谷成熟，人民得以养育。人如果在吃饱、穿暖、安居外却没有受到教育，那与禽兽有什么两样呢？圣人为此让契担任司徒的官职，专掌民政，以伦理道德教化百姓，让他们知道父子之间有亲爱，君臣之间有道义，夫妇之间有区别，长幼之间有先后，朋友之间有诚信。尧曾经说过：'激励他们，匡扶他们，辅助他们，使他们各自安身，再进一步振兴他们的人格，培育他们的道德。'圣人为人民忧患到这个地步，还来得及耕种吗？

尧以得不到舜这样的人作为自己的忧虑，舜以得不到大禹和皋陶这样的人作为自己的忧虑，而那些为了百来亩田地收成不好而担忧的人正是农夫。分给别人财物叫做惠，教导别人善良的道理叫做忠，为天下的苍生找到杰出的人才叫做仁。所以把天下让给别人容易，为天下苍生找到圣人难。孔子说：'尧做天下的君主实在伟大！只有上天最伟大，只有尧能效法上天，广阔无垠得无法形容！舜也是了不起的君主！崇高伟大地统治天下却不据为己有！'尧、舜治理天下，难道无所用心吗？只是他们的心思不花费在耕种上罢了！

我只听说过用华夏来改变蛮夷，没有听说被蛮夷改变的道理。您的老师陈良是南方的楚国人，可他向往周公、孔子的学说，到北方来向中国的学者学习。北方的学者还不见得能超过他，他就是所谓的豪杰之士啊！您兄弟两人跟从他几十年，老

Confucius died, his disciples mourned for three years, and when they all prepared their luggage to return home, they first went together to Zigong's house to bow in departure and to cry on each others' shoulders, choked with sobs, and then left in different directions. Zigong returned to Confucius' grave and constructed a hut, and lived by himself for another three years before returning to his homeland. After some time, Zixia, Zizhang, and Ziyou felt that You Ruo looked like Confucius, and wanted to treat him just they had treated Confucius and serve You Ruo; they insisted that Zengzi agree with this. Zengzi said, 'No way. Confucius' greatness is like being washed in the pure waters of the Yangtze River or Han River; or like tanning in the scorching heat of summer. Gleaming white light cannot be superseded, and nobody can compare to him!' At present, this guy Xu Xing, is a barbarian from the south, he has a heavy local accent like a bird's call; yet he still dares to slander the way of the former kings. You have betrayed your own teacher to study with him, greatly different than what Zengzi did. I have heard it chanted in the *Book of Poetry*, 'Birds fly out of the deep valley, and fly to a tall and great tree.' ❶ I have never heard of birds leaving a tall and great tree to fly down into a deep valley. The *Book of Poetry* praised the Duke of Zhou, saying, 'Attack the Rong and Di barbarians, Punish the Southern barbarians.' ❷ The Duke of Zhou only attacked the southern barbarians, you are trying to learn from them; you truly do not easily change yourself!"

Chen Xiang was not convinced; but defended himself, saying, "If Xu Xing's theories were to be implemented, prices in the market would all be the same, none of the commoners in a state would act falsely, even if a short child were to go to the market to buy something he would not be cheated by anyone. Fabric and silks would be priced the same as long as they were the same length; twine and silk floss would be priced the same as long as they were the same length. Foodstuff would all be the same price as long as they were the same amount; shoes would be the same price as long as they were the same size."

Mencius felt even more that he was laughable, so instructed him, saying, "The size, weight, or quality of something cannot be assigned a uniform price; this is the actual condition of things. Their prices vary by as much as double or five times, some by as much as ten or one hundred times; some vary by as much a thousand or ten thousand times. But you instead mix things up by

师死了，居然背叛他！从前孔子去世之后，弟子们守了三年丧，大家收拾行李准备回家时，一起到子贡的房里作揖告别，相向而哭，泣不成声，然后散去。子贡返回孔子的墓地筑了个庐屋，独自再守了三年才回家乡。过了些时，子夏、子张、子游觉得有若长得像孔子，便想用事奉孔子的方式来事奉有若，他们一定要曾子同意这样做。曾子说：'不行，孔子的伟大，就象用长江和汉水的清流洗濯过，就象用夏天的骄阳照晒过，洁白光明得无以复加，谁也比不上！'眼下这个许行，是个南方的蛮夷，满口土话如同鸟叫，居然还诋毁先王之道。您背叛自己的老师向他学习，和曾子大不一样了。我听《诗》里唱道：'鸟儿们从幽谷飞出，飞上高大的树木。'❶从来没听说鸟儿从高大的树上飞下幽谷的。《诗》里歌颂周公道：'攻击戎狄，惩罚南蛮。'❷周公尚且攻击南蛮，你却向他们学习，真是不善于改变自己啊！"

陈相还是有些不服，辩解道："如果实行许子的学说，那么市场上的物价就不会有差别，一国的民众都不会虚伪；即便让五尺高的儿童到市场上买东西，也没有人欺负他。布匹和丝帛只要长短相同，价格就一样；麻线和丝绵只要轻重相同，价格就一样；粮食只要多少相同，价格就一样；鞋子的大小相同，价格就一样。"

孟子更觉得他可笑，开导他说："事物的大小轻重精粗不能整齐划一，这是事物的实情。它们的价格有的相差一倍或五倍，有的相差十倍或百倍，有的相差千倍或万倍。可您却将它

❶《诗·小雅·伐木》："鸟鸣嘤嘤，出自幽谷，迁于乔木。"
❷《诗·鲁颂·閟宫》："戎狄是膺，荆舒是惩。"

❶ Literally, "Birds chirp *ying-ying*, leaving the deep valley; they move to a tall tree;" *Book of Poetry*, "Minor Elegantiae," "Hacking Wood."
❷ Literally, "The Rong and Di—— they should be resisted; the Jing and Shu——they should be punished;" *Book of Poetry*, "Lauds of Lu," "Closed up Palace."

regarding them as having the same price, this causes chaos for the world! Who would do such a thing as sell large shoes for the same price as small shoes? Therefore I say, if you follow the theories of Xu Xing, this would have the opposite effect of leading everyone to act falsely, in this case how can one govern the state?"

Among pre-Qin philosophers, Mencius is considered in the front ranks of debaters. He was good at guiding matters according to the circumstances, and tying his opponents up in knots. He used the matter of not being able to stand seeing an ox killed to entrap King Xuan of Qi, and made him sit nicely and listen to his discourse on the doctrine of humane government. He was good at setting up questions, leading opponents into untenable logical positions. He asked Gaozi whether all white things were able to be called white; he asked King Hui of Liang whether using a knife to kill someone was different from using a club to kill someone; he asked Chen Xiang whether Xu Xing personally wove—all were marvelous ploys. He patiently and systematically taught those who humbly sought instruction from him in a step by step and clear manner. He boldly deflected those who intentionally challenged him, and directly refuted them.

He was extraordinarily skilled at making metaphors and drawing analogies. He seemed to have a store of exquisite analogies and moving fables readily available which were as profound as they were apt, and humorous and lively. His reasonableness and persuasiveness were able to move men's hearts without leaving them fed up. Zhao Qi of the Eastern Han Dynasty praised Mencius for "being apt at metaphors, with easy, non-threatening diction that conveyed meaning in a singular way" ❶ .According to statistics, out of the entire 261 paragraphs in *Mencius*, 93 of them employed a total of 159 metaphors ❷. In addition to the lively metaphors we enjoyed above like the man of Song tugging on his rice shoots, and or clasping Mt. Tai and crossing the sea, or that man who stole his neighbors chickens every day, we can cite a few others examples.

King Hui of Liang complained to Mencius, saying, "I do my utmost in managing the state. When a famine occurs in the area within the Yellow River, I move the people to the area west of the river, and ship grain from the eastern region to the area within the river. If a famine occurs in the eastern region, then I do the same thing. But when I look at the government of a neighboring state, its ruler does not exert himself as much as I do by a wide margin. Yet the people of the neighboring state do not decrease in numbers, while mine do not increase; why is this?" Mencius answered, saying, "You, great king, like

们混同划一，这是扰乱天下啊！大鞋子和小鞋子卖一样的价格，谁会做这样的事？所以说，听从许行的学说，反而是率领大家做虚伪的事，这样怎能治理国家呢？”

在先秦诸子中，孟子堪称第一流的言辩家，他善于因势利导，让对手束手无策，他借不忍杀牛的事，让齐宣王上钩，乖乖地听他谈论一番仁政的道理；他善于设问，将对手逼入逻辑的死角，他问告子白色的东西是否都能叫做白；问梁惠王用刀杀人和用木棒打死人有何不同；问陈相许行是否亲自纺织……都是高超的手段；他对虚心请教的人循循善诱，条分缕析；他对有意挑战的人当头棒喝，直接否定。

他非常擅长取譬设喻，精采的比喻和生动的寓言俯拾即是，深刻贴切而又妙趣横生，所以他的说理和说教能够打动人心而不令人生厌。东汉的赵岐就赞叹孟子“长于譬喻，言辞从容不迫，而意思已经突显了出来”❶。据说《孟子》全书二百六十一章中，就有九十三章总共使用着一百五十九种譬喻❷。除了我们在前面几章中领略到的宋人拔苗助长、挟持泰山超越北海之类生动的比喻和有个人天天偷他邻居的鸡之类的寓言，我们还可以再举一些例子。

梁惠王向孟子诉苦，说：“寡人治理国家算得上是尽心了。河内地区闹饥荒，我就把百姓迁移到河东地区，将河东地区的粮食调运到河内地区。河东地区闹饥荒也这样做。可是我看看邻国的政治，远不如寡人这样尽心。可邻国的百姓不见减少，寡人的百姓不见增加，这是为什么呢？”孟子回答说：“大王

---

❶ 赵岐《孟子章句·题辞》。
❷ 李炳英《孟子文选·前言》，北京，人民文学出版社，1957，第9页。

❶ Zhao Qi, *Chapters and Verses of Mencius*, "Introduction."
❷ Li Bingying, "Preface," *Selected Passages of Mencius* (Beijing: The people's Literature Publishing House, 1957), p. 9.

warfare; let me use warfare to make an analogy. When war drums sound, weapons clash, yet the troops cast off their helmets and armor and drag their weapons as they flee. Some only ran off for a hundred steps before stopping; some ran for fifty steps before stopping. If those who only ran fifty steps jeered at those who ran one hundred steps, is this acceptable?" King Hui of Liang said, "It is not acceptable; it is just that they merely ran fifty steps. A fifty-step distance still constitutes running off." Mencius said, "If you, great king, understood this principle, then you would not expect that your population would be greater than your neighboring state!" ❶

When Mencius was in the state of Song, he said to the great minister Dai Busheng, "Do you want to help your lord of state learn well? I can tell you clearly how to do it. One grandee from the state of Chu wanted to let his son learn to speak the language of Qi. Should he let a man from Qi be his teacher, or let a man from Chu be his teacher?" Dai Busheng said, "Of course he should let a man from Qi be his teacher." Mencius said, "Even if you let a man from Qi teach him, all the people around are making noise in the Chu language; even if you whip him every day, and force him to speak the Qi language, it still would not work. The only thing you can do is take him to the bustling streets of the Qi capital of Linzi and live for a few years, then even if you beat him every day to speak the Chu language, it would not work! Before you told me that Xue Juzhou was a good man, and that you wanted to invite him to move into the palace. If all of the young and old, honorable and low are not good people like Xue Juzhou, then how could the King of Song exert any good influence? " ❷

Sometimes Mencius' metaphors are simply complete short stories ❸:

A man from Qi married a wife and kept a concubine at home. Every time this husband went on a trip, he ate and drank to his heart's content before returning home. His wife asked him with whom he was feasting. The names he mentioned were all rich, noble, and powerful men. His wife told the concubine, "Every time our lord returns home he has eaten

喜欢战争，就让我用打仗来打个比方吧。战鼓敲响，刀兵相接，士兵们却丢盔弃甲，拖着兵器往回逃。有的逃了上百步才停止，有的逃了五十步就停止了。如果逃了五十步的人讥笑逃了上百步的人，是否可以？"梁惠王说："不可以，只不过他没逃到上百步罢了，五十步也是逃啊！"孟子说："大王如果明白这个道理，那就别指望您的百姓比邻国多了！"❶

孟子在宋国的时候，对大臣戴不胜说："您想让您的国君学好吗？我可以清楚地告诉您怎样做。有个楚国的大夫，想让他的儿子学说齐国话，是让齐国人做老师呢？还是让楚国人做老师？"戴不胜说："当然让齐国人做老师。"孟子说："可是让一个齐国人教他，周围有那么多的楚国人喧哗，你就是天天用鞭子打他，逼他说齐国话也不行啊！只要把他带到齐国首都临淄城的闹市里住上几年，就是天天用鞭子打他，逼他说楚国话也不行了。您曾经说薛居州这个人是个好人，要请他住在王宫里。如果王宫里的长幼尊卑都是薛居州这样的好人，宋王还能和谁干出坏事呢？如果王宫里的长幼尊卑都不是薛居州这样的好人，宋王还能和谁干出好事呢？只有一个薛居州，又能对宋王产生什么样的影响呢？"❷

孟子的寓言有时简直就是一篇完整的小说❸：

齐国有位娶了一妻一妾在家的人。这位做丈夫的人每次外出，都酒足饭饱地回来。妻子问他和什么人在一起吃饭，他说出来的都是些富贵显要的人。妻子便告诉小妾说："夫君每次外出都酒足饭饱地回来。问他和什么

---

❶《孟子·梁惠王上》3章。
❷《孟子·滕文公下》6章。
❸《孟子·离娄下》6章。

❶ *Mencius,* "King Hui of Liang," Ⅰ3.
❷ *Mencius,* "Duke Wen of Teng," Ⅱ6.
❸ *Mencius,* "Lilou," Ⅱ6.

and drunk his fill, but I have never seen these men come to visit us. I plan to secretly follow him and see what's up."

Early the next morning, she followed her husband on his trip. He went throughout the entire city, but no one ever stopped to greet her husband or talk with him. Finally he went to a graveyard in the eastern suburb. Her husband ate the left-over food offerings from the funeral sacrifices. Before getting full, he went to another sacrifice and continued eating. This was the reason he ate and drank his fill every day.

His wife returned home, and told the concubine what she had seen, saying, "Our lord is the one we look up to and depend on for our entire lives, but he turns out to be this sort of man!" Thereupon, the two of them cried and cried in the courtyard, but the husband did not know this. When he returned home he was completely satisfied, and put on airs for his wife and concubine.

In the eyes of a gentleman, the method he used to seek out wealthy, noble, and powerful men will hardly ever not cause his wife and concubine to feel shame and cry and weep!

This book *Mencius* not only is one of the sources of thought for we modern people, it is also one of the sources of modern Chinese language. Both history and language have passed through more than two thousand years of refinement. Many of the words spoken by Mencius are still alive in our language and writing. In just the most common 4000 modern sayings as calculated by the *Small Dictionary of Chinese Sayings* [1], Mencius himself contributed more than 40 sayings or memorable phrases. Following are some examples: "Tug at shoots to aid their growth," "Try to put out a burning cart of firewood with a cup of water," "It goes without saying," "Not consider 1,000 miles too far to come," "Be head and shoulders above the rest," "You' ll say anything to get your way," "Careless and sloppy," "To search for a rainbow in a drought," "A just cause finds much support, while an unjust cause gets little," "To console the people and punish the wicked," "The advantage of the weather is not as good as the advantage of geography; the advantage of geography is not as good as group harmony," "Only cultivate oneself," "Feeling not disgraceful in looking down and up," "Resist when your back is against the wall," "Neither riches nor honors can corrupt him, neither poverty nor humbleness can make him swerve from principle, and neither threats nor forces can subdue him," "The poor and base cannot be moved, and cannot be subdued by force," "Impressed with one's own wisdom," "If you are going to believe the *Book of History*, it would be better to not have it," "Treat my elders and the

人在一起吃饭，都是些富贵显要的人，可是我从来没见这些人来造访我们家里，我打算暗地里跟踪他，看个究竟。"

第二天早起，她便尾随丈夫外出。走遍了城里，没有一个人停下脚步与他的丈夫打招呼说话。最后来到东郊外的墓地，她丈夫向那些祭祀的人乞讨残剩的祭品吃；没吃饱，又寻找别的地方乞讨——这就是他天天酒足饭饱的原因。

妻子回到家里，将看到的告诉小妾，说："夫君是我们终身指望和依靠的人，可现在他竟是这样的人！"于是，两人在院子里又骂又哭，可作为丈夫的这个人还不知道，仍然从外面心满意足地回来了，还向自己的妻妾摆威风。

在君子的眼里，那些乞求富贵显达的人们所用的方法，能不让他的妻妾引为耻辱而相向哭泣的真是少之又少！

《孟子》这本书不仅是我们现代人的思想源泉之一，也是现代汉语的源泉之一。历史和语言经过了两千多年的淘洗，许多孟子说过的话，仍然活跃在我们的语言和文字当中。仅以现代汉语中常用的4000多条成语而言❶，仅孟子一个人就贡献了40多条，诸如："拔苗助长"、"杯水车薪"、"不言而喻"、"不远千里"、"出类拔萃"、"出尔反尔"、"大而化之"、"大旱望霓云"、"得道多助，失道寡助"、"吊民伐罪"、"天时不如地利，地利不如人和"、"独善其身"、"俯仰无愧"、"负隅顽抗"、"富

---

❶ 以《汉语成语小词典》（北京，商务印书馆，1958年第一版）为计。

❶ First edition; Beijing: Commercial Press, 1958.

elders of others as your own, treat my young and the young of others as you own," "Perceive even the finest detail," "Undergo any hardship for the sake of goodness," "Sacrifice one's life for righteousness," "Thrive in adversities and perish in soft living," "The setter of a bad example," "Regard as an enemy," "Twice the work with half the results," "Abyss of suffering," "Heaven has assigned a great responsibility," "Evade the question by changing the subject," "Fifty paces laugh at one hundred paces," "The first to know and first to perceive," "Not lift a finger to help," "Expose something to sunheat for one day and to cold for ten days," "Regard neighbor's field as an outlet for one's overflow," "Draw but not shoot," "Climb a tree to look for a fish," "Cannot have your cake and eat it too," "Do violence to oneself and hurt oneself," "With single-minded devotion," "Win advantage from both sides," etc.

However, skill at debate and moving and rich metaphors are not enough to display the full range of Mencius' language. Each reader of *Mencius* is able to deeply feel his linguistic style: sustained parallelism, surging in all directions, replete with emotion, and full of vigor and strength. This type of power and strength derives not only from his ability to use language, but from his vast power of thought, profound cultivation, and broad emotional appeal. He claimed himself that he was good at nurturing his flood-like *qi*, saying, "This type of *qi* comes from the Way and justice in the heart that is collected, naturally and spontaneously, and grows over time." One time Xu Bi asked him, "Several times Confucius praised the fine virtue of water, saying, 'Oh water, oh water!' What kind of enlightenment did water afford him?" Mencius said that [1]

> the source of a spring kept welling up without stopping, day and night it flowed, covering land, ravines and gullies. It flowed on straight ahead until it entered the great sea. Something with a foundation and a source is like this, and Confucius was enlightened by it. Yet those things without foundations, such as a storm in July or August, pour down in sheets, filling every ravine and gully. After a few moments, it dries up. Therefore, if one's fame and prestige exceed his actual condition, a gentleman would be ashamed of this.

Even if Mencius at this point was discussing the question of name matching reality, he nevertheless revealed that one's external expression required an internal accumulation. In the Confucian view, language and virtue were the same, both were internally cultivated. The *Great Learning* which

贵不能淫，贫贱不能移，威武不能屈"、"好为人师"、"尽信书，不如无书"、"老吾老以及人之老，幼吾幼以及人之幼"、"明察秋毫"、"摩顶放踵"、"舍生取义"、"生于忧患，死于安乐"、"始作俑者"、"视如寇仇"、"事倍功半"、"水深火热"、"天降大任"、"王顾左右而言他"、"五十步笑百步"、"先知先觉"、"一毛不拔"、"一曝十寒"、"以邻为壑"、"引而不发"、"缘木求鱼"、"鱼与熊掌不可兼得"、"自暴自弃"、"专心致志"、"左右逢源"等等。

不过，言辩的技巧和生动丰富的譬喻还不足以彰显孟子的语言境界。每个阅读《孟子》的人都能够深切地感受到孟子的语言风格：排比递进，纵横激荡，感情充沛，充满了雄浑的气势和力量。这种气势和力量不仅仅来自于他运用语言的能力，还来自于他宏阔的思想，深厚的修养和博大的情怀。他自称善养浩然之气，"那种气是由存在于内心之中的道义集聚起来，自然而然，日久生成的。"一次徐辟问他："孔子多次称赞水的美德，说：'水啊！水啊！'水给了他什么启发呢？"孟子说❶：

有源头的泉水滔滔不绝，昼夜不息地注满大地上的沟沟坎坎，一直向前，注入大海。有本有源的东西就像这样，孔子在其中受到了启发。而那些没有本源的东西，好像七、八月间的暴雨，倾盆而下，注满了河沟；可站在那儿等一会儿，便干涸了。所以，如果一个人的声望和名誉超过了他的实际，君子就会引为耻辱。

尽管孟子在此谈论的是名实相符的问题，但他揭示了一个人外在的表现需要内在的积蓄。在儒家看来，语言与道德一样，

---

❶《孟子·离娄下》18章。

❶ *Mencius*, "Lilou" Ⅱ 18.

according to legend was composed by Zengzi contains a similar affirmation, "Insincere people cannot express well their own words." ❶

Mencius' viewpoint on nurturing the *qi* became the method for self-cultivation by later prose authors, and was especially venerated by ancient prose authors. The Northern Song Dynasty literatus Su Zhe said, "The essays of Mencius are generous and expansive, and fill the space between heaven and earth." ❷ Qing Dynasty literary critic Liu Xizai said, "Amassing the Way and righteousness and nurturing the flood-like *qi* are the special abilities of Mencius." ❸ As the text that records Mencius' speech and discourse, the *Mencius* is a brilliant classic of ancient Chinese prose.

都是内在的修养。在传说是曾子写作的《大学》里也有这样的断言："不真诚的人没办法表达好自己的言辞。"❶

　　孟子的养气观念，成为后世散文作家的修养方法，特别受到古文作家们的推崇。北宋文学家苏辙说："孟子的文章，宽厚宏博，充斥于天地之间。"❷清代文学评论家刘熙载说："聚集道义，培养浩然之气，是孟子的本领。"❸《孟子》作为记载孟子言论的文本，是中国古代散文的光辉典范。

---

❶ 《礼记·大学》："无情者不得尽其辞"。
❷ 苏辙《上枢密韩太尉书》："今观其文章，宽厚宏博，充乎天地之间，称其气之小大。"
❸ 刘熙载《艺概·文概》："集义养气，是孟子本领。"

❶ Or, as literally put in the *Record of Ritual*, "The Great Learning," "Those lacking in sentiment cannot express themselves in words."
❷ Su Zhe, "Letter to Grand Guardian Han of the Imperial Secretariat, Bureau of Military."
❸ Liu Xizai, *The Summary of Arts*, "The Summary of Prose."

泰山，体现儒家文化精神的中国名山
Mount Taishan, the famous mountain of China
embodying the spirit of Confucian culture

八　大道——儒家思想与人的发展

Chapter VIII　The Great Way: Confucian Thoughts and the Development of Man

The ancient Chinese manual of divination *Book of Changes* says, "Things beyond the level of the physical, that is, abstract things, are known as the Way. Things at the level of the physical, that is, concrete things, are known as implements." ❶ The "way" is the same as modern Chinese "roadway;" its extended meaning is the principle behind natural things or their laws of development. However, the character for "Dao" is constituted from the element for "head" and the element of "walking," pronounced *chuo*. "Head" is a picture of human hair and eyes, which represent the entire head. The meaning of *chuo* is walking and then suddenly stopping. We are justified in feeling that originally "way" expressed the picture of a person with his eyes wide open searching for the way. Therefore, the various philosophers during the Spring and Autumn and Warring States Periods on the one hand regarded the "Way" as the track and law for the development of all things in the universe; it is regarded as the natural reason for things being as they are. On the other hand, they also regarded the "Way" as the truth that humanity was continuously learning and the techniques to be mastered of ideological theory and its construction; it was the moral law that should be observed and put into practice.

Confucians also called the truth as they recognized it and ideological theories as the "Way." Confucians were concerned about human life and moral practice. Confucianism is the learning about how to be human, therefore, the "Way" of the Confucians can be called the "Human Way."

The Human Way is relative to the Way of Heaven. In 524 B.C., an astrologer from the state of Zheng warned the grandee Zichan who was in power in Zheng that a disastrous fire would break out. He requested that a jade implement be offered in sacrifice to the gods to eliminate this disaster of fire. Zichan was not willing, saying, "The Way of Heaven is far from us, the Human Way is close to us." ❷ Confucius admired Zichan who was a worthy gentleman older than himself; he also partook of this trend in thought, and never discussed matters concerning strange oddities, violence, disloyalty, or gods and spirits ❸. He felt that doctrine concerning human life was closer at hand and more feasible, and doctrine concerning Heaven above and nature was deep, distant, and abstract. His disciple Zigong said, "We can hear the master's theories concerning ritual, music, and literary remains, but we cannot hear the master's theories concerning the heavenly nature of man and the way of

中国古代的占卜书《易经》里面说："形而上的东西，也就是抽象的东西叫做道；形而下的东西，也就是具象的东西叫做器。"❶ "道"和现代汉语中的"道路"是一个意思，引伸为事物的自然之理或发展规律。但是，"道"这个字由"首"字和"辵"（音绰）字组成。"首"是人的头发和眼睛的图案，代表人的头部；"辵"的意思是忽走忽停。我们有理由认为，"道"原本表示一个人瞪大眼睛在不断地寻找道路。所以，春秋战国时代的诸子们一方面将"道"作为宇宙万物发展的轨迹和规律，当成事物之所以如此的自然道理；一方面又将"道"作为人类不断认识到的真理、掌握的技术和建构起来的思想学说，是人类应当遵守和履践的道德法则。

儒家也将他们认识的真理和思想学说叫做"道"，儒家关注人生，履践道德。儒学是如何做人的学问，所以，儒家的"道"可以称之为"人道"。

人道是相对于天道而言的。公元前524年，郑国的星占家警告郑国的执政大夫子产，说郑国将要发生火灾，请求用玉器祭神，禳除灾难。子产不肯，说："天道离我们很远，人道离我们很近。"❷孔子很钦佩子产这位比自己年长的贤人君子，他自己也有这样的思想倾向，从不谈论怪异、暴力、悖乱和鬼神的事情❸。他认为关于人生的道理切近可行，而关于上天或自然的道理幽深玄远。他的弟子子贡说："夫子关于礼乐文献方面的学说，我们能够听到；夫子关于人的天性和自然天道方

---

❶《周易·系辞上》。
❷《左传》昭公十八年。
❸《论语·述而第七》21章。

❶ *Book of Changes*, "Great Commentary," Ⅰ.
❷ *The Commentary of Mr. Zuo*, Duke Zhao, 18th Year.
❸ *Analects*, "Shu'er," 7.21.

nature." ❶ As far as the doctrine of man goes, what Confucius was concerned about was practical human life, and not matters concerning pre-moral life or life after death. His disciple Zilu asked him the method of serving the ghosts and spirits. He answered "You still are not able to serve man in a good manner, so how will you be able to serve the dead in a good manner?" Zilu pursued insensitively by asking again, "Let me boldly inquire from you master, what exactly is death?" Confucius said, "Before understanding the doctrine of life, how can you understand the doctrine of death? " ❷

　　Throughout his entire life of teaching, Confucius lectured most on the "Human Way," but he never presented an abstract, metaphysical disquisition on the concept of "Way;" he did provide a simple and feasible method for implementing it. He once said to Zengzi, "Zeng Shen, my Way can be synthesized into one concept." Zengzi answered, "You are right." After Confucius left, other students inquired of Zengzi about the master's words. Zengsi said, "The master's Way consists only in 'being loyal' and 'acting with reciprocity.' " ❸ Loyalty is to do one's best and exhaust one's strength for others. Zengzi claimed that every day he examined himself multiple times to see whether he was loyal in his planning with others and whether he was sincere in his interactions with friends. ❹ Loyalty is the outward performance of humane love, and helps others accomplish the Way. Reciprocity is another side of humaneness, it is the expression of sympathy toward others. Since the two words loyalty and reciprocity are different contents of humaneness, why didn't he directly describe the "Way" as humanness? Because "humaneness" is a noun and a concept, but "being loyal" and "acting with reciprocity" are both verbs, and are two means of extending humaneness towards others, and is the way to enact humanness. Therefore, what is important is not in what humaneness actually is, but how one puts it into practice and achieves it. He stressed that, "Men are able to broaden the 'Way,' the 'Way' is not able to broaden man. " ❺ From this we can tell that Confucius' "Way" was not some mysterious and profound or perfect and refined philosophical system, but was

面的学说，我们听不到。"❶就人生的道理而言，孔子关注的是现实的人生，而不是生前或死后的事。弟子子路问他事奉鬼神的手段，他却说："你还没能好好地事奉活着的人，怎能好好地事奉死去的人？"子路不知趣，又问："我斗胆地再请教老师，死到底是怎么一回事？"孔子说："还没把活的道理弄明白，怎能明白死的道理？"❷

孔子一生讲学，给学生说了那么多关于"人道"内容，但他并没有对"道"进行形而上学的抽象论述，而是提供简单易行的履践方法。他对曾子说："曾参啊，我的'道'可以用一个观念来贯穿。"曾子回答："是的。"孔子出去后，同学向曾子打听老师的话，曾子说："老师的'道'，只有'忠'和'恕'而已。"❸忠就是对别人尽心尽力。曾子自称每天多次反省，看看自己为别人谋事是否忠心，与朋友交往是否诚信。❹忠是仁爱的外施，是帮助别人成就道德，恕是仁的另一面，是对别人的同情。既然忠恕二字是仁的不同内涵，那为什么孔子不将他的"道"直接说成是仁呢？因为"仁"是一个名词和概念，而"忠"、"恕"都是动词，是对别人施予仁爱的两种做法，是行仁之道。所以，重要的不在于仁到底是什么，而是如何去实践仁、实现仁。他强调："人能弘扬光大'道'，'道'不能弘扬光大'人'。"❺由此可见，孔子的"道"不是玄远幽深或完

❶《论语·公冶长第五》13章。
❷《论语·先进第十一》12章。
❸《论语·里仁第四》15章。
❹《论语·学而第一》4章。
❺《论语·卫灵公十五》29章。

❶ *Analects*, "Gongye Chang," 5.13.
❷ *Analects*, "Xianjin," 11.12.
❸ *Analects*, "Inward Virtue," 4.15.
❹ *Analects*, "Xue'er," 1.4.
❺ *Analects*, "Duke Ling of Wey," 15.29.

a life journey of ceaseless study and practice. Confucius was worried over his disciples only trying to understand the content of "way" in its linguistic sense. He hoped that they would enact the "Way" in their normal daily lives, and transform it into the moral conduct and the wisdom of human life to be enacted individually. He intentionally said this to his disciples, "I do not want to speak any more." Zigong said, "If you do not speak, then what would we transmit?" Confucius said, "Can it be true that Heaven speaks? The four seasons keep operating, all things are born and grow, can it be true that Heaven speaks?" ❶

Even if Confucius' "Way" is extremely easy to put into practice, nevertheless his regards the "Way" as extremely lofty. He said that this kind of neutrality of the "Doctrine of the Mean" and its normal moral conduct is the highest form of virtue; however, it is constantly betrayed ❷. Confucius once sighed with deep emotion, saying, "Everyone who exits his house has to go out by the front door of their homes; why don't they walk along my "Way?" ❸ The "Way" is more important than life. Confucius said, "If one can understand the Way in the morning, then it would be worth it to die at night!" ❹ The difference between a gentleman and a petty person is whether one seeks the "Way" for his ideal life. He repeatedly stressed, "The gentleman seeks for the Great Way and does not seek for food or clothing. Even with plowing to sustain life, one will still be hungry sometimes, but studying principles will also bring one a salary. The gentleman is only worried over whether he is able to understand and enact the 'Way,' but is not concerned whether he has plenty of food or clothing." ❺ "A knight who sets his will on seeking the 'Way' but who feels ashamed at his shabby old clothing and his common food and drink is not worth discoursing with." ❻ Actually, the easier a "Way" is, the harder it is to put it into practice once you get started on it. Zengzi felt this type of difficulty; he said, "A knight cannot help being filled with willpower, because his burden is heavy but the roadway is distant. In shouldering humaneness, can

美细致的哲学体系，而是一个不断学习，不断实践的人生旅程。孔子担忧弟子们只顾从言语当中理解"道"的内涵，希望他们在日常生活中实践"道"，将"道"转变为自我的德行和人生智慧。他故意对弟子说："我想不再说话了。"子贡说："您如果不说，那我们还传述什么呢？"孔子说："难道天向我们说了什么吗？四季在运行，万物在生长，天难道说话了吗？"❶

　　尽管孔子的"道"极为平易可行，但他将"道"看得极为崇高。他说"中庸"这种中和、平常的德行是最高的美德，可是人们长久地背离它❷。孔子深深地感慨："每个人外出都要经过自家的房门，可为什么没有人从我的'道'上走呢？"❸"道"比生命还重要。孔子说："早晨明白了道，晚上死去都值得！"❹君子和小人的区别就在于是否以追求"道"作为人生的理想。他一再地强调："君子谋求大道而不谋求衣食。耕田谋生，也会饿肚子，学习道理也会得到俸禄。君子只担忧能否明白和履行'道'，而不担忧是否丰衣足食。"❺"士人有志于追求'道'，却为自己衣着破旧，饮食不精而感到耻辱，这种人不值得与他交谈。"❻事实上，越是简易的"道"，走起来越难。曾子感到了这种艰难，他说："士人不得不充满毅力，因为他的负担重而道路远。担负着仁，难道不重吗？一直担当到

❶《论语·阳货十七》19章。
❷《论语·雍也第六》17章。
❸《论语·雍也第六》17章。
❹《论语·里仁第四》8章。
❺《论语·卫灵公第十五》31章。
❻《论语·里仁第四》10章。

❶ *Analects*, "Yang Huo," 17.19.
❷ *Analects*, "Yongye," 6.17.
❸ *Analects*, "Yongye," 6.17.
❹ *Analects*, "Inward Virtue," 4.8.
❺ *Analects*, "Duke Ling of Wey," 15.31.
❻ *Analects*, "Inward Virtue," 4.10.

it be said to be light? Carrying it until death, can the road be said to be short?" ❶ Ran Qiu even wanted to abandon it; he said to Confucius, "It is not that I do not like what you master say, but I cannot put it into practice, as I feel that my strength is not enough!" Confucius said, "Those whose strength is insufficient will naturally give up halfway then stop, but you have set up a limit for yourself beyond which you are unwilling to move." ❷

While Confucians were emphasizing enacting the human way, those who came from the ranks of astrologists and historian officials were also developing their theories on the Way of Heaven; at length the Taoists constructed an entirely new set of concepts on the Way of Heaven that replaced the old belief in an all-powerful "Heaven" and the supreme god, ghosts, and spirits; the "Way" was explained as natural law, and abstraction became the foundation and essence of the universe. The Taoist classic *Laozi* described objectively and clearly this natural way, "There is something that is chaotic yet unified, that existed before the birth of heaven and earth. It lacks sound and form, is eternal without extinction, it operates without ceasing; it can become the matrix of heaven and earth. I do not know its name, but if forced I can call it the 'Way.' If forced again, I call it 'Great.' It expands its greatness and moves forward, as it moves forward it grows more distant; growing more distant it then returns. The 'Way' that I am talking about is great, heaven is great, earth is great, and man is great. In the universe there are four great things, and man is one of them. Man imitates earth, earth imitates heaven, heaven imitates the 'Way.' The 'Way' exists on its own and acts on its own, it is naturally so of itself." ❸ Following this, the Taoists attacked the Confucians, contending that humaneness and righteousness were the result of man not following the natural way; this is the thrust of the verse "When the Great Way was abolished then were humaneness and righteousness advocated; when wisdom emerged, then falsity was produced, only after relatives lacked harmony did filial piety and kindness emerge; only after the state turned dark and chaotic did loyal ministers emerge." ❹ This formed a challenge to the Confucian school, for if the "human way" of Confucianism lacked demonstrative proof of its philosophical thinking, then it would lose its foundation and become empty dogma.

Therefore, after Confucius, Confucians needed to explain the "Way of Heaven." It was probably in the school of Zisi that Confucians expanded Confucius' thought on the Doctrine of the Mean, and constructed it own

死，难道不远吗？"❶冉求甚至要放弃了，他对孔子说："不是我不喜欢老师您的学说，可是实践起来，感到力气不足啊！"孔子说："力气不足的人，走到半道自然会停止，可你这是划下界线不愿意走。"❷

就在儒家专注于实践人道的同时，那些出身于占星家和史官的思想家们也在发展天道的学说，终于由道家学派建构了一套全新的天道观念，代替了旧信仰中至高无上的"天"和上帝鬼神，"道"被阐述为自然规律，抽象为宇宙的根源与本体。道家经典《老子》就如此客观、清晰地描述自然之道："有个浑然一体的东西，在天地生成之前就存在，无声无形，永恒不灭，运行不止，可以成为天地的母体。我不知道它叫什么，勉强可以叫做'道'，再勉强叫做'大'。它广大而前行，前行而遥远，遥远而回返。所以说'道'大，天大，地大，人大。宇宙当中有四大，人居其中之一。人效法地，地效法天，天效法'道'，'道'自在自为，自然而然。"❸接着，道家抨击儒家的仁义正是人们不效法自然之道的结果，所谓"大道废弃了，才倡导仁义；有了智慧，就产生虚伪；亲戚不和睦，才有孝慈；国家昏乱，才有忠臣"❹。这对于儒家学派形成了挑战。如果儒家的"人道"没有这种哲学思辨的论证，便会失去根据，就成了空洞的说教。

因此，孔子之后的儒学必须讲"天道"。大概在子思学派

---

❶《论语·泰伯第八》7章。
❷《论语·雍也第六》12章。
❸《老子》25章。
❹《老子》18章。

❶ *Analects*, "Tai Bo," 8.7.
❷ *Analects*, "Yongye," 6.12.
❸ *Laozi*, 25.
❹ *Laozi*, 18.

concepts of the "Way of Heaven" and the "Human Way." The *Doctrine of the Mean* said, "Sincerity is the way of heaven, pursuing sincerity is the human way. The former spontaneously dwells in the middle in accordance with the Way, and does not require any external encouragement, and requires no thought to choose it; this is the realm of the sage. The later requires a choice to pursue it, and it must firmly hold on to goodness. It must be studied in a broad manner, and inquired after minutely, and carefully pondered, attentively scrutinized, and profoundly enacted." Sincerity is true and not fake, and not only is objectively truthful but is also the sensation and judgment of truth by man. In this way, the "Heavenly Way" as the basis of morality, is not like what the Taoists describe as something chaotic and mysterious that is beyond description. It is able to be pursued in a concrete sense, and does not exist in the abstractness of profound thought. The "Way of Heaven" is the realm reached by the sage, and the "Human Way" is the path to becoming a sage and becoming one with the "Way of Heaven." To this degree of significance, the "Way of Heaven" is the "Human Way," is the ultimate destination of the "Human Way, and is the perfection of the "Human Way." Since every man can reach this zenith through study and practice, the "Way" should be close at hand to men, and can be followed and put into practice. The *Doctrine of the Mean* says, "The gentleman seeks for a glorious and lofty realm but follows the middle and common path of the mean."

Since the "Way of Heaven" is the "Human Way," then what is the composite of them both? The *Doctrine of the Mean* says, "What Heaven above orders for us is nature, following nature to develop is called the Way. Causing human nature to preserve the developmental direction that it should have is called education. The Way is something that cannot be left for even a moment; if one can leave it for even a moment then it isn't the Way." The *Doctrine of the Mean* also contains two passages which appear in the *Mencius* almost intact, and have been recorded as Mencius' own words: "Bringing oneself to reach the realm of sincerity takes a method. One cannot reach the realm of sincerity without knowing what goodness is." "The goodness manifest from the ultimate in sincerity is called nature; understanding goodness, by a step reaches the realm of sincerity, and is called education. Sincerity will automatically manifest goodness, and understanding goodness will allow one to achieve sincerity. Only through understanding goodness will one be able to pursue sincerity. Only those of utmost sincerity will be able to 'exhaust nature,' that is, to perfectly understand, develop, and realize human nature; only those who perfectly understand and develop human nature will be able to

那里，儒学发挥了孔子的"中庸"思想，建构起了自己的"天道"与"人道"概念。《中庸》说："诚是天的道，追求诚是人的道。前者自然而然地居中合道，不需要外在的劝勉，不需要思索选择，这是圣人的境界；后者则需要选择追求，牢固地把握住善。需要广博地学习、周密地询问，谨慎地思考，仔细地辨察，笃实地践行"。诚就是真实不虚妄，不仅是客观的真实，而且是人对真的感知与判断。这样，作为道德根据的"天道"就不象道家说的"道"那样混沌玄虚，不可名状。它能够实实在在地去追求，不存在于抽象的冥想之中。"天道"既是圣人达到的境界，"人道"就是成为圣人，与"天道"合一的途径。在这个意义上，"天道"就是"人道"，是"人道"的极至，是完美的"人道"。既然每个人都可以通过学习和实践达到这个顶点，所以"道"就应该平易近人，可以行走履践。《中庸》说："君子追求崇高光明的境界却依循中和平常的中庸之道"。

既然"天道"就是"人道"，那么两者的统一体是什么呢？《中庸》说："上天命定给我们的就是性，依循性的发展就是道，使人性保持其应有的发展方向就是教化。道是不可以片刻离开的东西，能够片刻离开的东西就不是道。"《中庸》里还有两段话几乎原封不动地出现在《孟子》书中，被记录为孟子的言论："让自己达到诚的境界是有方法的。不知道什么是善，就不能使自己达到诚。""由至诚而昭示出的善，叫做性；明白了善，进而达到诚的境界，叫做教。诚自会显示出善，明白善就能够实现诚。只有明白善，才能追求诚。只有极其诚的人，才能'尽性'，即完全了解、发挥、实现人性。只有完全

perfectly understand and develop the nature of things; only those who perfectly understand and develop the nature of things will be able to assist heaven and earth in the transformation of all things, and reach the spiritual realm where heaven and earth are merged." ❶ Therefore, the "Way of Heaven" exists within human nature, and human nature becomes the pathway for communication between Heaven and man. "Exhausting nature" is to discover the universality and commonality between Heaven and man through moral practice; it is a kind of moral experience and process of self-confirmation.

From the exposition of the *Doctrine of the Mean*, we discover the occurrence of a clear revolution in thought, which is that Confucians made a philosophicalized exposition of their own "Way." They used the format of seeking a definition ("What is....") to offer their own definition, and also indicated just where the "Way" lay and how to seek this "Way." Another point worth noticing is that the theory of "exhausting the nature" and the mode of putting it into practice even more so became a type of individual moral life which had its own internal transcendental coloration that did not require seeking or relying on any external moral compass or the pressure of any educative force.

If we take all of this as background, and then tie it in to Mencius' theory of human nature and morality, we can understand that it is precisely the thought of the *Doctrine of the Mean* rendered more profound by Mencius. His "human nature is good" theory was expounded as the "sincerity" of the "Way of Heaven" that heaven had endowed to every human nature in the form of "humaneness, righteousness, ritual courtesy, and wisdom." The reason men were able to fuse with Heaven through "exhausting nature," was because the heart of man possessed an internal transcendental ability. This was a process of first understanding a theory then putting it into practice. *Mencius* said that ❷

> The complete understanding and development of one's own heart will enable one to profoundly understand the original human nature; understanding the original human nature will enable one to understand the heavenly order. Maintaining one's own spirit and nurturing one's own original nature is how we serve Heaven. Whether we live a long time or for a short spell does not matter, as long as we are steadfast in nurturing our own hearts, and wait for the arrival of the heavenly order. This is the method of remaining in repose and establishing the order.

地了解、发挥人性，才能完全地了解、发挥物性；只有完全地了解发挥物性，才能赞助天地化育万物，达到与天地并存的精神境界。"❶所以，"天道"存在于人性当中，人性成了沟通天人的通道，"尽性"就是通过道德实践来发现人性与天道之间存在的普遍性和共同性，是一种内在的道德经验和自我求证的过程。

从《中庸》的表述中，我们发现一个明显的思想革命发生了，那就是儒家对自己的"道"有了一种哲学化的论述，或者说，孔子提出来的"儒家之道"被阐明了。其中用"什么是什么"的语句对"道"下了定义，还指明了"道"在何处以及如何追求"道"。还有一点值得注意的是，"尽性"的理论和实践方式更多地是一种个体的道德生活，带有内在超越的色彩，不寻求、不依靠外在道德规范或教化力量的强迫。

如果我们以此为背景，再联系孟子关于人性和道德的学说，就可以明白：正是孟子大大地深化了《中庸》的思想。他的"性善说"阐明了作为"天道"的"诚"就是天赋予人性之中的"仁义礼智"，人之所以能够通过"尽性"来与天合一，是因为人的心灵具有内在超越的能力。这是一个先明白真理再付诸实践的过程。孟子说❷：

> 全部地了解、发挥自己的心灵，就能深刻地了解人的本性；了解人的本性，就明白了天命。保持自己的心灵，养护自己的本性，这就是我们侍奉天的行为。活得长也好，短也好，我只是坚持修养我的身心，等待天命的来临，这就是安身立命的方法。

---

❶《孟子·离娄上》12章。
❷《孟子·尽心上》1章。

❶ *Mencius*, "Lilou," Ⅰ 12.
❷ *Mencius*, "Jinxin," Ⅰ 1.

The transcendental process of "exhausting the heart to know one's nature and know Heaven" is the process of moral self-practice. *Mencius* said that❶

The gentleman depends on the "Way" to deeply penetrate into cultivation, and must make some gains for himself. What one gains on one's own will be able to repose peacefully within; doing this he is able to gather a rich supply; doing this will enable him to use it without exhaustion and to be resourceful and successful; therefore the gentleman is able to gain something on his own.

Mencius' "Way" can be encapsulated by the two words "humaneness" and "righteousness." He said that men should act in accordance with humaneness and righteousness and not try to purposefully implement humaneness and righteousness❷. Humaneness and righteousness constitute the correct way within human nature. He also said that ❸

You could not talk with men who harmfully went against themselves and could not work with men who rejected themselves. Saying words that slander ritual propriety and righteousness is called harmfully going against the self; the self and heart not being able to peacefully repose in humaneness or adhere to righteousness is called rejecting oneself. Humaneness is the residence in which men peacefully repose; righteousness is the correct roadway for men. It is very tragic to leave such a dwelling empty, or to abandon travelling on such a correct roadway!

Wangzi Dian of Qi asked instruction of Mencius, saying, "What do knights do?" Mencius said, "Make their ambitions lofty." Wangzi asked, "What are lofty ambitions?" Mencius said, "Only adhering to humaneness and righteousness. Killing an innocent man is inhumane, seizing something that does not belong to you then is unrighteousness. What is our dwelling? It is humaneness. Where is our road? In righteousness. Dwelling in humaneness and travelling in righteousness will accomplish the work of a great man or gentleman." ❹

Similar to Confucius, Mencius also considered that the "Way" is easy and close to men. He sighed once, "The 'Way' is right close at hand but men seek it in distant places; things that originally are easy to do men make hard to do. All

"尽心知性而知天"的超越过程完全是一个自我的道德实践过程，他说❶：

> 君子凭藉着'道'来深入地修养，要能够自己有所获得。自己得到的东西，就能安居于其中；安居于其中，就能积累深厚；积累深厚，就能取用不尽，左右逢源，所以君子要能够自己有所获得。

孟子的"道"也可以用"仁义"二字概括。他说，人应该顺着仁义前行，而不是去刻意地推行仁义❷，仁义是内在于人性中的正道。他还说❸：

> 自己戕害自己的人，不可以和他谈论；自己抛弃自己的人，不可以与他共事。说话诋毁礼义叫做自我戕害，身心不能居于仁、遵循义叫做自我抛弃。仁是人安居的住宅，义是人正确的道路。空着好宅子不住，放弃正道不走，真是可悲啊！

齐国的王子垫请教孟子："士人是干什么的？"孟子说："让自己志向高尚。"王子问："什么叫志向高尚？"孟子说："遵循仁义罢了。杀一个无罪的人就是不仁，不是他应该拥有的却去攫取就是不义。我们的居处是什么？是仁；我们的路在何方？在义。居处于仁，行走于义，大人君子的事情就做到了。"❹

和孔子一样，孟子也认为"道"是平易近人的，他感慨道："'道'就在近处可人们还往远处求，事情本来容易做可人们还

---

❶《孟子·离娄下》14章。
❷《孟子·离娄下》19章。
❸《孟子·离娄上》10章。
❹《孟子·尽心上》33章。

❶ Mencius, "Lilou," II 14.
❷ Mencius, "Lilou," II 19.
❸ Mencius, "Lilou," I 10.
❹ Menci Mencius, "Jinxin," I 29us, "Jinxin," I 33.

that is required is that men love their own parents, respect their own elders, and the world would then be at peace." ❶ But by the same token he also profoundly realized the height and depth of the "Way" and the difficulty in putting it into practice. He took the "orthodox transmission" as inherited from Yao, Shun, Yu, Tang, Kings Wen and Wu, the Duke of Zhou, and Confucius as his own lofty mission. He took the "Way" and called it the "Great Way of the Gentleman" ❷. His ideals were to dwell in humaneness, the broadest mansion in the world; to stand on ritual, this most correct position in the world; and to walk on righteousness, the most glorious and great roadway in the world. ❸ One time his disciple Gongsun Chou said to him, "The 'Way' is truly loft, beautiful, and seems similar to climbing to heaven, seemingly too high to climb. Why can't the 'Way' change into something that is attainable, letting men seek it every day?" Mencius answered arrogantly, "A high class carpenter would not change his tools for craftsmen lacking in skills; the great archer Houyi would not change the standard by which he drew the bow for a clumsy archer. When a gentleman draws a bow, he does not refuse to shoot, exhibiting an air of being anxious to shoot. He stands in the precise center of the roadway; those who are able will shoot with him." ❹ He harbors endless respect and praise for the beautiful scenery viewed on the "Confucian Way." ❺

Once Confucius climbed East Mountain; the state of Lu appeared quite small; he then climbed Mt Tai but the world did not appear any larger. Therefore, those who have toured the Eastern Sea find it hard to enjoy the watery scenery of others; those who have studied under the sages find it hard to accept other theories. To enjoy a watery scene takes a certain method, like observing the ripples. The glory of the sun and moon, will shine on even a crack. If flowing water does not collect in low places, then it would not flow ahead. The gentleman sets his resolve on seeking the Great Way, and if he is not brilliant and talented, and be successful, he cannot reach the realm of understanding.

往难处行。人们只要各自亲爱自己的父母，尊敬自己的长辈，天下就太平了。"❶但他同样深知"道"的高深与实践的艰辛。他以继承尧、舜、禹、汤、文武、周公、孔子以来的"道统"作为自己的崇高使命；他将"道"称作"君子之大道"❷；他的理想是居住在仁这座天下最宽阔的宅第，站在礼这个天下正中的位置，走在义这条天下最光明的大道上。❸有一次弟子公孙丑对他说："'道'真是崇高、美好，好像和登天一样，似乎高不可攀。为什么'道'不能变得可以企及的样子，让人们能天天去追求呢？"孟子骄傲地说："高级的工匠不会为了手艺差的人改变规矩，善射的后羿不会为了拙劣的射手改变拉弓的标准。君子拉开了弓，并不发出箭，作出跃跃欲试的样子。他站立道路的正中，有能力的人就会跟上来的。"❹他怀着无穷的敬意赞美在"儒家之道"上看到的壮美景色❺：

> 孔子登上东山，鲁国变得很小；他又登上了泰山，天下便不再广大。所以观览过沧海的人便很难欣赏别的水景；在圣人门下学习过的人便很难接受别的学说。欣赏水景是有方法的，一定要观察水的波澜。日月的光明，连缝隙里都会照亮。流水不灌满低洼的地方就不向前流淌；君子立志追求大道，不能斐然成章，有所成就，就不能到通达的境地。

❶《孟子·离娄上》11章。
❷《孟子·尽心下》29章。
❸《孟子·滕文公下》2章。
❹《孟子·尽心上》41章。
❺《孟子·尽心上》24章。

❶ *Mencius*, "Lilou," Ⅰ11.
❷ *Mencius*, "Jinxin," Ⅰ29.
❸ *Mencius*, "Duke Wen of Teng," Ⅱ2.
❹ *Mencius*, "Jinxin," Ⅰ41.
❺ *Mencius*, "Jinxin," Ⅰ24.

All in all, from Confucius to Mencius, Confucians expounded the way that they discovered to develop humanity, that is, the way of goodness for any age and any people. Its starting point was certainly the individual; its process followed an entire life and history, and extended into the future. To earnestly perfect the self and to help other perfect themselves, then, fulfilled the value of being human and accomplished the mission given by Heaven.

After Mencius died, close to a thousand years later, after the strong and prosperous Tang Dynasty went through a political storm and crisis of belief, Confucians once again discovered that what Mencius had expounded concerning the "Way of Confucianism" was an extraordinarily important spiritual tradition. No matter how beautiful the external world was, it would inevitably perish, they said, but if this great moral will and spiritual strength was ever lost, it would be impossible to rebuild the nation. Once again, a self-appointed inheritor of the Confucian orthodox tradition, the great literatus Han Yu, employed the linguist style of Mencius to compose his essay for the ages, "Tracing the Way." He systematically expounded the Confucian Way as established by Confucius and Mencius. As the conclusion of the present book, here is an extract:

> Charity is called "humaneness;" conduct that is correct is called "righteousness;" adhering to humaneness and righteousness is called the "Way." When it is internalized and completely independent of external things it is called "virtue." The classics are the *Book of Poetry*, the *Book of History*, the *Book of Changes*, and the *Spring and Autumn Annals*; their canons of conduct are the rites and music, the penal code, the political system. Their people are the knights, the farmers, the craftsmen, and the merchants. Their society and human relations and other ranks are the lord and minister, father and son, teacher and friend, host and guest, elder and younger brothers, and husband and wife. The clothing that was worn were linen cloth and silk. The houses in which they dwelled were palaces and homes. The food that they ate included corn, vegetables, fish, and meat. As a "Way," it was easy and plain; as a teaching, it was easy to enact. As the "Way" to fulfill the self, it brought peace and good fortune; as the "Way" to fulfill others, it brought humaneness and justice. As the "Way" for the spirit to follow, it brought peace and security; as the "Way" to govern the world and the state, it could be used in all the fours seas for all to measure up to.

总之，从孔子到孟子，儒家阐明了他们所发现的人类发展之道，即任何时代，任何人群的善道，其起点必定是他们自身，其过程伴随他们的生命、历史并延续至未来。认真地完成自己，并帮助他人完成自我，便实现了作为人的价值和上天赋予的使命。

孟子死后，时近千年，强盛的大唐王朝经历了一场政治风暴和信仰危机之后，儒家再次发现了孟子阐明的"儒家之道"是非常重要的精神传统。再美好的外部世界也会毁灭，但如果失去了伟大的道德意志和精神力量，就无法重建我们的家园。再度以儒家道统继承者自居的大文学家韩愈，用他那类似孟子风格的语言，写成了《原道》这篇千古垂范的文章，系统地阐述了孔子和孟子开辟的儒家之道，我们摘录其中的一段，作为本书的结束：

> 博爱叫做"仁"，行为正当叫做"义"，遵循仁义叫做"道"，全在乎自己不有待于外物叫做"德"。经典是《诗》、《书》、《易》、《春秋》；其法度是礼乐、刑法、政治；其人民是士人、农夫、工匠、商贾；其社会和伦理等级是君臣、父子、师友、宾主、兄弟、夫妇。穿的衣服是麻布、丝绸；住的房屋是宫殿、家室；吃的食物是粟米、果蔬、鱼肉。作为"道"，它简易明白，作为教化，它容易践行。作为成就自我的"道"，它带来和顺吉祥；作为成就别人的"道"，它带来仁爱公正；作为心灵遵循的"道"，它带来和平安适；作为治理天下国家的"道"，它放之四海而皆准。

图书在版编目(CIP)数据

孟子/徐兴无著;(美)霍尼(Honey, D.)译. ——
南京:南京大学出版社,2010.9
(中国思想家评传简明读本:中英文版)
ISBN 978-7-305-07583-4

Ⅰ.①孟⋯ Ⅱ.①徐⋯②霍⋯ Ⅲ.①孟轲(前372~
前289)—评传—汉、英 Ⅳ.①B222.5

中国版本图书馆CIP数据核字(2010)第178161号

出版发行 南京大学出版社
社　　址 南京汉口路22号　邮　编 210093
网　　址 http://www.NjupCo.com
出 版 人 左　健

丛 书 名 《中国思想家评传》简明读本(中英文版)
书　　名 孟 子
著　　者 徐兴无
译　　者 David B. Honey
审　　读 李 寄
责任编辑 芮逸敏　　　　编辑热线 025-83593947

照　　排 江苏凤凰制版印务中心
印　　刷 宜兴市盛世文化印刷有限公司
开　　本 787×1092　1/16　印张 16.75　字数 225千
版　　次 2010年9月第1版　2010年9月第1次印刷
ISBN 978-7-305-07583-4
定　　价 33.00元

发行热线 025-83594756　83686452
电子邮箱 Press@NjupCo.com
　　　　　Sales@NjupCo.com (市场部)